# Women in management

## A developing presence

## Edited by Morgan Tanton

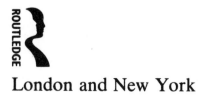

London and New York

First published 1994
by Routledge
11 New Fetter Lane, London EC4P 4EE

Simultaneously published in the USA and Canada
by Routledge
29 West 35th Street, New York, NY 10001

Reprinted 1995

Typeset in Times by
J&L Composition Ltd, Filey, North Yorkshire
Printed and bound in Great Britain by
Mackays of Chatham PLC, Chatham, Kent

*British Library Cataloguing in Publication Data*
A catalogue record for this book is available from the British Library

*Library of Congress Cataloguing in Publication Data*
A catalogue record for this book is available from the Library of Congress

ISBN 0-415-09728-2 (hbk)
ISBN 0-415-09729-0 (pbk)

# Contents

# Figures

# Tables

# Contributors

**Beverly Alimo-Metcalfe** is a chartered occupational psychologist who has worked extensively in public and private sector organizations. Her fields of interest include leadership and interpersonal skills, techniques of assessment, techniques for identifying development needs, career development and appraisal. She has strong interests in gender in relation to all of these topics and is currently investigating qualities of leadership amongst female and male managers in the NHS. Beverly has published extensively, and has presented papers at many international conferences in Europe, the USA and Canada, Australia and Thailand.

**Richard Boot** early in his career worked for a major oil company. Since that time he has had a range of academic posts (City University Business School, London Business School and Lancaster University), complemented by his own consultancy work. In 1990 he decided to opt for the freedom (and threat) of operating independently in order to change the nature of time and energy available for being a father, being a husband, being a friend, bird watching, writing and dreaming.

**Breda Gray** is a lecturer in sociology at the University of Central Lancashire. She lived in Ireland until she was twenty-four when she went to Canada to study with a view to returning to Ireland after a few years. She has moved from Canada to London to Lancaster and is not sure when/if she will return to Ireland. Her studies and work have been in social sciences, social work, development work and management learning. She is currently straddling the independent trainer and academic divide but leaning more towards the academic, with lots of questions as always.

**Alev Ergenc Katrinli** is married with one child and has a BA in business administration, MBA and Ph.D. in organizational behaviour. She is working as an associate professor in the Faculty of Economics and Administrative Sciences, Dokuz Eylul University, Turkey. Her area of interest is organizational behaviour and industrial psychology.

**Joanna Knight** is an independent consultant who specializes in enabling individuals, groups and organizations to learn and change in order to meet their goals. She uses experiential learning methods and works collaboratively with clients to achieve these changes. Prior to this, Joanna held senior positions with major private sector companies in personnel, line management and as an internal consultant focusing on management and organizational development. Supporting her wide practical experience of management and organization development, Joanna has an MA in Management Learning and has embarked on an MSc in Change Agent Skills and Strategies.

**Sue Marlow** is a senior lecturer in human resource management at the School of Business, De Montford University, Leicester. In her previous post as a research fellow at Warwick Business School, Sue contributed to a number of research projects focusing on fast growing small firms and ethnic minority entrepreneurs, publications from which are existing or forthcoming. Current research interests include women in the business environment and entrepreneurship. She is co-director of a funded research project examining the role of human resource management in the small firm sector.

**Judi Marshall** is a reader in organizational behaviour in the School of Management, University of Bath. She joined the School in 1978. Her main academic interests are women in management, gender, organizational cultures and qualitative, post-positivist research methods. Judi is married and has two children and a Siamese cat. She lives in a small Gloucestershire town and likes cycling and reading.

**Linda Martin** is a lecturer in management studies at SAUS, University of Bristol, where she undertakes research, teaching and consultancy with public sector organizations. She has local authority experience both as a consultant and as a senior officer for community development. Her particular interests include power issues in groups and organizations, local democracy and managing change and feminist theory. Linda has worked with women and women's learning in the community, in organizations, and higher education. She teaches on Master's programmes in gender and social policy, management development and social responsibility and comparative development and international policy. With Althea Efunshile she runs a programme for black and white women managers entitled 'Managing Power, Inequality and Change'. Linda is a member of the Standing Conference of Public Sector Training Agencies (SCEPSTA) where she leads the Equality network. She lives in Bristol with her partner and two daughters aged 17 and 21.

**Virginia E. O'Leary** is currently Chair and Professor of the Psychology Department at Indiana State University. She has served as Senior Research Fellow at the Massachusetts Institute of Behavioral Medicine and Director of the Radcliffe Conferences on the American Psychological Association and the American Psychological Society. She has numerous publications on a wide range of women's issues and has been credited with numerous awards and professional citations.

**Ömür Timurcanday Özmen** is married with one child and has a BA in Business Administration and Management from the University of Aegean where she now works as an associate professor in the Faculty of Economics and Administrative Sciences. Her area of interest is organizational theory, management and organizational behaviour and industrial psychology.

**Sue Pritchard** set up a small independent consultancy, Learning in Partnership Ltd, in 1991, following the birth of her daughter, in an attempt to enjoy work and family in more equal measure. She specializes in working with issues of personal, professional and organizational learning, particularly with women and with trainers and developers. In addition to her consultancy work, Sue has now embarked on a post-graduate research degree at Bristol University, exploring women's experience of organization change, and has added a son to the family.

**Maureen Ryan** is a doctoral student in clinical psychology at Indiana State University. She received her BA from the State University of New York at Albany. She has co-authored an article on gender awareness and group therapy and is currently working with Virginia O'Leary and colleagues to develop a heuristic model of resilience in women.

**Adam Strange** is a lecturer in the Department of International Studies at Nottingham Trent University. Formerly he was a research and associate lecturer in urban planning at Leeds Polytechnic, and research fellow in the Centre for small and medium-sized enterprises at Warwick Business School. Adam's current research interests include entrepreneurship and small business property. He has produced several publications in small business and planning.

**Elaine Swan** has worked in various retail contexts including working as training officer for Selfridges and as Training and Development Manager for Pronuptia Youngs. She recently completed her MA in Management Learning and is currently pursuing doctoral research in the area of representations of emotion in the sphere of consumption, i.e. advertisement, film and shopping.

**Morgan Tanton** is a lecturer in the Department of Management Learning in the Management School at Lancaster University. After an eclectic career, fifteen years of which were spent in Canada, she joined Lancaster University. She spent a number of years carrying out ethnographic research looking at Management Development practice in leading European business schools and more latterly completed a three-year study looking at the relationship between human resource management and financial performance in the UK. Her research interests are currently women in management, ethnobiography and the completion of her Ph.D. She has a son, John, who lives in Canada.

# Acknowledgements

I thank all those who contributed to, or supported the first Lancaster conference on Women in Management Learning and those who have made this book possible. In particular, I would like to thank Rosemary Nixon from Routledge who has been enthusiastic and helpful since the idea was first mooted and Sally Close for her care and support in the final stages of production.

# Introduction

**THE ORIGIN: WOMEN IN MANAGEMENT LEARNING**

This book has its roots in a conference organized at Lancaster University on the day following the launch of Opportunity 2000. Opportunity 2000 is a UK initiative launched on 28 October 1991 to increase the numbers of women in management and particularly at senior levels. The Lancaster event was advertised as a conference *on* Women in Management Learning but as the applications and papers started to arrive I began to realize it was becoming a conference *for* women in management learning. And as the telephone conversations of interest and concern for the future of women in management gradually increased as the conference drew near, I was reminded of the empassioned words of Bernice Reagon:

> [Sometimes] it gets too hard to stay out in that society all the time. And that's when you find a place, and you try to bar the door and check all the people who come in. You come together to see what you can do about shouldering up all of your energies so that you and your kind can survive . . . [T]hat space should be a nurturing space where you sift out what people are saying about you and decide who you really are. And you take the time to try to construct within yourself and within your community who you would be if you were running society.
>
> (Hartsock 1987: 163)

That is what the conference became, a place where those interested in the development of women could be together to see what could be done to shoulder up our energies to understand the issues for women in management and to improve the conditions for women in management learning.

This book is another facet of this drawing together. It is another space where the authors have sifted out ideas from the work they have been carrying out, and brought them together in order to share them with others.

The quotation from Bernice Reagon is given in a paper by Nancy Hartsock (1987) and she describes Bernice as 'civil rights movement activist, feminist, singer with the band Sweet Honey in the Rock, and social historian with the Smithsonian' (p. 163). The description is a good example of the variety of roles that we all have and yet there is a tendency to reduce ourselves to a one-word description or definition. Our status, our job, our role becomes the key to our presentation of self. At this conference all the participants were educators.

Yet within this one word there were university lecturers of many years experience, young women trainers from large organizations, women who were self-employed, women who were teachers, human resource specialists, developers, independent consultants, women from Norway, Northern Ireland, Sweden, Canada, the US, Bahrain, the UK and there were two men.

## THE CONFERENCE: WORKING WITH DIFFERENCE

One of the tasks was to create an environment in which all the participants and all the contributions would be valued. This meant exploring the conditions which make it possible for people who are different, and often separated from each other by institutional or societal structures, to speak and be heard.

Some papers attracted large attendance, others smaller interest and paradoxically (or predictably) a paper given by one of the male delegates was attended by almost all the conferees although his intention was to talk informally with a small group.

Although the conference was on women in management learning, there was considerable concern for men in organizations and I found myself wondering why men had not shown a similar concern for women. The perception by the conferees was that the organizational environment which is not healthy for women is similarly unhealthy for men. It was generally the perception that until women make the stand for authenticity, and the conditions which allow it, women will continue to leave and men will continue to reinstate the formidable hierarchical structures which eliminate the potential for individual respect, flexibility and difference.

But perhaps most disconcertingly, those who did not have English as their first language felt themselves to be marginalized at the conference. Although we had attempted to value difference across boundaries of status and experience we had created a significant 'other' within the essentially female community.

## THE BOOK: WOMEN'S VOICE

Although in my role as editor and as an academic pursuing my own career I have imposed a structure to this volume which constructs meaning, I have not attempted to homogenize or influence the styles of the contributors for the danger in Gilligan's (1982) singular 'different voice' is that it threatens individuality.

It seems crucial that women's voice and style remain heterogeneous in order to counteract the view that a single category 'women' has been created and that such women may be to blame for what is described as a decline in educational standards:

Various national reports conclude that there is a crisis in education defined as the erosion of academic standards and the collapse of traditional values in education. In all of these appeals, the decline of academic standards is clearly linked to the proliferation of scholarship and educational programs in women's studies and black studies. And though seemingly different in tone and intent, conservative academic arguments about the need to 'return to basics' and to claim the legacy of 'the classics' are actually attempts to reinstate partriarchal authority.

(Anderson 1988: 46)

Possibly this is the latent threat which lies low and influences women writers and possibly editors to adopt a style which Roberts (1981: 26) describes as 'a type of academic discourse that can only be understood by a "coterie of sociologists"' (1981: 26).

However, I have chosen to be influenced by June Purvis who says of feminist research:

the research itself should be written up in an 'accessible' style that can be read by the primary audience of women rather than an 'academic' style that will be read mainly by an elite of experts.

(Purvis 1985: 185)

In the last session of the conference a question was raised about the level of challenge during the three days. We had all been supportive and worked long hours happily together but had we been sufficiently challenging and rigorous?

How do we judge rigour when, according to McAuley (1987), it is achieved in the male-dominated academic culture by 'the cut and thrust of academic debate', which he calls 'destructive criticism'. Do we need more challenge when, as Belenky *et al.* (1986) point out, women already get so much challenge from their everyday engagement with the world? And isn't there already in women a strong self-critiquing voice which has secured the success of assertiveness training courses?

## THE SUBJECT: A NAMELESS CHARACTER IN TWELVE CHAPTERS

For someone considering entering management this book could be read as the story of a woman manager in the 1990s, through her entry into a leadership position in the organization, until she leaves her employment.

But it is also a challenge to human resource specialists because the hypothetical central character leaves mid-career as a result of fatigue, frustration and illness. She is a lost resource because the conditions within which she works are unacceptable.

The sixteen contributors to this volume have addressed several questions about the future for women managers. For example: Will they stay in senior management and survive this second wave of women's liberation? Will they choose to leave management to be controlled, disciplined and managed by men, or will another alternative be found?

In Chapter 1 I look at the practice of management development and document the elements which improve education for women, touching briefly on the implications of different philosophical feminist approaches for education.

In Chapter 2 appraisal and assessment to leadership position is explored by *Beverly Alimo-Metcalfe* who uses her work within the National Health Service to show how such systems prevent women's progress into senior positions in management.

An account of Women's Development Programmes initiated and implemented from within the organization, possibly as a 'salve to the organizational conscience', is given in Chapter 3 by *Joanna Knight* and *Sue Pritchard*.

*Virginia O'Leary* from the US has contributed Chapter 4, written with *Maureen Ryan*, which looks at changes over the last decade in the roles of women bosses and assesses the significance of these changes for future generations of women.

*Elaine Swan* focuses on an issue frequently omitted from management texts although found in psychology and sociology and one which is arguably central in human relations. In Chapter 6 she explores Managing Emotion, raising the spectre of reason set in opposition to emotion as the source of its banishment.

*Linda Martin* (in Chapter 7) reviews the case of black and white women managers in Local Government and, by deconstructing their experiences, exposes previously-hidden knowledge suggesting that women's strategy for equality is to engage by making hidden discourses visible.

*Joanna Knight's* own experience of motherhood was the catalyst for her research which studied senior managers' experiences of motherhood on their careers (Chapter 8).

Two papers have had to represent the voices of the under-represented. In Chapter 5 *Alev Katrinli* and *Ömür Özmen* describe the initial findings of their longer study of Turkish women's experience of management. Although I am pleased that their paper is included I am unhappy at the seeming tokenism of this single inclusion by non-English speaking contributors.

A similar but different concern surrounded *Richard Boot's* chapter (Chapter 9). Should this volume include the issues that men experience or should that be left for another book? Richard's paper provokes both women and men to create what he calls global sanity which would include, amongst other things, new criteria for success.

In Chapter 10 *Sue Marlow* and *Adam Strange* have looked at success and what it means for women entrepreneurs. They found that current policies aimed at small firm owners are inappropriate for females.

To end the story and ground the challenge to human resource specialists, *Judi Marshall* in Chapter 11 previews her forthcoming book by referring to the initial results of her recent study which reveals why women leave senior management jobs.

Finally, *Breda Gray* has used a review of Women Only Management Training since the 1960s to set this volume in a social, legislative and political context. She has also included a useful appendix which lists significant events from the 1960s to the 1990s.

## REFERENCES

Anderson, M. L. (1988) 'Changing the curriculum in Higher Education', E. Minnich, J. O'Barr and R. Rosenfeld (eds) *Reconstructing the Academy*, London: University of Chicago Press, 36–68.

Belenky, M. F., Clinchy, B. M., Goldberger, N. R. and Tarule, J. M. (1986) *Women's Ways of Knowing*, New York: Basic Books.

Gilligan, C. (1982) *In A Different Voice*, Cambridge, Mass: Harvard University Press.

Hartsock, N. (1987) 'Foucault on power: a theory for women?', M. Leijenarr (ed.) *The Gender of Power – A Symposium*, Leiden: Vakgroep Vrouwenstudies/Vena.

McAuley, J. (1987) 'Women academics: a case study in inequality', A. Spencer and D. Podmore (eds) *In a Man's World*, London: Tavistock Publications.

Purvis, J. (1985) 'Reflections upon doing historical documentary research from a feminist perspective', R. G. Burgess (ed.) *Strategies of Educational Research: Qualitative Methods*, London: The Falmer Press.

Roberts, H. (1981) 'Women and their doctors: power and powerlessness in the research process', H. Roberts (ed.) *Doing Feminist Research*, London: Routledge & Kegan Paul.

# Chapter 1

# Developing women's presence

*Morgan Tanton*

## INTRODUCTION

The phrase 'developing women's presence' was created by a colleague, Vivien Hodgson, when she and I were designing a series of workshops. The word 'presence' had a ring of rightness for us. Later, looking at the dictionary I see more clearly why:

> presence (z), n. Being present, *as your presence is requested, in the presence of a large company*; . . . place where person is, as *admitted to, banished from, his presence, in this (august etc.) presence*, in the presence of this (etc.) person; . . . *the presence*, ceremonial attendance on person of high especially royal rank, as *remained in, retired from the presence*; carriage, bearing, as *a man of (a) noble presence; presence of mind*, calmness and self command in sudden emergencies.
>
> (Fowler and Fowler 1975)

Presence does not only mean being bodily present, it also indicates position, acceptability, importance, rank, bearing, self-command. Our educational objective was 'developing women's presence'.

## THE QUESTION

Since that time I have been asked to run a number of gender workshops and recently I was negotiating the details of a workshop at a management school with the teaching director when he suddenly asked falteringly 'What is different about management development for women?'

As a lecturer in the Department of Management Learning I am often asked this question and it is always posed by a male. The question appears to me to be 'shot out' in the middle of another conversation: 'Is there really any difference in the way women learn?' – And it seems to require an equally rapid response.

This chapter is my response, consciously laboured, pondered, taking time and space, because the issue of women's education is complex:

(a) because women are individuals, just as different from each other as they are from men: 'Burton (1985) argues that the differences between women of different classes are more significant than their common gender identity' (Alvesson and Billing 1992: 84);

(b) because some of the differences between men and women refer to values – not only personal or organizational values, but societal values and 'research show[s] how certain values, more common to male socialization, [have] come to be accepted as the standard for human beings' (Calas and Smircich 1990: 10);

(c) because there are different attitudes to women, women's place or the philosophy of 'feminism' which influence teachers. I want to develop this theme at the end of the chapter.

To answer the original question I will refer to what others have said about women's experience of tutors as well as my own research with women managers and teachers of women managers. But I begin by allowing the voices of some other women to speak in answer to another question.

## IS THERE A NEED TO DEVELOP WOMEN'S PRESENCE?

In a workshop with some fifteen management education specialists (mostly women) I asked them for their reasons for developing women's presence in their organizations. The answers came quickly and a list of reasons emerged. As the women spoke some comments were coloured by frustration, resignation or anger, but there was general understanding and agreement in the comments which each made. There were no disagreements. I have selected some of these to capture the issues which they described.

We need to Develop Women's Presence because:

1 the power-oriented context in which we work gets lost;
2 women and men start from different places, with different pictures in their heads;

3 women develop men's presence within the family, within society and as trainers in the way we take responsibility for *process* in teaching;

4 women's values are labelled emotional while men's are seen as real;

5 women are still numerically disadvantaged in management;

6 the physical settings in which training takes place are often uncomfortable for women;

7 issues for men and women within organizations are complicated by issues of culture;

8 women's needs are diverse but still stereotyped as unified;

9 women's values, qualities and talents, if allowed to flourish, will be beneficial to organizational performance;

10 there is still opposition to women in positions of high status.

Some other reasons were given as to why we need to develop women's presence. These referred to particular characteristics which women needed or lacked, for example, assertiveness, aggression, self-esteem, confidence, and so on. For example, they said 'women are less aggressive', 'women lack self-esteem'. The focus of the group was on woman as 'other' to the characteristics of a male norm. This could be interpreted as pragmatic given that they worked in what they described as 'male-dominated' organizational cultures.

Alternatively it could be seen as a measure of the depth of the entrenched values within society that even this group of women concentrating their attention on the issue of women's development approached it from the perspective of the 'centred male'.

According to Kirkham (1985), one of the key differences between being a member of a majority group and being a member of a minority group is that majority group members do not think about what it means to be a member of that majority group, whereas minority group members give much thought to the meaning and effect of being in that minority and to the dynamics of the majority group.

If, as Kirkham (ibid.) suggests, women as a minority group spend a great deal of thought understanding the meaning and effect of being in the minority but their focus is (like those in this workshop) always from the perspective of their 'otherness', they may be inadvertently confirming their differentness as deficit.

By naming the stereotypes that we wish to discourage, for example, 'Masculinity . . . for example, as rational, analytical, achievement-oriented, problem-solving, independent, self-reliant and resourceful. Femininity, on the other hand . . . as receptive, nurturant, empathetic, intuitive, emotional, supportive and sub-missive' (Alvesson and Billing 1992: 75), (sic) are we simply colluding by re-creating and re-presenting once again words which, as Spender (1980) has shown, have now taken on additional meaning as either negative or positive depending on their connection with female or male stereotypes?

Conscious of this paradox I have attempted to write from a 'woman-centred' perspective. Instead of highlighting how women are different from men I have described how women are. I have omitted reference to men or, where this was unavoidable, I have endeavoured to refer to men as 'other' to the female norm. This has not always been possible because in much of the literature men's values, style and organization are the norm.

I am reminded of the dilemma outlined by Calas and Smircich, at the end of their paper to the conference 'Re-Thinking Organization':

> As we close our chapter . . . we should have been happy . . . But we're skeptical . . . we realize that we have written as women can write in a writing that is already gendered. Thus it seems we have come to occupy 'the women's position' which was written for us before we came into this text. We were asked to fill the space on women and organizations for the conference and the book and so we did.
>
> (Calas and Smircich 1990: 32)

They realized that by contributing they were also helping to sustain the circumstances and conditions of the gendered organiza-tion which they and the other contributors were attempting to re-think.

Is this chapter and this volume one more affirmation of women's marginality? Or by stating women's ways of knowing, women's ways of learning, women's ways of being, are we developing women's presence?

## WOMEN'S EXPERIENCE AS LEARNERS

A body of research is developing which studies adult women's experiences as learners which will enable tutors to improve their practice. For example, Sullivan and Buttner refer to studies which observe that:

Instructors sometimes inadvertently treat male and female students differently. For example, instructors may focus eye contact on men, allow interruptions of women's comments, rephrase women's comments, give greater public praise to men and ask women 'lower-order' factual questions while reserving the 'higher-order' critical thinking question for men (Belenky, Clinchy, Goldberger and Tarule 1986; Hall and Sandler 1982).

(Sullivan and Buttner 1992: 81)

It may be useful for trainers, teachers or tutors to know that, according to some research, 'male students may be less likely to recognize the contributions of their female colleagues to work with them collegially, or to offer support' (Hall and Sandler 1984). This might explain why Sternglanz and Lyberger-Ficek (1977) found that women in educational settings tend to be less assertive in class discussions than men. If women in a small (syndicate) group feel overlooked or devalued they may react by becoming 'quieter'. Alternatively, it is possible that some women react to being unrecognized by reverting to more assertive behaviour which when demonstrated by women is sometimes labelled as aggressive.

Tutors may find it useful to discover that 'men are more likely to attribute their successes to ability whereas women attribute theirs to luck or effort' (Nieva and Gutek 1980) and that there seems to be some indication that such views may be reinforced by instructors who tell high-achieving males that they are competent and high-achieving females that the work was easy (Sandler 1986).

One explanation of success may create an impression of more ability than the other which may influence how the next question from the tutor is phrased or to whom it is phrased.

Tutors may find it valuable to learn that

Instructors tend to wait longer for men than for women to answer a question before moving to another student, coach men but not women by asking for additional elaboration or explanations to questions, call directly on male students but not on women students even when women volunteer and respond more fully to men's than to women's comments.

(Sullivan and Buttner 1992: 83)

Instructors may find it challenging to know that Sandler (1986) also found that tutors are 'more likely to call male students by name more often than female students and usually know the names of proportionately more male than female students'.

In the United States, 'The Project on the Status and Education of Women' studied the atmosphere in classrooms and identified instructor behaviours that treated women differently from men, that is, tutors maintaining more eye contact with men, frequently interrupting women, making sexist jokes and adopting a posture of attentiveness when talking with men (for example, leaning forward), but the opposite when talking with women (Sullivan and Buttner 1992: 84). These differences 'may lead women to lose confidence, lower their academic goals, and limit their career choices' (Hall and Sandler 1984: 2).

The women I worked with described their experience of learning with men as problematic. For example: 'When women express their knowledge it is put down'; 'There are often either jokes or confrontational responses after women speak'; 'Many women feel threatened in teaching sessions so don't speak'; 'There are different standards for men and women'; 'Women are accused of personalizing issues'; 'Women get tired of being the only female'; 'Men say the sessions are different when I am there'; 'Men say they think of me as just another man, but I'm a woman'.

These comments begin to create a picture of women's experience of reality which a number of writers describe. They assert that men's version (of reality) is different (McAuley 1987; Jones 1988; Addelson 1983 and Belenky et al. 1986).

But it is men's reality which controls what counts as knowledge and in my research with women it is the power exercised through ownership of knowledge which causes the strongest feelings of frustration; the frustration that women's knowledge is not incorporated or valued until it is spoken by a man.

## WORKING WITH ONLY MEN'S KNOWLEDGE

The content of what is taught to women is still (apart from in women's studies) largely as a result of male research on male subjects. And 'men have often made their own knowledge and their own sex, representative of humanity' (Spender 1985: 1).

This has meant that 'women's achievements and political struggles are, by and large, omitted from recorded history and have little place in men's and women's consciousness' (Shotter and Logan 1988: 72). It is not only the achievements and struggles themselves which are omitted but the presence of women in history and as a result of such omissions, 'there is nothing by which she can orient herself to bring her personal experience into continuity with the past' (Janssen-Jurreit 1982: 33). This may be the most powerful sense of loss. Not only is the individual woman in a learning situation unrecognized by her male colleagues (Hall and Sandler 1984), but her sense of belonging to a heritage of other women is lost. She is isolated on a lone raft in a sea of knowledge without a history to support her, without an ally or mentor to guide or teach her, and without a voice that will be heard or understood when she calls for help. These three elements are key to her development and survival.

## KEYS TO DEVELOPING WOMEN

The lack of women's heritage in knowledge, the importance of relationships, and ways of talking are well documented, and should be considered in the design and implementation of any course which women will be attending.

### Content – an untapped heritage of knowledge

Women's knowledge and work is largely missing from the field of management. The content or curriculum is created and controlled by what has been determined as suitable or adequate knowledge and women's historical contribution to management education has been omitted. To put this in a historical context, when the origin of management education in the USA at university level was inaugurated at the Wharton School of Finance and Commerce in 1918, women in the UK still did not have the vote (Wheatcroft 1970: 85).

In attempting to influence today's curriculum women find it difficult, if not impossible, for example, to teach a session which has not been carried down through this biased heritage. For example, sessions on emotion in management, motherhood in management, bereavement or sexism in management would not only be treated with skepticism and raised eyebrows by many male teachers within the management schools, but also by the students, possibly even some female students. Because they have come to accept knowledge which in the terms of Spender (1985) and Daly (1973) is 'false or partial knowledge' because it has excluded women as producers and subjects of knowledge.

McAuley (1987) describes how a woman had brought into her organizational studies department an interest in the development of curriculum changes to understand gender differentiation. However, most of the men were relatively indifferent about the introduction:

> This indifference tended to be either slightly hostile or passively uninterested; the hostility arose out of an attitude that there was no particular issue to discuss, as attention to gender was essentially somewhat marginal in its thrust and distracted from the major issues of understanding organizations, while the passive indifference suggested a gentle puzzlement that such an area of concern could exist, together with an acceptance that it might – as long as it did not involve them.
>
> (McAuley 1987: 175)

The dilemma of appropriate content is poignantly portrayed by Beetham (1989). Although the excerpt describes her work with an English class, it is relevant here as it demonstrates the difficulty of overcoming attitudes which accept a content couched in traditional, and therefore partial, knowledge:

> And once again I feel the familiar contradictions; the tension between the self I feel I am and those explanations of the self which I can give. And that other set of tensions around the text, which is on the table in all its particularity but which is also the product of social and narrative conventions. In an abstract way I know what I want to do in reading the text in the seminar. It is in part to set the idea of the self-explanatory text and the self-sufficient reader against the argument that the reader and the text are constructed. These ideas, however are potentially threatening to me, as well as – I suspect – to the students.
>
> The seminar discussion of *The Mother's Magazine* therefore, begins against a resistance from some students. One of them says to me, only half-jokingly, that she has come to do English because she wants to read Jane Austen, not some obscure woman whose writing was so dreadful that no one has bothered to reprint it since 1843 or whenever. Her particular enthusiasm is not shared by the others in the group, but they understand what she means. They want access to the culture, self-improvement or even pleasure which is vested in recognised works of genius like *Emma* or *Hamlet*. These non-canonical

texts threaten their sense of literature and of what studying literature is for.

(Beetham 1989: 183–4)

It is difficult for women to contribute gendered issues to the curriculum and for some female students to accept such topics, because the view of what is appropriate is one of those values referred to previously, which is more common to male socialization but now accepted as the standard for all.

As an example the suggestion by Bowen *et al.* (1987) that emotional arousal resulting from discussion of sexism can enhance learning and that it should be encouraged, has not been taken seriously and I know of no management school that has included such an approach in their core programmes.

However, women have much more to add to the field of management education than simply additional content.

## The context – relationships

There are now a number of talented senior women assuming positions of influence within organizations and their awareness of the limited nature of knowledge extends beyond the content of the curriculum. For example, a director of training recently recounted to me that she had been negotiating with a business school to run a Masters in Business Administration (MBA) for her organization. She had requested that in order to redress the imbalance in numbers of men and women in senior positions in her organization she would like there to be a majority of women teachers on the programme. One of the male teachers from the business school retorted that he would be worried about the bias in such a policy.

If that particular male teacher reads this account with embarrassment he need not feel alone. According to Deem, 'gender consciousness is lower in male teachers' (Deem 1980). A study carried out within an MBA class in the United States (Sullivan and Buttner 1992: 86) found that women in the class believed that discrimination frequently occurs and 50 per cent had themselves experienced such discrimination. However, most of the male MBA students thought that only older men (defined by them as over 45) still discriminated against women. Again, the results show how differently men and women perceive the same world.

Women appear to be affected, interested, influenced by attachment or relationships with others. For women:

[d]evelopment is tied to understanding and strengthening the self in relation to others. For women, attachments and relationships play a central role in both identity formation and conceptions of developmental maturity (Chodorow, 1974; Douvan and Adelson, 1966; McClelland, 1975), colouring how women see themselves, their lives, their careers and their ongoing responsibility to those around them.

(Gallos 1989: 115; and see Bardwick 1980; Eichenbaum and Orbach 1988; Gilligan 1982; Josselson 1987)

This emphasis on the relationship with others affects all aspects of women's learning. For example:

*Self-evaluation* – 'Women tend to judge themselves by standards of responsibility and care towards others, with whom affiliation is recognized and treasured' (Ferguson 1984: 159).

*Moral judgement* – 'Women's moral judgements are closely tied to feelings of empathy and compassion for others' (Ferguson 1984: 159; Gilligan 1982; Chodorow 1978).

*Freedom of expression* – 'Growing up female has often meant relinquishing freedom of expression and choice in order to sustain relationships' (Eichenbaum and Orbach 1988; Miller 1976; Schaef 1981).

*Relationships with advisors* – 'Female students focus on the importance of a personal relationship with an advisor to enhance their learning experience, whereas male students focussed on the instrumental value of an advisor to "know the facts" or "how to get them"' (Harvard Assessment Project 1990).

*Learning from others* – 'Although a manager's tendency to learn from assignments and hardships does not appear to be gender-related, the capacity of the women to learn from other people is remarkable' (Velsor and Hughes 1990).

*Power* – 'Women perceive power issues very differently because of their concern for relationships' (McClelland 1975; Gallos 1989).

*Attentiveness* – 'women display greater attentiveness . . . to the needs of subordinates, in other words, they are better at listening and taking into account what they hear when they act' (Hammond 1992: 7).

This emphasis on relationships must signal an important consideration for teachers, trainers or developers of women and should be reflected in the design of any educational experience. If teachers are aware of such a focus from the minute a programme begins, that is, the first advertising of the programme until the evaluation is completed, there might be changes in methods and styles of delivery.

For example, after a programme for junior/middle managers of a leading building society I was told by a senior executive that women did not 'get on' in their company. The programme in question was the first that the managers had attended. Women were in the minority. Some of them had not been away from their families before in this manner. On arrival they were individually left in the lobby of a large impersonal hotel, sitting with bags in hands, waiting for someone from the company to arrive to give them instructions and information.

The sessions which followed were formal and 'traditional' in that the instructors (who were all males) spoke from a raised platform at the front of the hall-like room. The participants sat in rows listening. No women asked any questions and no woman responded to any questions. Women did not get on in that building society.

Opportunities for relationships in this setting had been quashed from the moment the managers arrived. No thought had been given to creating a climate which was conducive to building relationships with either tutors or colleague-managers, neither in terms of the setting for the event, nor the processes which took place during the programme. Most successful companies are well aware of the importance of such scene setting, and although it may have been introduced initially because it facilitated women managers, this 'user-friendly' atmosphere has been found to be equally valuable to men.

### The voice – ways of talking

The third characteristic which must be understood is women's way of talking. There are a number of studies about the way women talk and behave in conversations which it is useful to report. For example, women talk less and feel more restricted in mixed-gender groups than in all-female groups (Josefowitz 1984). Sullivan and Buttner (1992) explain that when women do speak, they often use a hesitant and question-posing style.

According to Hall and Sandler (1984), Sandler (1986), Zimmerman and West (1975), men not only talk more than women in mixed-sex groups, but they also interrupt women more frequently than women interrupt men. Men are also seen to exert more control over the topics of conversation (Eakins and Eakins 1978; Hall and Sandler 1984; Sandler 1986; West and Zimmerman 1983; Zimmerman and West 1975).

Belenky *et al.* (1986) report that many women are reared to believe that 'women should be seen and not heard'.

Confusingly, women who talk equally with males are thought to talk more (Spender 1980; Edelsky 1981; Sadker and Sadker 1986).

According to Fishman (1983) and Hirschman (1973), women ask more questions and give more listening responses. Cultural and societal norms reinforce women as listeners rather than speakers according to Belenky *et al.* (1986) and Tannen (1991) has constructed a model of men as lecturers 'report talking' whilst women use talk for rapport.

One of McAuley's (1987) interviewees commented on the way women typically conducted themselves at conferences and in academic debate:

[She] emphasized how women attempt to be supportive of each other in debate. She referred to ways in which comments on each others' papers are designed to be facilitative and constructive . . . She saw the approach of women to intellectual activity as being just as rigorous as that of her male colleagues, but that it came from a different conception of the nature of the pursuit of the scientific debate.

(McAuley 1987: 167)

In order to develop their careers women have to learn to talk in ways that men value so that their feminist ideas will be understood. They therefore not only have to be experts in the 'old' men's studies and in the 'new' feminist ideas on the traditional academic disciplines (Spender 1985). They have also to influence the curriculum and communicate in a manner which is alien to them. It needs to be said that this demands energy and courage because:

the feminist working to change her discipline will not find it advantageous to support and work in Women's Studies. Most probably her participation in Women's Studies will not add to her chances of keeping her job or being promoted.

(Bowles and Duelli Klein 1983: 7)

For women in management the constraints and challenges are particularly grave. Management is still very much a male discipline with all the stereotypical characteristics of excellence being embedded within a male character. As an example, there is currently no journal on the topic of women in management that is acceptable to the recent academic audit system. Women wishing to publish their work in this field must write for one of the 'malestream' journals if their academic rating is to be upheld. Such systems, structures, attitudes and values lead women in management to a state of isolation.

## ISOLATED WOMEN

Given that the key characteristic attributed to women is their valuing of relationships, it seems almost unacceptably cruel that according to many studies, women in management positions (particularly senior management) are lonely (Davidson and Cooper, 1983; Asplund 1988; Marshall 1984; Powell 1988).

Such loneliness leads to their further isolation as 'tokens' of proof of organizational equality, or tokens of proof of women's managerial competence (Marshall 1984; Kantor 1977; Freeman 1990; Scase and Goffee 1989).

Sheppard cites the lack of support from male colleagues, the need for a network of women managers, and a fear of being identified with the other women who are in clerical positions and of lower organizational status as a recurrent theme from her respondents, managerial women, in a variety of contexts (Sheppard 1992: 139–57).

The experience of loneliness at work can also raise a number of further uncomfortable roles or issues for women:

- *boundary-marker* (Marshall 1984; Scase and Goffee 1989) – 'where she treads the men may not wish to go' – 'she represents the outside';
- *extra-visible manager* (Kantor 1977; O'Leary and Johnson 1991) – 'if she puts a foot wrong she'll be noticed';
- *traitor* (O'Leary 1988) – 'other women criticize my differentness [through promotion] from them';
- *martyr* – 'I have to go on and on or I'll let my women colleagues down';
- *one of the boys* (Marshall 1984 and Tanton 1992) – 'I don't have any problems – I feel just like a man';

- *conformist* – 'conformity and the abandonment of critical consciousness are the prices of successful performance in the bureaucratic world' (Ferguson 1984: 29);
- *unrecognized explorer* – 'I have to go where no other women have been but there's little recognition when I get there'.

One obvious way to counteract such isolation is to increase women's presence in organizations. By this I do not mean simply increasing the numbers of women, nor even increasing the numbers of senior women. Increasing women's presence means something more.

Developing women's presence within organizations would be an opportunity to develop brilliance in organizations by maximizing the talents of difference. It would be the creation of a place where women's ways of being would be valued: a culture of flexibility and adaptability and therefore creativity.

Such an organization would find place for women's ways of talking and value the processes of communication as much as content of communication. Explanations and feedback would be regular and rigorous. Discussion across differences (status and gender) would be common. Women would be promoted to senior positions by retaining their own ways of working.

Commitment to working relationships would replace commitment to power relationships. Systems and structures would be reviewed regularly to guard against 'taken for granted' assumptions and the normalizing of patterns of discrimination and prejudice to ensure relationships of support and opportunity.

The isolated raft with its solitary survivor referred to previously would become a flagship within a regatta of brilliance and difference and in order to ensure the successful launch of such a vessel, educators before designing programmes should ask two questions: 'How do we facilitate learning relationships?' and 'How will talk be heard on this course?'

## THE FOUR FACES OF FEMINISM

Early in this paper I referred to different approaches to feminism and the effect that such different approaches would make to educational development. I want to finish by expanding on this briefly.

Feminism does not express a unified discourse or approach. It is now a network or cobweb of attitudes (for example, liberal feminism, socialist-feminism, radical feminism and, latterly, post-structuralist feminism). Any design for women's learning should address the effects of different views of feminism because whether we are aware of them or not, these are the cushions which embed our interpretations and decisions.

Although the topic deserves fuller attention, I want to refer briefly to these different values and the effects they have on our educational practice in order to highlight the complexity of the original question.

To begin with the *liberal feminist* whose view is that the nuclear family is a 'taken-for-granted' stresses:

> women's rights as individuals to choice and self-determination, irrespective of biological sex, and their key political objectives are to create the material conditions necessary to ensure women's self-determination, given her role as mother and primary childcarer.
>
> (Weedon 1991: 16)

In terms of education for women as a result of these values liberal feminists'

> prescription for education, with its stress on access to provision, access to men's knowledge and access to management roles, can be seen to conform to the residual model of adult education . . . [which] treats women by and large as members of a temporarily disadvantaged group who must be handed out compensatory courses in order to permit them to 'catch up' with men.
>
> (Blundell 1992: 203)

A *socialist-feminist* most commonly takes the Marxist or psycho-analytic view that human nature is socially produced:

> They do not prioritize the oppressive structures of capitalism, patriarchy and racism, but see them as discrete forms of oppression which are often interrelated, as in the case of the family . . . Socialist-feminist objectives have profound implications for family life. They include the elimination of the sexual division of labour and the full participation of men in child-rearing etc.
>
> (Weedon 1991: 17–18)

In terms of education the Marxist and socialist feminist would take the view that the school is a key institution in the socialization of gender differences and

> It is probably true to say that by the time women arrive in adult education classes, they have already been thoroughly schooled into an acceptance of their subordinate position in the family and workplace, and that adult education serves only to reinforce that acceptance.
>
> (Blundell 1992: 211)

For the *radical feminist* the biological difference between men and women is seen as the basis of the subordination of women and

> the fundamental form of oppression, prior to class or race, there is no room for the family as it currently exists. Patriarchy is seen as a trans-historical, all-embracing structure, which necessitates women's withdrawal into a separatism from which to develop a new women's culture independent of men. The family is identified as the key instrument in the oppression of women through sexual slavery and forced motherhood.'
>
> (Weedon 1991: 17)

The radical feminists 'are concerned with constructing a new, women-centred knowledge to replace the old male-centred variety; and with getting women into a position where they can distribute and reproduce this knowledge' (Blundell 1992: 206).

The *post-structuralist feminist* is the most difficult to define briefly and instead I give three pointers to distinguish its field:

1 Post-structuralists hold that meaning and subjectivity are constituted within language, rather than language reflecting meaning: 'a feminist poststructuralist must pay full attention to the social and institutional context of textuality in order to address the power relations in everyday life.' (Weedon 1991: 25).

Post-structuralists take the view that an individual is both the subject of and is subjected to the language within which she lives. The individual is not a 'conscious, knowing, unified, rational subject' (Weedon 1991: 21) but is 'a site of disunity and conflict, central to the process of political change and to preserving the status quo' (Weedon, ibid.).

2 Michel Foucault (although he would probably have denied the label post-structuralist) has been heralded by many post-structuralist feminists as offering a way out of the male-engendered academic desert because he pointed out, that 'the

production of knowledge is always bound up with historically specific regimes of power and, therefore, every society produces its own truths which have a normalizing and regulatory function' (McNay 1992: 25).

3 Foucault also 'named the body as the point where power relations are manifest in their most concrete form' (McNay, ibid.: 16) thereby giving a focus to the experience that many women had known but were unable to have recognized.

Post-structuralist feminist educators would begin with a deconstruction of educational philosophy, educational theory, the language of education and the power/knowledge discourse which underpins it. They would recognize multiple models and work through exploration, uncertainty, flexibility. The objective would be 'a beginning all over again', a complete *tabula rasa* in which men's as well as women's knowledge and reality could be incorporated into our management organizations and hence into our educational practice.

## CONCLUSION

I have attempted in this chapter to put together information for those who are interested in the development of women managers, both women and men. Communication with male colleagues is important since according to Kirkham (1985) the majority group does not think much about what it means to be a member of that majority group and there will be little understanding from most men neither of their own privileged position nor of women's experience of work.

I have included details of practice which may influence teachers but I have set these 'micro-techniques' alongside a brief introduction to the more fundamental issue of the philosophy which underpins the education of women in management. Perhaps the next phase should be a more thorough exploration of such feminist philosophies and their relevance to education.

## REFERENCES

Addelson, K. (1983) 'The man of professional wisdom', in S. Harding and M. B. Hintikka (eds) *Discovering Reality*, Dordrecht, Holland/Boston, USA: D. Reidel, 165–86.

Alvesson, M. and Billing, Y. D. (1992) 'Gender and organization: towards a differentiated understanding', *Organization Studies* 13(12), 73–102.

Asplund, G. (1988) *Women Managers – Changing Organizational Cultures*, Chichester: Wiley.

Bardwick, J. (1980) 'The seasons of a woman's life', D. McGuigan (ed.) *Women's Lives: New Theory, Research, and Policy*, Ann Arbor: University of Michigan Center for Continuing Education of Women.

Beetham, M. (1989) in A. Thompson and H. Wilcox (eds) *Teaching Women*, Manchester, Manchester University Press, 180–9.

Belenky, M., Clinchy, B., Goldberger, N. and Tarule, J. (1986) *Women's Ways of Knowing*, New York: Basic Books.

Blundell, S. (1992) 'Gender and the curriculum of adult education', *International Journal of Lifelong Education* 11 (3), 199–216.

Bowen, D., Seltzer, J. and Wilson, J. (1987) 'Dealing with emotions in the classroom', *Organizational Behavior Teaching Review* 12 (2), 1–14.

Bowles, G. and Duelli Klein, R. (1983) *Theories of Women's Studies*, London: Routledge & Kegan Paul.

Burton, C. (1985) *Subordination, Feminism and Social Theory*, Sydney: George Allen & Unwin.

Calas, M. B. and Smircich, L. (1990) 'Rewriting gender into organizational theorizing: directions from feminist perspectives', M. I. Reed and M. D. Hughes (eds), *Rethinking Organization: New Directions in Organizational Research and Analysis*. London: Sage.

Chodorow, N. (1974) 'Family structure and feminine personality', M. Rosaldo and L. Lamphere (eds) *Woman, Culture and Society*, Palo Alto, Cal.: Stanford University Press.

Chodorow, N. (1978) *The Reproduction of Mothering*, Berkeley: University of California Press.

Daly, M. (1973) *Beyond God the Father*, Boston, Mass.: Beacon Press.

Davidson, M. J. and Cooper, C. L. (1983) *Stress and the Woman Manager*, London: Martin Robertson.

Deem, R. (1980) *Schooling for Women's Work*, London: Routledge & Kegan Paul.

Douvan, E. and Adelson, J. (1966) *The Adolescent Experience*, New York: Wiley.

Eakins, B. W. and Eakins, R. G. (1978) *Sex Differences in Communication*, Boston, Mass.: Houghton Mifflin.

Edelsky, C. (1981) 'Who's got the floor?', *Language in Society* 10, 383–421.

Eichenbaum, L. and Orbach, S. (1988) *Between Women*, New York, Viking.

Ferguson, K. (1984) *The Feminist Case Against Bureaucracy*, Philadelphia, Temple University Press.

Fishman, P. M. (1983) 'Interaction: the work women do', B. Thorne, C. Kramarae and N. Henley (eds) *Language, Gender and Society*, Rowley, Mass.: Newbury House, 89–101.

Fowler, H. W. and Fowler, F. G. (1975) (eds) *The Concise Oxford Dictionary, 5th edn*, Oxford: Oxford University Press.

Freeman, S. J. M. (1990) *Managing Lives – Corporate Women and Social Change*, Amherst: University of Massachusetts Press.

Gallos, J. V. (1989) 'Exploring women's development: implications for career theory, practice, and research' M. B. Arthur, D. T. Hall and B. S. Lawrence (eds) *Handbook of Career Theory*, Cambridge: Cambridge University Press.

Gilligan, C. (1982) *In A Different Voice*, Cambridge, Mass.: Harvard University Press.

Hall, R. and Sandler, B. (1982) *The Classroom Climate: A Chilly One for Women?*, Washington, DC: Association of American Colleges.

Hall, R. and Sandler, B. (1984) 'Out of the classroom: a chilly climate for women?', Washington, DC: Association of American Colleges.

Hammond, V. (1992) 'Gender: what does the research tell us?', *Target-Management Development Review* 5 (1), 6–7.

Harvard Assessment Project (1990) *Explorations with Students and Faculty about Teaching, Leading and Student Life*, Cambridge, Mass.: Harvard University Press.

Hirschman, L. (1973) 'Female–male differences in conversational interaction', paper presented at the annual meeting of the Linguistic Society of America, San Diego, CA.

Janssen-Jurreit, M. (1982) *Sexism: The Male Monopoly on History and Thought*, London: Pluto Press.

Jones, K. (1988) 'On authority: or why women are not entitled to speak', I. Diamond and L. Quinby (eds) *Feminism and Foucault: Reflections on Resistance*, Boston: Northeastern University Press, 119–33.

Josefowitz, N. (1984) 'Teaching managerial skills to women: the issues of all-female vs mixed-sex groups', D. M. Hai (ed.) *Women and Men in Organizations: Teacher Strategies*, Washington DC: The Organizational Behavior Teaching Society.

Josselson, R. (1987) *Finding Herself: Pathways to Identity Development in Women*, San Francisco: Jossey-Bass.

Kantor, R. B. (1977) *Men and Women of the Organization*, New York: Basic Books.

Kirkham, K. (1985) 'Managing diversity in organizations: teaching about majority group behavior', presentation at the 12th Annual Organizational Behavior Teaching Conference, University of Virginia.

McAuley, J. (1987) 'Women academics: a case study in inequality', A. Spencer and D. Podmore (eds), *In a Man's World*, London and New York: Tavistock Publications, 158–80.

McClelland, D. (1975) *Power: The Inner Experience*, New York: Irvington.

McNay, L. (1992) *Foucault and Feminism*, Cambridge: Polity Press.

Marshall, J. (1984) *Women Managers: Travellers in a Male World*, Chichester: Wiley.

Miller, J. B. (1976) *Toward a New Psychology of Women*, Boston, Mass.: Beacon.

Nieva, V. and Gutek, B. (1980) 'Sex effects on evaluations', *Academy of Management Review* 5, 267–76.

O'Leary, V. E. (1988) 'Women's relationships with women in the workplace', B. A. Gutek, L. Larwood and A. Stromberg (eds) *Women and Work: An Annual Review* 3, Beverly Hills, Ca.: Sage, 189–213.

O'Leary, V. E. and Johnson, J. L. (1991) 'Steep ladder, lonely climb', *Women in Management, Review and Abstracts* 6 (5), 10–16.

Powell, G. N. (1988) *Women and Men in Management*, London: Sage.

Sadker, M. and Sadker, D. (1986) 'Sexism in the classroom: from grade school to graduate school', *Phi Delta Kappa* 67, 7.

Sandler, B. (1986) *The Campus Climate Revisited: Chilly for Women Faculty, Administrators, and Graduate Students*, Washington, DC: Association of American Colleges.

Scase, R. and Goffee, R. (1989) 'Women in management – towards a research agenda', paper presented at British Academy of Management Conference, September.

Schaef, A. (1981) *Women's Reality: An Emerging Female System in a White Male Society*, Minneapolis, Minn: Winston.

Sheppard, D. (1992) 'Women managers' perceptions of gender and organizational life', A. J. Mills and P. Tancred (eds) *Gendering Organizational Analysis*, London: Sage.

Shotter, J. and Logan, J. (1988) 'The pervasiveness of patriarchy: on finding a different voice', M. M. Gergen (ed.) *Feminist Thought and the Structure of Knowledge*, New York: New York University Press, 69–86.

Spender, D. (1980) *Man-Made Language*, London: Routledge.

Spender, D. (1985) *Men's Studies Modified*, Oxford: Pergamon Press.

Sternglanz, S. and Lyberger-Ficek, S. (1977) 'Sex differences in student-teacher interactions in the college classroom', *Sex Roles* 3(4), 345–52.

Sullivan, S. E. and Buttner, E. H. (1992) 'Changing more than the plumbing: integrating women and gender differences into management and organizational behavior courses', *Journal of Management Education* 16(1), 76–81.

Tannen, D. (1991) *You Just Don't Understand*, London: Virago.

Tanton, M. (1992) 'Developing authenticity in management development programmes', *Women in Management Review* 4, 20–6.

Velsor, E. and Hughes, M. (1990) *Gender Differences in the Development of Managers: How Women Managers Learn from Experience*, Greensboro, North Carolina: Centre for Creative Leadership.

Weedon, C. (1991) *Feminist Practice and Poststructuralist Theory*, Oxford: Basil Blackwell.

West, C. and Zimmerman, D. H. (1983) 'Small insults: a study of interruptions in cross-sex conversations between unacquainted persons', in B. Thorne, C. Kramarae and N. Henley (eds) *Language, Gender and Society*, Rowley Mass.: Newbury House, 103–17.

Wheatcroft, M. (1970) *The Revolution of British Management Education*, London: Pitman.

Zimmerman, D. and West, C. (1975) 'Sex roles, interruptions and silences in conversation', B. Thorne and N. Henley (eds) *Language and Sex: Differences and Dominance*, Rowley, Mass.: Newbury House, 105–29.

# Chapter 2

# Waiting for fish to grow feet!
## Removing organizational barriers to women's entry into leadership positions

*Beverly Alimo-Metcalfe*

If I had US $10 dollars for each time someone had remarked to me over the last ten years that there cannot be that many problems for women in Britain, given that until recently it had a female Prime Minister, I would have a wardrobe of exclusive clothes. Sadly, this is not the case. In fact Britain, if not her ex-Prime Minister, should be shuddering with shame after reading the most recent report of the Equal Opportunities Commission, which includes statistics relating to the employment of women and men in Britain (EOC 1991a).

The report states that, despite the fact that women comprise a higher proportion of the work-force in Britain than in any other European Community country except Denmark, the earnings gap between women and men is wider, with women in Britain earning an average of 77 per cent of their male counterparts' salaries. This earnings gap is up to 10 per cent wider than in the rest of the European Community.

The EOC report and a recent article on 'European Women in Business and Management' (Alimo-Metcalfe and Wedderburn-Tate 1993) also contain the now-familiar tables of statistics showing how under-represented women are in senior managerial positions, and I am well aware that there is little to celebrate in other European countries.

But I refuse to be fatalistic, and I also see an opportunity provided by the growing concern of organizations for the problems that will be presented by demographic changes and drastic reductions in the numbers of young people in the work-force.

Large British organizations now realize how much they *need* to attract and retain women, but I fear that without a serious and critical examination of their selection and assessment procedures, little will change with respect to women's representation in either non-traditional female occupations, or senior management positions. Moreover, the irony is that research indicates that in order to pull organizations through the turbulence that the future promises, organizations will need to recognize, encourage and nurture those qualities and skills in their leaders that are more strongly associated with females than males.

## ASSESSMENT PROCEDURES: HOW MIGHT THEY DISCRIMINATE AGAINST WOMEN?

Assessment of potential has always been a complex procedure for those who insist on using techniques that are respectably reliable and valid. Unfortunately, the most popular selection technique, namely the selection interview, is highly susceptible to the influence of stereotyping and prejudice on the part of the assessor. Both the instrument of assessment, and the final assessor are one and the same. For women interviewed by men there is substantial opportunity for discrimination, particularly when applying for out-of-role jobs (for example, management, engineering, computing). Assessors have notions of the 'ideal' candidate who often bears a striking resemblance to themselves.

Whilst assessment theory suggests that assessors should have a clear idea in their head as to the skills and traits required for the job, and then use the selection interview as a means of 'objectively' collecting relevant data in order to inform the final decision, research suggests that when it comes to interviews of women applying for traditionally-male jobs, type of dress, physical attractiveness and even the wearing of lipstick significantly affect the assessor's decision (Iles and Robertson 1988).

Fortunately, organizations are becoming increasingly aware of the poor reputation that the selection interview has, and many are attempting to adopt more systematic and rigorous approaches to selection and assessment. As these become more sophisticated and complex my concern increases, since any potential discrimination becomes enmeshed in the complexity and terminology of the process.

My concern centres on the three major aspects of the assessment process:

the criteria
the techniques/instruments
the assessors

## THE CRITERIA

The essential first stage of an assessment process whether for selection, promotion or career placement, is determining the dimensions against which one will make assessments. In order to identify these dimensions one seeks out job 'experts', individuals who are very familiar with the job and its demands. Clearly, this often includes current jobholders and usually their bosses.

These people describe the qualities and skills that are involved and give examples of effective and ineffective behaviours, and these are later used to establish a job profile against which candidates are assessed. In the case of senior management jobs, these providers of criteria are highly likely to be male.

Much has emerged from the feminist literature on organizational theory, on the subject of men's dominant position in society, describing the resultant construction of institutions created in their own image, which utilize patriarchal power that devalues women (for example, Calas and Smircich 1989, 1990). Most organizational theorists have omitted any mention of women, including, for example, Weber (1947), and 'central elements of bureaucracy (which organizational design has taken for granted) are founded on assumptions about the subordination of women' (Martin 1990: 2). Implicit assumptions of the value of certain concepts have been summarized as:

| Valued | Devalued |
|---|---|
| Objective | Subjective |
| Rational | Irrational |
| Expert | Untrained |
| Abstract | Case-by-case |
| Dehumanized | Humane |
| Detached | Involved |
| Impersonal | Personal |
| Unemotional | Emotional |
| Authoritarian | Nurturant |
| Unequal | Egalitarian |
| Graceless | With grace |
| Unsympathetic | Sympathetic |
| Untouched by gratitude | Moved by gratitude |

As Martin (1990) remarks: 'Inspection of these columns reveals the hidden assumptions; the devalued characteristics are all, traditionally, more likely to be associated with women than with men' (p. 12).

Models of career progression reflect the male pattern of continuous employment, high workload which frequently overlaps into family life, age requirements – that can only be achieved without interruptions for child-rearing – and freedom to be geographically mobile (NEDO/RIPA 1990).

There is evidence that there are distinctions between masculine and feminine management styles (for example, Loden 1985). The former emphasizes control, use of power to dominate others and separatedness of personal and work issues; the latter emphasizes integration, process, communication, co-operation, openness and contact.

Clearly only obtaining data on criteria from males is more likely to perpetuate the male model of management at the expense of devaluing the female.

It is interesting to note that studies of excellence in management, namely John Kotter's (1982) study of general managers and Peters and Waterman's (1982) best seller *In Search of Excellence* emphasize views of management that appear at times directly to contradict the textbook or 'espoused theories' of management with an emphasis on task rather than process. A later section will cite reasons that make the distinction even more important.

## THE TECHNIQUES

### The selection interview

This has already been criticized for its susceptibility to bias, much of which is due to the lack of rigour in basing questions on carefully-established job analyses, but also because the interviewer's judgements are affected by his/her perceptions of the subject and their 'suitability' for a particular job. In fact, the technique has been significantly improved with respect to its validity in the model called the behavioural/situational interview (Latham *et al.* 1980). Based on thorough job analyses, interviews are structured to standardize the procedure as far as is feasible. Questions are asked of candidates with respect to how they have behaved, or would behave, in specific situations, and responses are scored against a behaviour-based rating scale. Such improvements in criteria identification and data-gathering are to be welcomed. However, let us hope that as much attention is devoted to the creation of the behaviourally-based rating scale. For example, do the situations include a range of traditionally male-or-female-type activities, such as those relating strongly to task, versus those relating strongly to people or process dimensions? Were the variety of possible situations sought from both female and male 'job experts'?

The importance of these additional questions will be explained more fully in the next section on the assessment centre methodology.

**The assessment centre**

This methodology has attracted considerable growth in popularity over the last two decades (Robertson and Makin 1986). The reason has been the increasing realization that a technique with a high validity-rating is most likely to be the most cost-effective (for example, Cook 1988). In addition it has a variety of potential uses. It can be used for recruitment, selection, promotion, identifying individuals for fast-track career programmes, and for identifying development needs and strengths. It can also be used as a vehicle for 'selling' the organization to what will become an increasingly 'precious' group – high-flying graduates. It therefore provides entry into the most cosseted organizational positions. However, for women it may present hidden obstacles.

Assessment centre exercises reflect the commonly-held 'espoused' views of managerial activity, portraying leadership more in terms of directing, controlling, decision-making and informing, rather than Kotter's findings that some of the key characteristics related to interpersonal skills of creating co-operative networks, of walking-the-patch, and seeking information rather than telling. One may be forgiven for considering such characteristics as more typically practised by women than men.

Relating this to the design of an assessment centre, which since they are so costly are inevitably only a few days long at most, it is difficult to create opportunities for such complex interpersonal behaviour to be witnessed, with the result that it is perhaps not surprising that greater attention is often given to the achievements of a task rather than a process which necessarily requires individuals to work together over a much longer period of time.

The actual methodology of the assessment centre, bringing

participants together in groups, can place women at a distinct disadvantage. Since assessment centres are so expensive they are typically used for elite groups in organizations or for making senior management appointments. This means that frequently women participants are in the minority. There is substantial evidence from the group dynamics literature that being a minority member of a group imposes pressures on the individual which inhibit her/ his potential contribution (Rosenberg *et al.* 1955). Eskilson and Wiley (1976) found in an experimental situation that the sex ratio (that is, proportion of females to males, or vice versa) of problem-solving groups significantly affects the rate of leadership activity performed by males and females. Female and male leaders exhibited similar and high rates of leadership when in groups comprised exclusively of members of their own sex. However, female leadership activity dropped drastically in male-dominant groups even in those cases where the female was the formal leader of the group.

A field study which attempted directly to test Kanter's theory, that being in a numerical minority in an unbalanced sex ratio group (that is, unequal numbers of females and males) would inhibit performance in a group (Finigan 1982), found that the results confirmed the hypothesis for three sex ratio situations; male-dominant groups, female-dominant groups, and those in which there were equal numbers of both sexes. However, under-achievement was particularly pronounced for females in male-dominant groups. The reasons suggested for this state might be due to what has been called 'feminine modesty effect' identified by Gould and Stone (1982). Finigan (1982) offers three possible reasons why individuals in a minority group appeared to be inhibited from contributing to group discussion. These are:

1 Techniques whereby members of the majority sex inhibit contributions of the token by restricting opportunities for input. Males tend to ask fewer, and only specific kinds of questions of females. Also they most frequently asked women for information rather than opinions. Consequently, the majority sex may be seen to direct the nature of the minority response.

2 A second source of inhibition might stem from the minority's perception of the illegitimacy of their contribution; thus, feeling that they are 'outside' may result in self-imposed inhibitions by

the females. An extension of the 'modesty effect' (Gould and Stone 1982) may also be exacerbating the situation.

3 Inhibition due to cultural gender-role norms. This relates to the experiences of females in male-dominant groups of not being valued for their contributions as highly as the male members.

Male members of female-dominant groups contributed actively to the leadership roles in the group and their contributions were valued as highly as those of female members. Finigan interprets this as due to the high status attributed to males overcoming any stigma associated with being a minority member.

An interesting study by Megargee (1969) paired males and females who rated themselves high on a dominance scale with males and females who rated themselves low, using combinations of mixed and same-sex dyads. Males who were 'high dominants' adopted the leader role in the majority of cases, regardless of their partner's gender. However 'high dominant' women paired with 'low dominant' men assumed the leader role only 20 per cent of the time. This study has been repeated by other researchers who obtained similar findings. However, a more recent study argued that the results were a consequence of the type of task. Carbonell (1984) argued that when a 'feminine' as opposed to a 'masculine' task was used, the 'high dominant' individual always led. She concluded that while dominance is likely to predict leadership roles in same-sex pairs, the nature of the task can influence sex-role conflict.

In view of these findings how would one describe the content of managerial assessment centres with respect to the gendering of tasks? Presumably by definition they are mainly male-gendered.

## THE ASSESSORS

As has been stated earlier, it is far more likely to be the case that males will be assessors for jobs offering entry to senior management. What then are the perceptions that men hold of women with respect to their suitability for management?

## WHAT DO MEN THINK OF WOMEN?

In 1975 Broverman et al. noted that men held a stereotyped perception of women as:

dependent
passive
non-competitive
illogical
less competent
less objective

They also felt that it is desirable for women to be less ambitious. Other studies have found that males tend to underestimate the importance of motivators for females. These included:

desire for responsibility
advancement
challenging work
a voice in decision-making

Virginia Schein (1973, 1975) investigated the existence, or lack thereof, of a relationship between sex-role stereotypes and perceived requisite personal characteristics for middle managers. She asked 300 male middle managers and 167 female middle managers to complete an index of 92 descriptive items and rate each on a five-point scale as to whether they were or were not characteristic of (a) women in general; (b) men in general; (c) successful middle managers. Schein found highly-significant similarities between the ratings the males gave of men and of managers ($r=0.62$), but a mean zero rating in resemblance between their ratings of women and managers ($r=0.06$). Amongst the women sampled there was also a highly-significant resemblance between their ratings of men and managers ($r=0.54$); and whilst there was also a significant resemblance between their ratings of women and managers, it was significantly smaller than that between men and managers ($r=0.30$). She concluded that 'successful middle managers are perceived to possess these characteristics, attitudes and temperaments more commonly ascribed to men in general than to women in general' – in other words, 'think manager, equals think male'. Schein (1989) and colleagues wondered whether equal opportunities laws and affirmative action requirements had modified perceptions some fifteen years after the original research (Brenner *et al.* 1989). Although noting that as only 2 per cent of women held senior management positions in the US at that time, there was little evidence of any positive outcomes, whilst for the females their perceptions had changed markedly in that there was little difference in the degree of resemblance between their perceptions of men and successful middle managers ($r=0.59$), and women and successful middle managers ($r=0.52$), the men's attitudes were remarkably similar to those of the earlier sample. Perhaps even more depressing are the two most recent studies using Schein's descriptive index with US management students (Schein and Mueller 1990 – see Table 2.1) and with British and German management students – the data may be seen as depressing, particularly for the German sample.

Table 2.1 German, British and US intra-class coefficients, managerial sex-typing

| | Sample | | |
| Source | German | British | US |
| --- | --- | --- | --- |
| **Males** | | | |
| Managers and men | 0.74** | 0.67** | 0.70** |
| Managers and women | –0.04 | 0.02 | 0.11 |
| **Females** | | | |
| Managers and men | 0.66** | 0.60** | 0.51** |
| Managers and women | 0.19* | 0.31** | 0.43** |

Source: Schein and Mueller 1990.
\* <0.05.
\*\* <0.01.

As the researchers state, 'the results reveal that males in all three countries perceive successful middle managers as possessing the characteristics, attitudes and temperaments more commonly ascribed to men in general than to women in general. Within each country there were large and significant resemblances between the ratings of men and managers and mean zero resemblances between the ratings of women and managers' (Schein and Mueller 1990: 9).

If these samples of management students are representative of the views of future senior managers, there is little basis for hope that managerial sex typing will change in the foreseeable future.

One hopeful sign may, however, be gleaned from a separate British study of female and male managers (Alban Metcalfe and Nicholson 1984). This study, which comprised 1,497 male and 805 female mainly middle managers, obtained data from a self-concept scale. The managers were asked to describe themselves at work, and in general. It contained fewer items than Schein's descriptive index, fifteen in this instance, some of which bore a close resemblance to Schein's items. These data, which are reported more extensively elsewhere (Alban Metcalfe 1987), suggested that, controlling for age effects, female and male managers in Britain perceive themselves at work very similarly. Only three significant differences emerged; these were that the women felt more tense and perceived themselves as more intellectual than the men perceived themselves, and the women were also less likely to keep their feelings to themselves. Otherwise they perceived themselves as equally creative, forceful, confident, ambitious, controlling, trusting, happy, fulfilled, optimistic, contented with themselves, and equally disliking uncertainty.

Whilst this British study cannot be directly compared with Schein's studies, it offers data on perceptions of one's self, as opposed to women, men, or managers in general. And whilst it might be interpreted by some as offering some hopeful findings it may also be interpreted as providing more evidence of how women have to adapt to the expectations of male-dominant cultures.

## APPRAISAL

Organizations' appraisal systems vary considerably, none the less, irrespective of whether they are primarily evaluative or developmental, since they are concerned with reviewing performance they contain an element of assessment. They are also considered to be an important method for ensuring the creation of personal development plans and ensuring that they are monitored (for example, Fletcher and Williams 1985). Research by Corby (1982) highlighted the different quality of appraisals for women and men in the British Civil Service. Whilst the men generally speaking received critical feedback, the women were far more likely to receive innocuous non-specific criticism if indeed they received any. This suggested the discomfort male bosses felt in relation to female subordinates. Since the quality of information exchanged in the appraisal was crucial for development purposes, and indeed is used either intentionally or unintentionally for the purposes of making recommendations for promotion, it is a procedure not to be overlooked when investigating organizational procedures in women's career development. Corby's study of promotion in the Civil Service (Corby 1982) drew attention to the relationship between such practices and her findings that women were far less likely to be identified and placed in highly visible mainstream general management positions.

The author recently conducted a survey for the Management Executive of the British National Health Service (IHSM 1991; Alimo-Metcalfe 1992a), which is the largest employer of women in Europe, employing nearly one million women, but does not have a proud track record with respect to equal opportunities (Alimo-Metcalfe 1991; Equal Opportunities 1991b). The research looked at the effect of introducing appraisal some six years after the introduction of general management, and three years after the introduction of performance-related pay (PRP). Among the analyses were some relating to gender (Alimo-Metcalfe 1992b). It was interesting to note that of the five bands used to rate general and senior managers for PRP, there were significantly smaller proportions of women in the two highest bands, but significantly larger proportions of women than men in the third and fourth bands. Of the general managers, though the sample of women was small, 27 per cent of males were given the highest rating but only 13 per cent of female general managers shared the same high assessment.

With respect to the process of the interview there were significant gender differences. Women found the interview significantly more difficult than men, with respect to:

talking freely about what they wanted to discuss;
discussing their relationship with their appraisor;
giving feedback to their appraisor;
identifying their areas of strength.

Clearly the difficulties faced by women in the interview will affect not only their satisfaction in their job but also their performance and opportunities for development.

A study by Thomas (1987) of anonymous narrative accounts of appraisals of the job performance of female and male US naval officers, investigated whether gender influences the judgements of the job behaviour of individuals. Her results demonstrated that different words were used to evaluate the performance of female and male line officers. The differences were with respect to both the content of the evaluations and also the accuracy of information imparted, and suggested among other things that women were 'less competent, logical, and mature', and their performance appeared to 'warrant fewer recommendations and only nebulous praise'. She concludes:

This research focused on women in a single organization, but there are implications for all women who compete with men in the professions, particularly those dominated by men. Schein (1978) identified several probable consequences of stereotyping on women's careers in management. First, if women are viewed as being more sensitive to the needs of others than are men, they are likely to be placed in staff versus line positions. As a result, they are less likely to acquire the skills and knowledge of the upwardly mobile. Second, if supervisors feel they lack the traits valued among managers and leaders (i.e., ambition, competitiveness, aggressiveness), women will be denied developmental tasks and their promotional potential will suffer. Third, women will be excluded from the organizational power network and thus be limited in their ability to function as effective managers.

(Thomas 1987: 107)

This paper stated at the beginning that women may have particular and important contributions for modern organizations. Why?

## MODERN ORGANIZATIONS – IN SHAPE FOR THE FUTURE?

Much has been written recently about the need to drastically change the shape, structure, organization and climate of modern organizations.

The old bureaucratic monoliths with military-type, rigid hierarchies, multi-layered and which place people in tight boxes in specific functions that prevent cross-specialism and cross-functional boundaries, are dying or dead. To succeed in times of unparalleled change organizations need to be slimmer and flatter, decentralized, creative fluid shapes ever adapting to new challenges and demands. The buzz word is the 'learning organization'. To benefit from experience the organization must create a culture which supports risk-taking and encourages reflection, analysis and learning from mistakes. A learning organization is one that 'continuously transforms itself in a process reciprocally linked to the development of its members' (Burgoyne 1991). Such organizations will require very different leaders from those who controlled the structures of the past. The old-style leader, referred to in some sources as the 'heroic leader' will find himself (most are male) redundant, out of touch, and abandoned. The traditional model of manager as 'expert' with all the answers directing others, exploiting power by considerable use of status and authority, and who demands conformity and obedience, will become a relic to be replaced by the post-heroic, transformational leader who leads by exciting enthusiasm in employees to share and own her/his vision.

S/he influences staff by establishing a high level of personal credibility and encourages openness, consultation and collaboration within the cross-functional teams in the organization. As a transformational leader s/he turns the organization away from old habits to new, recognizing the need for revitalization. Bradford and Cohen (1984) talk about the post-heroic leader whose primary role is as developer of staff, asking how problems can be solved in ways that further develop her/his subordinates' commitment and capabilities.

The major change in the organizational culture is from previous emphasis on creating a 'task' culture to creating a 'being' culture which reflects the importance of values such as co-operation, belonging, caring, responsibilities and receptivity.

One might be forgiven for responding with some degree of cynicism to this rather rosy image of the modern organization; however, there now exists evidence that such organizations do exist. A recent study jointly sponsored by Ashridge Management College and the Foundation for Management Education sought companies in the UK, other European countries, and North America which were cited as examples of innovative or excellent practice (Barnham *et al.* 1988). The account of what characterized them bore a strong resemblance to the description given above. They were certainly decentralized and flatter using multi-skilled project teams to work on complex tasks. Most notable in the Scandinavian companies was the emphasis on openness and trust, informal communication and 'a suspicion of paper and structure'; absence of hierarchy and open access to managers and staff throughout the organization. Participative management was crucial with considerable emphasis on the belief in the potential of each individual and a commitment to supporting and nurturing growth and development of staff. Two quotes in particular from the study come to mind: 'Developing people's capabilities is the key to survival' (Shell manager) and 'One of the key skills for managers in the future will be people management skills: the capacity to form and develop people' (ICI manager). 'Doing' and 'being' skills were celebrated and, perhaps most surprisingly to many traditional managers reading the report, 'love' was mentioned. An Electrolux manager stated 'People must work with their heart. You have to love them. The only way to empower people and develop consciousness is if you believe in it' (Barnham *et al.* 1988: 28).

What were the characteristics sought for 'doing' and 'being' skills and techniques?

## 'DOING' AND 'BEING'

Cunningham (1987) provides a framework which distinguishes between action-oriented management skills and techniques – the 'doing' – and the more qualitative aspects of management, that is, the attitudes, perceptions and values with which the manager approaches her or his job – the 'being'.

It seems that, although 'doing' skills and techniques still need to be acquired by the manager of the future, just as many, if not more, of the desired characteristics suggested by interviewees actually refer to 'being' factors. The following patterns of 'doing' and 'being' characteristics emerge from the analysis:

### Doing

- Good technical specialist skills in own area
- Analytical skills and ability to think things through clearly
- Financial skills and understanding
- Marketing skills and techniques
- Planning skills
- Project management skills and techniques
- Information technology skills – how to acquire, select and understand the information one needs
- Decision-making skills – how to sell ideas and gain consensus.

Whilst the skills and techniques above are considered to be important, virtually all respondents emphasized that 'doing' is dependent upon people, and that a wide range of 'people skills' will be required for management in the future.

These skills include:

- Communicating
- Negotiating
- Motivating
- Listening (not doing all the talking)
- Involving people at all levels
- Counselling and appraisal skills
- Delegation

So what has this to do with women and leadership? Few would disagree that the 'being' skills are qualities more closely associated with women than men, but to avoid simple stereotyping evidence should be sought.

Two recent studies in particular provide such evidence. The first by Judy Rosener (1990) surveyed prominent female leaders in diverse organizations in the USA using members of the *International Women's Forum* as a sample, and a comparable sample of men. Included in her findings was the following: women are more likely than men to use transformational leadership, namely, motivating others by transforming their self-interest into goals of the organization. Women are also much more likely than men to use power based on charisma, track record, and contacts (personal power) as opposed to power based on organizational position, title, and the ability to reward and punish (structural power).

The second study was conducted in the UK by Susan Vinnicombe (1987) at Cranfield School of Management. She used an instrument which integrated Mintzberg's notion of the three major sets of managerial roles of interpersonal, informational, and decisional, with the Myers-Briggs type indicator to create a taxonomy of management styles which were described as 'traditionalist', 'trouble shooter/negotiator', 'catalyst', and 'visionary'. The most significant difference was the marked lack of 'traditionalists' among the female managers. Whereas 57 per cent of the male managers tended to be 'traditionalists', there was an average of only 26 per cent amongst the females. 'In general, significantly more women managers were "visionaries" and "catalysts"' and she adds

It is useful to reflect on what Bates and Kiersey have to say about the effectiveness of 'catalysts' in organizations: 'Catalysts are excellent in public relations and shine as organizational spokespersons since they work well with all types of people.

They can sell the organization to its customers and can make employees feel good about themselves and the organisation. They are excellent in the top positions if given free reign to manage, but they may rebel and become disloyal if they perceive themselves as having too many constraints. They can easily nurture a following which is loyal to them personally rather than to the organization. They may have authority-figure problems and thus may unintentionally undermine the organization if they see authorities as being in conflict with their personal values and belief systems.'

This may relate to Steiner's observation that women tend to define power differently, that is, as the ability to use their own talents and to control their own lives. 'In working with people, they are much more collaborative and co-operative and far less hierarchical and authoritative than men.'

(Vinnicombe 1987: 20)

Perhaps it is not surprising then that men who may have a preference for the 'traditionalist' style feel uncomfortable when faced by women who are 'visionaries' or 'catalysts'? Worse still if they are assessing women's performance.


## CONCLUSION

It has been suggested in this paper that modern processes of assessment which may be used for selection, promotion, spotting potential for fast-track programmes, and for regular discussion of performance which inform decisions in career opportunities, may well operate against women's chances and choices of career development.

It was further argued that as such techniques become more complex, potential discrimination may become eclipsed from view. At a time when the need for new leaders requires qualities frequently associated with, and found to be more common amongst, females, organizations must scrutinize their practices. This is particularly true given Rosener's conclusions from her recent study of leadership, namely that:

[Women] are succeeding because of and not in spite of certain characteristics generally considered to be 'feminine' and inappropriate in leaders. The women's success shows that a non-traditional leadership style is well suited to the conditions of some work environments and can increase an organisation's chances of surviving in an uncertain world.

(Rosener 1990: 120)

However, it is not difficult to see that many men who cannot modify their old stereotyped views, or who do not wish to relinquish their power in the current situation, will feel threatened. The challenge therefore becomes even greater.

In the words of a recent title on a related subject 'It's like waiting for fish to grow feet!'

## REFERENCES

Alban Metcalfe, B. (1987) 'Male and female managers: an analysis of biographical and self-concept data', *Work and Stress* 1 (3), 207–19.

Alban Metcalfe, B. and Nicholson, N. (1984) *The Career Development of British Managers*, London: British Institute of Management Foundation.

Alimo-Metcalfe, B. (1991) 'What a waste! Women in the NHS', special issue of *Women in Management, Review and Abstracts* entitled 'Breaking the glass ceiling' 6 (5), 17–24.

Alimo-Metcalfe, B. (1992a) 'Appraisal appraised: lessons from a national survey in the NHS', *Local Government Management Journal* autumn, 18–19.

Alimo-Metcalfe, B. (1992b) 'Gender and appraisal: findings from a national survey of managers in the British National Health Service', paper presented to the 'Global Research on Women and Management Conference', 21–3 October, Carleton University, Ottawa, Canada.

Alimo-Metcalfe, B. and Wedderburn-Tate, C. (1993) 'Women in business in the UK', M. J. Davidson and C. L. Cooper (eds) *European Women in Business and Management*, London: Paul Chapman Publishing.

Barnham, K., Fraser, J. and Heath, L. (1988) *Management For the Future*, Ashridge Management Research Group and the Foundation for Management Education.

Bradford, D. L. and Cohen, A. R. (1984) *Managing for Excellence*, Chichester: John Wiley.

Brenner, O. C., Tomkiewicz, J. and Schein, V. E. (1989) 'The relationship between sex role stereotypes and requisite management characteristics revisited, *Academy of Management Journal* 32, 662–9.

Broverman, I. K., Vogel, R., Broverman, D. M., Clarkson, F. E. and Rosenkrantz, P. S. (1975) 'Sex-role stereotypes: a current appraisal', M. T. Schuch Mednick, S. S. Tangri, and L. W. Hoffman (eds) *Women and Achievement: Social and Motivational Analyses*, New York: Hemisphere Publishing.

Burgoyne, J. (1991) 'The management of management learning', paper presented at the 1991 *Annual Conference of the National Association of Health Service Personnel Officers: 'Meeting the Challenge'*, 20–2 September, Bristol, UK.

Calas, M. B. and Smircich, L. (1989) 'Using the "F" word: feminist theories and the social consequences of organizational research', paper presented at the *Academy of Management Meeting*, August, Washington, DC.

Calas, M. B. and Smircich, L. (1990) 'Rewriting gender into organizational theorizing: directions from feminist perspectives', M. I. Reed and M. D. Hughes (eds) *Rethinking Organization: New Directions in Organizational Research and Analysis*, London: Sage.

Carbonell, J. L. (1984) 'Sex roles and leadership revisited', *Journal of Applied Psychology* 69, 44–9.

Cook, M. (1988) *Personnel Selection and Productivity*, Chichester, UK: John Wiley.

Corby, S. (1982) *Equal Opportunities for Women in the Civil Service*, London: HMSO.

Cunningham, I. (1987) 'Patterns of managing for the future', paper presented to *Positioning Managers for the Future Conference*, January, Ashridge Management College.

Equal Opportunities Commission (EOC) (1991a) *Women and Men in Britain 1991*, London HMSO.

Equal Opportunities Commission (EOC) (1991b) *Equality Management: Women's Employment in the NHS*, Manchester: EOC.

Eskilson, M. G. and Wiley, A. (1976) 'Sex composition and leadership in small groups', *Sociometry* 39, 183–94.

Finigan, M. (1982) 'The effects of token representation on participants in small decision-making groups', *Economic and Industrial Democracy* 3, 531–50.

Fletcher, C. and Williams, R. (1985) *Performance Appraisal and Career Development*, London: Hutchinson.

Gould, R. J. and Stone, C. G. (1982) 'The "feminine modesty" effect: a self-presentational interpretation of sex differences in causal attribution', *Personality and Social Psychology Bulletin* 8 (3), 477–85.

Iles, P. A. and Robertson, I. T. (1988) 'Getting in, getting on, and looking good: physical attractiveness, gender and selection decisions, *Guidance and Assessment Review* 4 (3), 6–8.

Institute of Health Service Management (IHSM) (1991) *Individual Performance Review in the NHS: A Report by the IHSM for the NHS Management Executive*, London: Institute of Health Services Management.

Kotter, J. P. (1982) *The General Managers*, London: The Free Press.

Latham, G. P., Saari, L. M., Pursell, E. D. and Campion, M. A. (1980) 'The situational interview', *Journal of Applied Psychology* 65, 422–47.

Loden, M. (1985) *Feminine Leadership or How to Succeed in Business Without Being One of the Boys*, New York: Times Books.

Martin, J. (1990) 'Re-reading Weber: searching for feminist alternatives to bureaucracy', paper presented at the *Annual Meeting of the Academy of Management*, August, San Francisco.

Megargee, E. I. (1969) 'Influence of sex roles on the manifestation of leadership', *Journal of Applied Psychology* 53, 377–82.

National Economic Development Office/Royal Institute of Public Administration (NEDO/RIPA) (1990) *Women Managers: The Untapped Resource*, London: Kogan Page.

Peters, T. and Waterman, R. H. (1982) *In Search of Excellence*, London: Harper & Row.

Robertson, I. and Makin, P. J. (1986), 'Management and selection in Britain: a survey and critique', *Journal of Occupational Psychology* 59 (1), 45–58.

Rosenberg, S., Erlich, D. E. and Berkowitz, L. (1955) 'Some effects of varying combinations of group members on groups' performance measures and leadership behaviour', *Journal of Abnormal and Social Psychology* 51, 195–213.

Rosener, J. (1990) 'Ways women lead', *Harvard Business Review* 68, 119–25.

Schein, V. E. (1973) 'The relationship between sex-role stereotypes and requisite management characteristics', *Journal of Applied Psychology* 57 (2), 95–100.

Schein, V. E. (1975) 'Relationships between sex-role stereotypes and requisite management characteristics among female managers', *Journal of Applied Psychology* 60 (3), 340–4.

Schein, V. E. (1978) 'Sex-role stereotyping, ability and performance: prior research and new directions', *Personnel Psychology* 31, 259–68.

Schein, V. E. (1989) 'Sex-role stereotypes and requisite management characteristics past, present and future', paper presented at the *Current Research on Women in Management Conference*, September 24–6, Queen's University, Ontario, Canada.

Schein, V. E. and Mueller, R. (1990) 'Sex-role stereotyping and requisite management characteristics: a cross-cultural look', paper presented at the *22nd International Congress of Applied Psychology*, 22–7 July, Kyoto, Japan.

Thomas, P. J. (1987) 'Appraising the performance of women: gender and the naval officer', in B. A. Gutek and L. Larwood (eds) *Women's Career Development*, London: Sage.

Vinnicombe, S.(1987) 'What exactly are the differences in male and female working styles?' *Women in Management Review* 3 (1), 13–21.

Weber, M. (1947) *The Theory of Social and Economic Organization*, translated and edited by A. M. Henderson and T. Parsons, New York: Oxford University Press.

# Chapter 3

# Women's development programmes – 'No, we're not colour consultants!'

*Joanna Knight and Sue Pritchard*

There were fourteen women, twelve participants and ourselves as facilitators on each of the programmes described in this chapter. The quality of personal disclosure and sharing, and the attendant risk in so doing, was high. We used lovely country house hotels to reinforce our message that this was important work, worthy of investment, and to indicate that we wanted the participants to feel comfortable, safe and that we thought they were worth valuing. On one occasion in the hotel lounge, some bemused men, observing us working together, asked, 'Are they colour consultants?'

## INTRODUCTION

Much is being written and discussed about development programmes for women, in response to the increasingly urgent need for businesses to make full use of women's potential in the workforce. Many interesting and exciting courses are being offered for women, building on the experience of the last twenty years of Equal Opportunities work. Often, such courses are run outside businesses – or run in-house but by external consultants.

This chapter is an account of women's development programmes within Thorn Home Electronics International and an exploration of the issues around their setting up and implementation. The programmes were initiated and implemented from *inside* the organization and we want to explain the effect that this work has had, both at an organizational and at a personal level.

The fact that these kinds of programmes have been taking place for some years as part of the 'first wave' of women's development does not negate their importance to us. The very notion of a 'second wave' may imply that the time for such work is over, that it is somehow passé. But, in our experience, the need for this type of women-only development work is as strong as ever. It is our belief that most organizations pay mere lip-service to the notion of equality for women. While chief executives and directors make grand proclamations through mission statements and publicity-conscious new initiatives, the experience of the majority of women changes little. Despite the fact that by 1986 women represented 44.5 per cent of the total labour force (Coyle 1988) they are still to be found in the lower echelons of most organizations and senior women managers remain a rarity. Indeed, the evidence suggests that vertical segregation of women from men is increasing. Sadly, in our view, the proportion of full-time top managerial positions held by women has declined during the last ten years, falling from 9.7 per cent to 5.8 per cent, and only 15.2 per cent of middle and junior management jobs are held by women (Watson 1989). It is in this context that we are convinced more than ever that women-only work is relevant and important – both for individuals *and* for organizations.

We are writing from *our* perspective, believing that 'all writing is autobiographical in some sense' (Marshall 1984). This paper tells the story of our work in one organization and the impact that this work has had on us. Equally, though, we believe that our story has a wider relevance – for management and organization development practitioners, managers and women in work.

## THE CONTEXT

We both joined Thorn in 1986 – Joanna as an internal consultant working across a number of operating companies within Thorn Home Electronics International (THEI), but based at their newly-established development centre, and Sue as management development manager in a division of one of the operating companies. It was a time of great upheaval – a fundamental restructuring was taking place across the business resulting in several reorganizations and large numbers of redundancies. These structural changes were underpinned by a desire to achieve a significant cultural shift from a paternalistic, hierarchical, insular, technically-biased organization to a 'people-driven, marketing-led, results-orientated, customer-focused' (THEI mission statement) decentralized and outward-looking collection of businesses. This new *enabling* culture was perceived to incorporate what have been called more feminine styles of management – based on co-operative, facilitative, team-based and creative ways of working. Bringing about this new culture was seen as not merely congruent with, but instrumental in achieving the business vision and specific objectives.

Integral to the reorganization and the striving towards an enabling culture was a new commitment to management and organization development (indeed our appointments reflected this). As management and organization development specialists, we were very much involved in the development and implementation of the strategy and policies designed to progress the structural and cultural changes. Much was made and talked of the company mission statement and the new values underpinning this. The language of organization change became the new currency and was reflected in activities such as regular 'time-outs' for the boards of the operating companies and team-building throughout the businesses, and an emphasis on communication, quality, training and development.

A prominent feature of this new culture was the shift in focus away from the technical and service functions of the businesses towards the customer-focused showroom functions. Raw data taken from the businesses at the time of these early changes illustrates an almost 50–50 split between men and women employed; but closer examination revealed a divide between the traditionally high status, male-dominated service side and the low status, low-paid, female-dominated showroom side. The overwhelming majority of senior line managers throughout the business had, historically, been drawn from the service function.

The structural changes were greeted with greater or lesser degrees of optimism. Particular attention was paid by staff and junior managers to getting 'evidence' confirming – or more often not confirming – behaviours on the part of senior staff which were perceived to be congruent with the desired culture. For example, in meetings, staff paid a disproportionate amount of attention to verifying whether senior managers were *really* being open and inviting participation in decision-making, or whether they were merely pretending to share power whilst behaving in familiar autocratic ways. The whole process of change was protracted and often painful; for some the changes represented new opportunities, but many managers clearly felt that they were 'losers' in this new scheme of things.

All managers, whether supportive of, or threatened by, the changes (or both!), needed help in bringing about this new working environment. As management and organization development specialists we worked with them, identifying and responding to business needs which were tightly prescribed by the new culture. New training and development initiatives had to be firmly anchored in business policy and direction. At a philosophical level this is laudable: at a practical level, it resulted in some important initiatives being talked out or obstructed. This was because many senior decision-makers were, in our view, motivated by fear and discomfort, and were therefore seeking to negate or undermine the organization change or were simply unsure how to respond.

All this had many implications for the development of women managers. They were required to handle the growing scope of their role as showroom managers within an uncertain and changing environment; facilitate the changing relationships between service and showroom managers, particularly as they tended to have more highly-developed interpersonal skills; manage the career development of junior and middle managers (including their own) in a flattening organization structure, and so on. In addition, other women had been brought in as functional specialists to support the organization change, and were now working at middle management levels, as well as those who benefited from the increased importance now attached to their showroom experience. With no or little support coming from their bosses, and working in what was still seen as a 'macho' organization, many of these women needed help in coping with their new responsibilities.

We were both especially aware of – and increasingly provoked by – the incongruence between the espoused business vision and how this translated into reality in relation to women's development, promotion and employment. This was especially galling at a time when it looked as though opportunities for women had a real chance to be improved. The general view of women across the businesses is indicated by what was a commonly used term, 'the girls in the shops', which certainly does not suggest strong, assertive and competent managers! In addition, those women working at senior levels (including ourselves) often found themselves isolated, their views devalued or ignored by their male colleagues. Indeed, in the light of the mission statement and business needs, Sue had introduced, with some difficulty and little support, a pilot programme of outdoor development for women managers within the division where she worked. When the event proved to be a success, the process was 'commandeered' by local managers and became a reward for (largely) male managers in return for good performance. The plan to provide space for women to deal with the issues in being a woman manager in this particular division was thus thwarted.

We were determined to address these issues. Moreover, we were concerned to pay attention to women's needs in other aspects of the business, such as marketing strategy, flexible working arrangements and working hours, and so on. However, our motivation for women's development work did not stem solely from a moral imperative to offer equal opportunities for all. We also held the view that businesses limited themselves by marginalizing their women managers. By harnessing the potential of *everyone* in the workplace, we firmly believed that THEI could become more competitive, profitable, healthy and vibrant. This was very much in keeping with the mood and language in the mission statement and we were keen to apply the philosophy to that disadvantaged group, women.

Furthermore, as women managers ourselves, and as developers, we felt we should act on our own advice – and take responsibility for initiating a process in which we believed, without waiting for permission or approval. This was unlike our normal operating procedure, as we have indicated earlier. But the history of failure in the protracted negotiations normally required to get major human resource initiatives off the ground motivated us to try another approach. Similarly, in another organization, Miranda Lowe *et al.* shared our experience that:

> it is essential for us as a team of trainers to be proactive in making our own diagnosis of the key issues facing Sun Alliance and to take leadership in meeting these needs.
>
> (Lowe *et al.* 1988: 228)

We decided to take such leadership. We also felt encouraged by Roger Plant's assertion (Plant 1987) that change begins with the individual and, as such, anyone can attempt to exert their power and influence over an organization.

Our introduction of women's development programmes was low key in that we did not do massive marketing but it was strategically sound. For example, we canvassed support through established networks and found a small number of significant champions, people in respected and visible positions who explicitly supported us and what we were trying to do. We used their names liberally to give weight to the programme and to counter potential opposition. The first programme was marketed to the organization via a personal letter to all senior managers and human resource and training and development specialists. It was also included as an addendum to the main development centre brochure, accompanied by a brief explanation as to why a women-only programme was on offer. The response was encouraging. Not only were sufficient numbers nominated for the advertised programme, but a waiting list was created giving rise to strong arguments for continuing the process. The first programme ran in October 1989 and was judged to be a successful and rewarding event by the participants, their line managers and ourselves.

## THE PROGRAMME

### Objectives

We had two main objectives, one of which focused on the development of individual women and another which focused on wider organizational issues (for we hoped this would prove to be the start of a long-term and far-reaching process). These were:

To offer a process of empowerment for women managers to help them:

- identify and value their skills and strengths;
- develop a wider range of choices in managing their interpersonal relationships;
- learn/develop assertive skills and the ability to handle aggressive/ passive behaviours;
- set stretching and attainable goals for their work and their personal lives;
- enhance their self-confidence and sense of self-worth;

To raise the profile of women's needs and development in Thorn, as a prelude to further action.

### Participants

The programme was aimed at women with some degree of managerial experience either of specialist functions or as line managers. In practice, we drew a broad cross-section of women from the young high-flying graduate to the long-serving and experienced manager with no higher education.

### Outline

In order to meet our objectives for the programme, we felt it was essential to begin by raising participants' self-awareness, since we believe that understanding where you are now is a vital starting point to moving forward. These women needed an opportunity to consider the past and current influences on their lives, which had helped shape them, in order to determine whether these were still appropriate in the light of what they decided they wanted for themselves. We were concerned not to be prescriptive, by implying that one path in life was somehow preferable to or better than another, but to allow women space to consider their futures and to decide what was really important to them. Then, in order to help them to realize the goals which they identified for themselves, we felt it was important that these women develop sound assertive behaviours. Finally, we wanted to help them start moving towards the realization of their goals in practical ways, with enhanced self-esteem and a strong sense of what they could achieve. Throughout, emphasis was given to both personal and professional life and goals, and to our inner landscapes as well as our outer achievements. An outline of the programme is given in Table 3.1.

Participants continued to meet and to work with us after each programme, at their request, and according to the needs of the group. Some groups continued to meet for a year after the original programme had taken place.

Throughout the programme we worked substantially on participants' own issues, which included:

- lack of confidence/assertiveness;
- women managing men/older people;
- being women in a male world;

*Table 3.1* An outline of the programme

**Introductions**
- Ourselves and participants
- Why have a women-only programme?
- Outline of content and style

**Theme: 'Raising Self-Awareness'**
- What does it mean to be a woman in business?
- Identification of what we want from this programme
- Raising our self-awareness by:
  - looking at our self-image: what it is and what we'd like it to be
  - examining the influences on this
  - developing confidence in our abilities

**Theme: 'Developing Practical Skills'**
- What does it mean to be assertive?
  - values and beliefs about ourselves and others on which assertiveness is based
  - understanding and learning assertive behaviour skills
  - self-influence – 'internal dialogues' and saying 'no'
- Practical workshops: examining 'real live' issues and practising good assertive behaviours, using role play or rehearsal

**Theme: 'Moving Forward'**
- What are the fears holding us back – and overcoming them
- Giving and receiving feedback
  - sharing perceptions of self and others
- Setting goals and achieving them – sharing personal commitment to make changes
- Ways forward:
  - for this group
  - for other groups/individuals
- Re-entry issues and how to manage these for ourselves/others
- 'Messages by hand' – a closing technique to give some final feedback and leave a memento of the event

*Follow-up*
Themes were revisited and developed during the follow-up days. The long-term and ongoing nature of the work was thus emphasized. In keeping with the philosophy of the programme, the frequency and duration of these were determined by the participants. With certain groups we continued to meet for a year after the initial programme.

- negotiation/influencing skills;
- handling uncertainty;
- handling tensions between family and work;
- sexuality in work;
- managing upwards;
- career planning;
- managing change.

**Participants' stories**

In order to illustrate some of the results of the programme we want to share the stories of three participants. One woman had initially been reluctant to attend the programme at this particular point in her life, as she was concerned about her ability to deal with the issues which were then facing her. Her husband had just left her, after many years of marriage, and she was waiting for his decision as to whether or not this was to be a permanent arrangement. By using the programme to look at what she really wanted for herself, she started to take charge of her life again. While her situation did not change initially, she started to feel positive and to value herself. Over time, she decided not to take her husband back, coped well with the additional stress and pain of her mother's death, got a new job within the same company and started to develop new work and social relationships. She commented that she felt 'stronger inside' and more confident in herself after attending the programme.

One of the older women who attended the programme said that she felt intimidated by her director and unsure of whether she was valued at work. Her self-esteem was low. She was helped during the programme to have the confidence and the skill to discuss any difficult (in her perception) work relationships with the other parties involved. She found that her fears had been groundless and she received the confirmation of her abilities which she had so badly needed. Her self-confidence increased and she reported that she was becoming more receptive to hearing good feedback, rather than focusing, as she had done previously, on what she thought were her weaknesses.

Another younger woman, who had recently joined the company in a functional position, felt somewhat frightened of using her managerial authority and consequently felt that her staff perceived her as nice, but ineffectual. She was helped to see that she could be both strong and likeable (qualities which she had previously perceived as incompatible) and to have more confidence in her own abilities, by acting out the management of some difficult situations with her staff. She was consequently promoted and found herself with the strength to support others through a difficult period of redundancy and uncertainty. She reported increased confidence in her own management style, to which others were now responding positively.

These are just a few examples of participants' stories, but they serve to illustrate some important points. Generally, women reported that they felt stronger and more confident and more able to be themselves at work as a result of attending the programme. They were particularly appreciative of how much they had gained from each other, finding that other women's issues typically 'spoke' to them too.

### Process

As the participants themselves indicated, the way in which we worked together had a profound impact on the programme itself. As facilitators, we were concerned to allow women to determine what was important to them, rather than attempting to put yet more expectations and constraints on them. We therefore encouraged participants to exercise choice about what they wanted to work on and how. We also took time to build good relationships which acted as a useful means of support to women engaged in tough and challenging work on themselves. Some key features of our way of working are outlined in Figure 3.1.

### Developments and diversions

Four programmes ran over a period of three years against a background of increasing restructuring activity and poor performance on the part of the rental businesses within THEI – traditionally one of Thorn EMI's key profit generators. Training budgets came increasingly under threat although, due to the success of the programme, it continued to receive funding against the odds. The reorganization of September 1989 affected us particularly and following this the development centre was closed in order to reduce costs. Joanna took the opportunity to establish her own consultancy business and Sue was promoted to management development manager of the newly-formed Thorn UK Rentals. We continued to collaborate on training and develop-

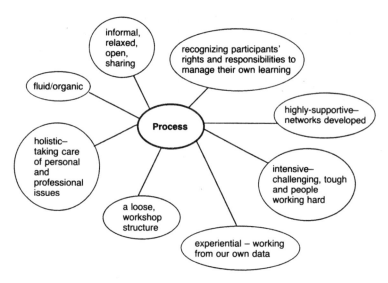

*Figure 3.1*   Key features in the way we worked

ment activity – particularly the women's development programme, with Joanna now participating as an external consultant.

In April 1991 a further significant restructuring took place – and the movement towards a decentralized, empowering corporate culture ended with the businesses being streamlined and pulled back to strong central control. The training culture reverted to a traditional 'back to basics' approach, laying much emphasis on taught courses of narrow management skills. When the opportunity arose Sue took redundancy and set up her consultancy business.

However, some eighteen months after these events, development for women has resurfaced, albeit in a slightly different style, and it is encouraging that, even against a background of poor business performance, a national recession and a 'back to basics' training plan, the impetus of women's development has persisted.

## THE IMPACT ON THE ORGANIZATION

On the whole there was a powerful positive effect on those who participated in the programme and, in turn, on those within their sphere of influence (see Table 3.2). Participants themselves and their bosses reported many changes for the better as a result of attending the programmes. Sometimes these benefits were not immediately apparent to the organization. In a number of cases participants made positive decisions to leave their jobs and move on. We felt that if this was what the participant wanted then it was far better to allow them to explore ways of leaving 'well'; and from the organizational perspective, a message may be drawn from the fact that numbers of able women did, indeed, choose to leave.

*Table 3.2* Positive and negative impacts on participants and the organization

| Positive impacts | Negative impacts |
| --- | --- |
| – participants themselves rated the programme highly<br>– the techniques and philosophy spread to participants' colleagues and teams<br>– we saw and heard of many examples of women taking control, making changes and being promoted<br>– the 'good press' created a (sometimes grudging) acceptance of the programme<br>– increased nominations meant maintaining funding for the work against a backdrop of severe cut-backs in training budgets<br>– we received an increasing number of requests from men who wanted to work on similar issues<br>– the programmes reinforced the message that development isn't simply about training courses and that working holistically does impact on participants' work lives<br>– some colleagues who had been opposed to the work (including women) changed their views as a result of the feedback<br>– the work developed a strong reputation and became highly regarded across the whole of Thorn | – a number of personal disappointments – some who we had thought of as allies didn't support us as we had hoped<br>– the initiative was tolerated rather than supported in the early stages<br>– it became a salve for the organization conscience – 'we *are* doing something on women's issues' – and allowed many to avoid addressing the myriad other issues around women's position in work, for example, terms and conditions, career development, sexual harassment at work and so on<br>– as success grew, criticism went underground and always behind our backs! This added to the personal disappointment we faced and didn't allow us to tackle criticisms head on<br>– even against obvious and acclaimed successes, we had to keep justifying the work and our continued funding<br>– its continuity always felt tenuous – the usual criteria applied to successful training events seemed to be suspended in this case |

A subtle side-effect of running these programmes was that the profile of what we are calling 'holistic' development work, that is, where the focus of attention is on the individual's personal as well as professional self, was raised on the training agenda. Whilst work of this nature was on offer elsewhere (and both of us were involved in other examples of this), it tended to be concentrated at more senior levels. The very typical employment profile of women in THEI meant that we were working with women across hierarchies and with a high proportion of women in functional and advisory roles, including trainers. They appreciated, on the whole, the style and values of the process they experienced on the programme and adopted some of the techniques, where appropriate, within their own work. Women line managers also began to question the traditional type of course work they had hitherto experienced. For example, an increase in the number of learner-centred programmes became apparent. This spilled over into many working environments and we received an increasing number of requests from men who wished to work on their own issues in a similar way.

These positive messages meant that our work with women developed a strong reputation across the Thorn group, and some people who had been initially unconvinced as to the value of women-only work changed their views. Even in an increasingly rigorous financial climate, funding was preserved for these programmes, despite the fact that virtually all other training had been suspended.

Other initiatives too began to materialize: our (private) agenda – to raise the profile of women's development throughout the businesses – seemed to be bearing fruit. For example, a programme to encourage women returners was set up; a Thorn EMI conference, at director level, on the employment of women took place in June 1990; and a small number of women (Sue included) managed to negotiate for themselves more 'women-friendly' employment packages, taking into account their family choices.

## LEARNING AND DEVELOPMENT

### At a personal level

One of the richest sources of inspiration and encouragement came from the participants themselves. They shared with us insights into their lives illustrating tremendous power, courage, competence and commitment to their work. We were repeatedly impressed with the calibre of the women attending the programmes. Often they came with the fairly typical problems of low self-esteem and poor self-image and, frequently, tales of difficult and un-helpful work environments. Despite this, we found evidence of tremendous strength and skill in the strategies used by women to survive in what was a particularly stressful and complex business at that time.

The level of openness and willingness to share quite personal and intimate experiences and feelings was frequently astonishing and inspiring. It gave us insights into the difficult and complex situations in which most women were operating. Sometimes these situations simply smacked of poor management ability on the part of their boss. At other times it seemed that these women were victims of sexual discrimination or sexual harassment either from their bosses, peers or staff. For example, a woman managing in a predominantly-male environment for the first time, attempting to assert her authority, was subjected to comments that she was over-reacting because it was 'the wrong time of the month'. This type of comment was not uncommon and there were numerous accounts of unwanted personal attention from men.

All this reinforced our commitment to continue to work with women on their development and to raise women's issues on the organization agenda at the most senior levels. Indeed, hearing about so many moving experiences provoked a 'righteous anger' in us and reinforced our resolve in the face of difficult circumstances.

Whilst we knew that this work would not necessarily be easy to do in this organization, we were surprised and disappointed at just how tough it was at times. Even in the face of repeated and public successes we got little support or encouragement from senior managers – unless such support appeared politically prudent! Time and again we were dependent on our own commitment and that of a small number of individuals who supported us. The importance of networks and support structures here cannot be over-emphasized; we were fortunate in that by working together we were able to sustain each other, and we also sought support from our other networks both inside and outside the organization.

Working with participants on such profound issues of a personal and professional nature impacted on us both. We were also undergoing many changes in our own lives. The programmes prompted us to think about how we defined success in our own lives, and what that might mean in terms of careers and families. Both of us produced our first offspring during the life of these programmes and we have firmly established our own consultancy businesses, believing that this gives us increased control over what we work on, how we work and the way in which our work integrates with our personal and family lives.

### At a professional level

Our view that organizations limit their growth by the profligate waste of their human resource was reinforced by the calibre of the women attending the programme. It was our view then that many able and competent women languished in posts below their capacity because they did not fit the narrow organization view of the 'manager' – male, white, technically experienced, aged 30–40 and, surprisingly, *not* educated to degree standard.

More ominous perhaps is our view that the organization would not come to grips with the fact that it had to change at a fundamental level to recognize and accommodate the wealth of talent in the diverse range of people it employed. As organization development specialists it was challenging for us to discover just how obdurate an organization and the individuals within it can become when they do not want to face unpalatable 'truths'. Even the (quite toothless) Equal Opportunity policy, stated in the employee handbook, was potentially limiting and over simplistic. It tended to foster two poles of opinion that *restricted* opportunity for women: either 'We *do* offer opportunities for women – they just don't take them', or 'We recognize that women have different needs and responsibilities – so they'd better not try and tackle the tough management stuff too'.

We were reminded that we have to work with the holders of power – in this case male executives – to increase their awareness and, importantly, to change their behaviour. We observed that for many the shift from statements of policy to real concrete changes in practice was just too tough to make. We found ourselves faced with a familiar paradox: should we 'hang fire' until all the precursors to successful change management were in place – commitment from senior managers, appropriate structural and procedural policies, a holistic view of management and organization development? But, as we indicated earlier, we had already experienced the inertia which this striving for organizational perfection could produce. We therefore chose to carry on working with women at an individual level – all the time paying attention to the organization they came from and to which they returned – believing that at the very least we were making some difference to the individuals who attended these programmes. However, we felt then and still do that attention must be paid to systemic, structural discrimination, policies, procedures, attitudes and behaviours, at specific and organization levels, as well as to the personal development of participants on a programme.

We are left with many questions on which we reflect in the light of our experiences. Our 'big question', the one which we debate frequently, is about how we manage the frustration and tension in continuing with slow but sure incremental learning and change (acknowledged as being most likely to succeed) and our wish to confront the discrepancies between words and actions and see large-scale change soon. How can we strive towards radical ends through pragmatic means? We are aware that there are no easy answers, but we retain our commitment to bringing about a situation where women's contribution to and participation in the work-force is fully valued.

Particularly pertinent at the moment is our observation that, whilst many organizations espouse the value of developing women, in times of economic hardship it becomes an optional extra, an overhead to be cut back. We wonder how committed to change they really are. It is curious that an apparently fundamental and widely-accepted social shift is still subject to the vagaries of the year-end accounts. Perhaps it is only those organizations which truly internalize the need for a radical shift in attitudes which will reap the benefits of the 'second wave' of development work with women.

## REFERENCES

Coyle, A. (1988) 'Continuity and change: women in paid work', in A. Coyle and J. Skinner (eds) *Women and Work: Positive Action for Change*, London: Macmillan Education.

Lowe, M., Silverosa, C. and Woollard, J. (1988) 'Developing women leaders in a traditional insurance company' in 'Lessons from Success', Journal of the Association of Management Education and Development (MEAD) Special Issue, 19 (3).

Marshall, J. (1984) *Women Managers: Travellers in a Male World*, Chichester: John Wiley.
Plant, R. (1987) *Managing Change and Making It Stick*, London: Fontana/Collins.
Watson, S. (1989) *Winning Women*, London: Weidenfeld & Nicolson.

# Chapter 4

# Women bosses: Counting the changes or changes that count

*Virginia E. O'Leary and Maureen M. Ryan*

## INTRODUCTION

It has been six years since the US Department of Labor reported that, for the first time in history, more than 50 per cent of adult women were in the labour force. It is estimated that by the year 2000 women's participation rate in the labour force will reach 63 per cent (US Department of Commerce 1991). Paralleling the feminization of the US work-force is the reduction in the number of men, especially white men, available to assume positions in upper management. This increase in available women, coupled with the decline in available men suitable for managerial roles, mandates a better understanding of women managers, particularly as it is estimated that between the years 1990 and 2005 the US will need 600,000 new managers and top executives (US Department of Labor 1991). In addition, as women workers constitute an increasingly large proportion of the labour force in the roles of both subordinates and superiors, the need to understand how the dynamics of women's relationships at work are affected by issues of gender increases as well.

A review of the proportion of women in executive, managerial, and administrative positions in the United States reveals a rapid increase. According to the Department of Labor, the percentage of women managers has increased from 16 per cent in 1970 to a current level of approximately 40 per cent (Aburdene and Naisbitt 1992). Most of these 'new' women managers are in entry-level managerial positions. They swell the ranks of lower management, likely to encounter the glass ceiling without even advancing into middle management (Kleiman 1992). The height of the glass ceiling has been found to be much lower than first thought. The glass ceiling has been used 'to describe a barrier so subtle that it is transparent, yet so strong that it prevents women and minorities from moving up the management hierarchy' (Morrison and Von Glinow 1990: 200).

For example, one study by the US Department of Labor investigating the employment and promotion practices of nine Fortune 500 companies found only 16.9 per cent of the 31,184 managers at the nine firms were women (Sugawara 1991). Of the 4,491 executive-level managers (defined as assistant vice-president and higher) only 6.6 per cent were women. Most women who were in management were working in areas of human resources, research or administration, as opposed to 'fast-track' positions that lead to rapid promotion and executive status (Sugawara 1991). According to the Feminist Majority Foundation (1991), of the 6,502 corporate officers in Fortune 500 at the level of vice-president or higher, only 175 were women.

Although these changes have begun to erode the stereotypes of the corporate woman as low in status, and relegated to clerical or support positions, they have not been as profound as the media imply. The introduction of women into upper management has produced some positive change. However, there have also been adverse effects. For example, women have gained entrance into previously male-dominated areas at the cost of isolation and loneliness (O'Leary and Johnson 1991).

It has long been held as conventional wisdom that real institutional change would be possible if women occupied a greater proportion of corporate director and management jobs and owned more companies (Gordon 1991). While it is indisputable that some women in power have made more than cosmetic changes in the workplace, it is unclear whether substantive transformations of the workplace can be obtained through simply increasing the proportion of women in upper management.

To the extent that substantive institutional changes in the workplace have not occurred, the workplace will continue to be characterized by the maintenance of negative relationships, stemming from inappropriate expectations in the absence of clear-cut norms regulating women's relationships (O'Leary 1988).

The purpose of this chapter is to document the changes that have occurred over the last decade in the roles of women working as bosses, and to explore the reactions of their subordinates, both female and male, in the context of assessing the significance of these changes for future generations of powerful women.

Despite the plethora of popular literature on women's working relationships, little is empirically known about the quality and the dynamics of these relationships (see O'Leary 1988, for a review). Much of the early writing on women bosses is not a statement about women bosses *per se*, but rather a reflection of sex-role stereotypes operating in organizational systems. Female sex-role stereotypes – inaccurate or partially inaccurate beliefs about women – provide the foundation upon which prevailing notions of women's inability to manage or lead effectively as executives were laid. The depiction of women, defined according to traditional sex-stereotypic traits, led inevitably to the conclusion that women did not possess the requisite characteristics to manage outside the home (cf. Schein 1973, 1975).

## SEX-ROLE STEREOTYPES

Social scientists define stereotypes as sets 'of beliefs about the personal attributes of a group of people' (Ashmore and Del Boca 1981: 16). In order to make sense of the social environment, perceivers group people into categories and associate attributes with those categories. Sometimes these attributes or traits are generalized from direct experience, at other times they are based on culturally transmitted information, because they refer to groups with which perceivers have little direct experience. Therefore, bias inevitably enters the process by which people's observations become represented in sex-stereotypic beliefs.

Belief formation regarding groups of people is a continuous process, occurring with little if any monitoring or conscious awareness (Eagly 1989). It most often occurs when any given characteristic of an individual is particularly obvious or salient – such as sex or race. Given the salience of categorization by gender (Grady 1977), it seems almost inevitable that people are perceived in terms of sex-role stereotypes.

### 'That's no lady, that's my boss'

The stereotypical view of the woman boss is as someone for whom no one, man or woman, wants to work (cf. Bowman *et al.* 1965; Feber *et al.* 1979; Kahn and Crosby 1985; Sutton and Moore 1985). Fuelling the negative image of women executives are a number of trade books such as *Women versus Women: The Uncivil Business*

*War* (Madden 1987), *Woman to Woman: From Sabotage to Support* (Briles 1987), *Success and Betrayal: The Crisis of Women in Corporate America* (Hardesty and Jacobs 1986), and *How to Work for a Woman Boss* (Bern 1987). The latter details 'over 280 coping strategies that will help you to adjust to this new phenomenon in the workplace' (p. 3). The book contains seven self-administered questionnaires designed to assist those whose bosses are women in identifying their bosses' management styles as 'nonlisteners, power brokers, nonmanagement managers, or hesitant decision-makers, etc.'. Clearly, the underlying premise is that working for a woman is problematic, a situation with which one must learn to cope.

Historically, women bosses have been viewed as being more like men than men themselves. Schein (1973, 1975) assessed the requisite characteristics perceived as determining managerial success. As the profiles of male and manager overlapped to a much greater extent than either did with the female profile, Schein (ibid.) concluded that 'to think manager was to think male'.

Nieva and Gutek (1981) suggest that the price extracted from women even peripherally included in a predominantly male work group includes a willingness to turn against other women, to ignore disparaging remarks about women, and to contribute to the derogation of other women. The label 'queen bee' has been applied to such women who have achieved professional success and are antifeminist (Staines *et al.* 1973).

Contrary to some of the early literature suggesting that women's relationships in the workplace are negative and unhealthy (Goldberg 1968; for a review see Nieva and Gutek 1981; Staines *et al.* 1973), more recent evidence suggests that these relationships can be positive and productive (O'Leary and Ickovics 1987, 1990; Slade 1984).

## Some good news

O'Leary and Ickovics (1990) interviewed twenty-three women secretaries working for women supervisors at a prestigious women's academic institution. Each was asked about a variety of aspects of her job and the job environment, her boss and her relationships with boss and co-workers. Despite the many objectively negative aspects inherent in the secretaries' descriptions of their jobs (for example, low pay and lack of opportunity for promotion, lack of prestige and challenge, limited decision-making power), the majority of them were positively disposed toward their overall work experiences. This positive disposition was often expressed in terms of interpersonal relationships, and the secretary-boss dyad was characterized by co-operation, communication, support, and mutual respect. The secretaries liked and admired their bosses in large part because they exhibited both sensitivity and competence – characteristics of a successful manager (Rosener 1990).

Other studies of female secretaries and their bosses provide further confirming evidence that women who work for women like both their bosses and their jobs. In one of the few empirical studies of the secretaries' perceptions of their bosses that has been conducted, Stratham (1985) found that women supervisors, in contrast to men, were seen as more competent (for example, more hard-working and thorough) and more considerate (for example, more sensitive and appreciative) and more likely to treat their secretaries as equals and inquire about their career goals.

## NEW LEADERS AND WAYS OF LEADING

Recently, Schein and her colleagues (Brenner *et al.* 1989) replicated their classic study in which they demonstrated that 'to think manager is [was] to think male'. The objective was to determine if there were any changes in middle managers' perceptions of women and men bosses. The results indicated that associations between sex-role stereotypes and requisite management characteristics has not diminished over the years for male managers' ratings. However, the passage of time has affected the female managers. In 1989 women managers rated the degree of resemblance between 'men' and 'manager' as identical to 'women' and 'manager'.

Today, women managers see some of the traits necessary for successful managerial performance as more likely to be held by women and some as more likely to be held by men (Brenner *et al.* 1989). Perhaps this is due to the confluence of a number of factors: women's personal investment in a management career, their personal experience as effective managers, and an expanded definition of successful managerial traits that encompasses feminine traits.

Rosener (1990) conducted a survey of the International Women's Forum, whose membership consists of prominent women leaders across the world. Rosener suggests that these women consitute a second generation of executive women who are 'succeeding because of – not in spite of – certain characteristics generally considered to be "feminine" and inappropriate in leaders' (p. 120).

The survey indicated that the leadership style of the women respondents emphasized interpersonal skill – as opposed to organizational stature – and having subordinates transform their own self-interest to correspond with the interests and goals of the organization. This new approach of women leaders is often referred to as 'participatory management' or 'transformational leadership'.

Transformational leadership is deeply rooted in women's socialization experience and represents an adaptive response on the behalf of women who 'entered the business world . . . in positions consistent with the roles they played at home' (Rosener 1990: 124). Rosener further states that given the fact that most women have lacked formal authority over others and control over resources, by default women had to find alternative means to accomplish their work. Women have chosen the 'path of least resistance' and transferred 'behaviors that were natural and/or socially acceptable for them' to the workplace (p. 124). By utilizing their unique socialization as a 'survival tactic' in the work world, women have shifted behaviours that were once construed as liabilities into assets.

### The big picture and women's ways of leading

The changing composition of top management and recent interest in women's distinctive leadership style can be viewed against the backdrop of larger changes in corporate America, such as consolidation and globalization of corporations (Fryxell and Lerner 1989). Western countries are increasingly being challenged by the productivity and industrial efficiency of Japan and other Pacific Rim countries (Aktouf 1992). In response to this threat, many of the leading proponents of management and organizational theory have called for a total re-evaluation of traditional western management. Aktouf (1992) argues that traditional management is not prepared for this change, due to management's lack of conceptual and theoretical means to grasp the magnitude of the coming upheavals.

Pierce and Dunham (1978) found that formalization and centralization (organizational structures traditionally preferred by men) were significantly and negatively associated with employee descriptions of the amount of autonomy, identity, feedback, and variety in their jobs. In contrast, employees in flat organizational hierarchies report more satisfaction with their responsibilities than employees in tall hierarchies (Gannon and Paine 1974).

The clear need to abandon management based on authority and on order imposed by the organization has resulted in a trend towards flattened organizations and 'centrarchies' versus hierarchies. Managerial practices that permit the development of the employee's desire to belong and to use their intelligence to serve the organization are currently favoured (Aktouf 1992). Recently, women have been identified as potentially better suited than men to run the companies of the nineties, which require transformational leadership. Helgasen (1990), in her book *The Female Advantage*, suggests that women's superior management instincts should earn them the designation of 'the new Japanese'.

Numerous articles in business-related journals echo Helgasen's sentiment that women executives bring more than just equal skill to those of their male colleagues. Women leadership is often associated with enhanced negotiating skills, a talent for consensus building, and a more balanced world view (Johnson 1990). Rosener (1990) does, however, warn against linking transformational leadership directly to being female and encourages organizations to expand their definition of effective leadership.

**Are the new ways of leading really new?**

While women executives and their abilities are presently seen in a more favourable light, managerial behaviours continue to be viewed in a dichotomous fashion according to gender. The work of Rosener and others supports the perpetuation of gender distinctions. Post-structuralist feminist theorists, however, contend that as long as organizational practices 'construct the identities of men and women very differently', women will be 'cast as marginalized actors who participate in only certain dimensions of organizational life' (Mumby and Putnam 1992: 466). Sonnenfeld, the head of the Centre for Leadership and Career Studies at Emory business school, says 'there's a scary orthodoxy about this new wave of feminism. It dictates that all women should behave in certain ways' (cited in Fierman 1990: 116). He suggests that women executives are adrift in a new sea of sex-role stereotypes. Fierman (1990) characterizes the work on women's leadership styles as 'new quick-

and-easy distinctions' of questionable merit. For example, the distinction between men as hoarders of information and women as natural disseminators of it has not been empirically demonstrated.

Aburdene and Naisbitt (1992) pose the following scenario:

> suppose that after a string of male bosses, your new supervisor is a woman. The trend toward a Women's Leadership style is one you will want to know about to help decide what she expects of you.
>
> (Aburdene and Naisbitt 1992: xiv)

This is reminiscent of Bern's (1987) *How to Work for a Woman Boss*, in which she identifies how to 'adjust to this new phenomenon [women bosses] in the workplace' (p. 3). The assertion that women are ideally suited to flattened organizations by virtue of 'natural management skills' – once applied solely to families and households – transfer[ed] smoothly to the corporate environment (Huggins, cited in Johnson 1990: 96) has generated significant controversy.

It is clear that when men incorporate in to their characteristically (male) behavioural repertoire behaviours that stress co-operation and participation (female), they are rewarded for their flexibility (cf. O'Leary and Donoghue 1978). It is less clear that women enjoy a parallel experience, particularly when their constituents are women.

## WHEN THE BOSS IS A WOMAN

There is some evidence to suggest that when women supervise other women they are required to demonstrate the basis of their authority. In a series of interviews conducted with young women in a co-operative secretarial training programme O'Leary (1987) found evidence that the evaluative criteria women use to evaluate women bosses may be distinctly different from those used to evaluate men. For example, women reported making immediate judgements about women supervisors to whom they were assigned to work for a week based on feelings of competition. In contrast, their evaluations of men supervisors took longer to make and were not based on competitive feelings about tangential issues such as mode of dress and grooming. Style of dress and grooming, as well as age, provided a symbolic means of assuring that the power differential between the two women was justified.

Among women, status differentials are difficult to discern. Women bosses should be older, more formally or professionally attired, and more severely groomed than their women secretaries. When they do not meet these criteria it is not clear that they have 'the right' to exert authority over a similar, same-sex peer. When the boss is a man there is no doubt about who has the higher status, regardless of dress or demeanour. Needless to say, traditional sex-role stereotypes reinforce the assumption that women and power are incompatible.

When women do behave atypically by gaining power and prestige their performance is subjected to scrutiny by observers who assume that their deeds are not those of an individual woman but are instead representative of 'their kind'. Obviously, women are not a monolithic group. Women (as well as men) must learn to acknowledge and value each other as individuals, rather than representatives of status categories.

Bardwick (1977) views the disparity between the concept and experience of power among powerful and powerless women as fundamental to understanding the conflict so frequently observed between the two groups. In her view, women who have personal power are secure in their relationships with others, lack the need to gain at others' expense, and have confidence in themselves. They do not see themselves as having or as holding on to power. Rather, they think of power in terms of increased responsibility. They therefore find it difficult to understand the animosity they engender among those women who view power as a zero-sum game, that is, if power is held by one woman in an organization, it is therefore not available to other women. Perhaps as increasing numbers of women attain positions of power and authority over other women (and men) the ways in which they wield their power will cease to be representative of women as a group, and be interpreted idiosyncratically, paralleling the interpretation now afforded to the behaviour of powerful men.

## When she is good, she is very, very good, but when she is bad she is horrid

One of the characteristics of women's relationships with women in the workplace that most differentiates them from those found between men and women appears to be their affective intensity (O'Leary 1988). O'Leary and Ickovics (1987), for example, found that although most of the women secretaries who worked for women business owners liked both their bosses and their jobs, those who did not were very negatively disposed toward them. The same kind of affective intensity marks girls' relationships with other girls during childhood and early adolescence, and may be an example of the 'spill-over' of sex-role socialization into the workplace (Gutek 1985).

Sex-role spillover is the carry-over of gender-based roles that are usually irrelevant and inappropriate to the work setting (Gutek *et al.* 1990). Regardless of the occupational role, men and women are expected to behave in a manner that is consistent with established gender roles. This phenomenon is exacerbated in work settings that have highly-skewed ratio of sexes. Gutek and Cohen (1987) suggest the sex roles associated with the majority sex become incorporated into work roles such that 'in male-dominated jobs, activity, rationality, and aggressiveness are emphasized, whereas nurturance and passivity are associated with "women's work"' (p. 97). Furthermore, sex-role spillover affects people in traditional work when their sex role and work role merge together, and affects people in non-traditional work when they are a visible minority and their sex does not correspond to the sex roles normally associated with their jobs (ibid). Women in non-traditional work are role-deviant.

There are no established norms governing women's relationships with women at work. The norms that govern women's relationships with one another were derived to regulate their interpersonal behaviour in the private arena. When women encounter women at work, their normative expectations for one another illustrate sex-role spillover at its worst. Women subordinates expect their women bosses to be more understanding, more nurturant, more giving and forgiving than men. These expectations are not only high, they are unrealistic. As Keller and Moglen (1987) so aptly observe, 'just as women are never good enough mothers or, for that matter, grateful enough daughters, neither are we good enough mentors or colleagues or students' (p. 23). Women subordinates often expect their women bosses to provide both mothering and mentoring as well as supervision. When these expectations are violated, as they almost inevitably are, the response is swift and intensely negative. Lips (1992) suggests that some of the negative reaction stems from positive stereotypes of women as warm, caring people – and as people who are especially likely to be supportive of other women. Thus, when women react negatively toward powerful women, part of that negativity may come from dashed hopes and unfulfilled expectations born of these positive stereotypes. Women have not consciously articulated norms for boss/subordinate interactions, especially when the boss is a woman. As a result it is not surprising that women at work tend to react to women bosses as 'women', and to men bosses as 'bosses'. For example, when a woman boss fails to accept childcare difficulties as a legitimate excuse for tardiness on the third day it is offered in a row she is a 'bitch'. When a male boss behaves identically he is an 'angel' the first two days and on the third he is simply 'doing his job'.

Interestingly, in O'Leary and Ickovics's (1990) study, a good deal of the secretaries' criticism of their women bosses centred on the ways in which they failed to meet their secretaries' expectations either because they were not behaving enough like (male) bosses or because they were acting too much like women and therefore not maximizing the role distinction between themselves and those who worked for them. Morrison and her colleagues (Morrison *et al.* 1987) concluded that women's success in upper management required them to 'constantly monitor their behavior, making sure they are neither too masculine nor too feminine' (p. 18).

## OLD HABITS ARE HARD TO BREAK

Treating women as inferior is an old habit and one that is difficult to eradicate at the individual, organizational and societal levels. Recently, Gersick and Hackman (1990) have identified the importance of habitual behaviours in maintaining both group structures and processes. Paralleling Langer's (1989) distinction between 'mindful' and 'mindless' cognitive processing, Gersick and Hackman suggest that 'a habitual routine exists when a group repeatedly exhibits a functionally-similar pattern of behaviour in a given stimulus situation without explicitly selecting it over alternative ways of behaving' (p. 69). Furthermore, it is the group's perception or coding of a situation that elicits the habitual behaviour. When gender is involved, coding occurs along sex-role stereotypic lines resulting in the tendency to define women and power antithetically. Thus women are habitually relegated to secondary status.

All organized social systems require some routinization of behaviour to get work done. In addition, routinization contributes to predictability and members of a group must be able to predict the response of other individuals in their workplace if they are to engage in co-ordinated action. From this perspective, routinization may be viewed as functional. It saves time and energy, and it obviates the need for active management of a whole range of associated behaviours. Because habitual behaviour follows automatically from recognition of the evoking stimuli, a group need not spend time creating and choosing the behavioural strategy that will guide its work.

Routinization also contributes to individual members' comfort with the group by reducing feelings of uncertainty about how the stimulus should be handled. In this regard, sex-role spillover operates as a mechanism to minimize the effort and reduce the anxiety associated with individuals perceived to be acting 'out of role'.

However, not all of the consequences of routinization are potentially beneficial. For example, routinization may result in the failure to recognize a novel stimulus situation, or to identify changes in a familiar situation. Subtle dysfunction may occur when the stimulus stays the same (women) but the surrounding situation changes (workplace). This results in the failure to recognize that the context has changed and that routines which heretofore have been appropriate for those stimuli are no longer appropriate. For example, despite little or no experiential exposure to bosses who are women, workers hold a clear stereotype of the 'woman boss' (O'Leary 1988). This stereotype is based on interactions with women in contexts outside the workplace.

When a group task is novel and there is no prespecified appropriate routine, the group must somehow derive a way of operating. This is the position in which women (and men) who work for women often find themselves. Faced with uncertain norms and expectations, groups quickly establish patterns and planning versus action. The process of creating comfort-enhancing routines can itself be anxiety-arousing. Thus, it has often been easier (and less anxiety-arousing) to import behavioural strategies that have been used successfully in the past but are inappropriate in the current context.

Gersick and Hackman (1990) have identified a number of factors that maintain habitual routines. They include the political costs or risks associated with altering a routine, group norms, behavioural norms and meta-norms, which inhibit collective reflection and lessen the chances that a group will acknowledge (or change) its first-level norm.

The tendency for social systems, including groups, to close down rather than open up under stress and threat is well documented. Under stressful conditions, when variation is perhaps most needed, conservative tendencies tend to be exaggerated. Groups that are threatened, such as males who are losing their statistical superiority within the work-force, often intensify their adherence to existing routines rather than reconsider the appropriateness of those routines.

To the extent that the status quo is maintained by automatic processing mechanisms, it may prove rather impervious to change. However, cognitive theorists maintain that conscious processing can override the automatic-processing phenomena. One key to change is to force automatically processed information into consciousness (O'Leary and Hansen 1985) by making workers aware of the inappropriateness of their stereotypes.

## CONCLUSION

Aburdene and Naisbitt (1992) suggest that women are 'transforming the different arenas . . . by building a new social order or paradigm that will eventually replace the old order' (p. xv). Indeed, much attention has recently been given to the feminization of the work-force and women's ways of leading. It has also been proposed that women's labour force participation has reached the point of 'critical mass' such that women's gains will now be self-sustaining (Aburdene and Naisbitt 1992).

The mechanisms of sex-role spillover and habitual routines, however, challenge the conventional wisdom that real institutional change will occur if women simply occupy a greater proportion of corporate director and management jobs. Critical mass alone is not sufficient for substantive transformations of the workplace. As long as sex continues to be a major defining characteristic of workplace interactions, women's relationships at work will continue to be characterized negatively (O'Leary 1988). We must move beyond counting the numbers and begin effecting changes that count.

## REFERENCES

Aburdene, P. and Naisbitt, J. (1992) *Megatrends for Women*, New York: Villard Books.

Aktouf, O. (1992) 'Management and theories of organizations in the 1990s: toward a critical radical humanism?' *Academy of Management Review* 17 (3); 407–31.

Ashmore, R. D. and Del Boca, F. K. (1981) *The Social Psychology of Male-Female Relations*, New York: Academic Press.

Bardwick, J. M. (1977) 'Some notes about power relationships between women', A. G. Sargent (ed.) *Beyond Sex Roles*, St Paul, MN: West.

Bern, P. (1987) *How to Work for a Woman Boss*, New York: Dodd, Mead.

Bowman, G., Wortney, B. N. and Greyser, S. H. (1965) 'Are women executives people?' *Harvard Business Review* 43: 14–28, 164–78.

Brenner, O. C., Tomkiewicz, J. and Schein, V. E. (1989) 'The relationship between sex role stereotypes and requisite management characteristics revisited', *Academy of Management Journal* 32: 662–9.

Briles, J. (1987) *Woman to Woman: From Sabotage to Support*, Far Hills, NJ: New Horizons Press.

Eagly, A. H. (1989) *Gender Stereotypes: Their Content, Sources and Consequences*, paper presented at conference on 'Restructuring for Reality: An In-Depth Look at Selected Issues', Radcliffe College, March.

Feber, M., Huber, J. and Spitze, G. (1979) 'Preference for men as bosses and professionals', *Social Forces* 58: 466–76.

Feminist Majority Foundation (1991) 'Study finds few women hold top executive jobs', *Washington Post*, 26 August.

Fierman, J. (1990) 'Do women manage differently?' *Fortune* 122 (15): 115–8.

Fryxell, G. E. and Lerner, L. D. (1989) 'Contrasting corporate profiles: women and minority representation in top management positions', *Journal of Business Ethics* 8: 341–52.

Gannon, M. J. and Paine, F. T. (1974) 'Unity of command and job attitudes of managers in a bureaucratic organization', *Journal of Applied Psychology* 59: 392–4.

Gersick, C. J. and Hackman J. R. (1990) 'Habitual routines in task-performing groups', *Organizational Behavior and Human Decision Processes* 47: 65–97.

Goldberg, P. (1968) 'Are women prejudiced against women?' *Trans Action* 5: 28–30.

Gordon, S. (1991) 'Every woman for herself', *New York Times*, 19 August, 15.

Grady, K. E. (1977) 'Sex as a social label: the illusion of sex differences', unpublished doctoral dissertation, Graduate Centre, City University of New York.

Gutek, B. A. (1985) *Sex and the Workplace*, San Francisco: Jossey-Bass.

Gutek, B. A. and Cohen, A. G. (1987) 'Sex ratios, sex role spillover, and sex at work: a comparison of men's and women's experiences', *Human Relations* 40 (2): 97–115.

Gutek, B. A., Cohen, A. G. and Konrad, A. M. (1990) 'Predicting social-sexual behavior at work: a contact hypothesis', *Academy of Management Journal* 33 (3): 560–77.

Hardesty, S. and Jacobs, N. (1986) *Success and Betrayal: The Crisis of Women in Corporate America*, New York: Simon and Schuster.

Helgasen, S. (1990) *The Female Advantage: Women's Ways of Leadership*, New York: Doubleday.

Johnson, M. (1990) 'The feminine technique in IS', *Computerworld*: 24 (50), 95.

Kahn, W. A. and Crosby, F. (1985) 'Discriminating between attitudes and discriminatory behaviors: change and stasis', L. Larwood, A. Stromberg and B. A. Gutek (eds) *Women and Work: An Annual Review* 1: 215–38, Beverly Hills, CA: Sage.

Keller, E. F. and Moglen, H. (1987) 'Competition: a problem for academic women', V. Miner and H. Longino (eds) *Competition, a feminist taboo?*: 21–37, New York: Feminist Press at the City University of New York.

Kleiman, C. (1992) '"Right stuff" can bump against the glass ceiling', *Chicago Tribune*, 6 January, 6.

Langer, E. J. (1989) *Mindfulness*, Reading, MA, Addison-Wesley.

Lips, H. M. (1991) *Women, Men, and Power*, Mountain View, CA, Mayfield.

Madden, T. R. (1987) *Women Versus Women: The Uncivil Business War*, Washington, DC, American Management Association.

Morrison, A. M. and Von Glinow, M. A. (1990) 'Women and minorities in management', *American Psychologist* 45 (2): 200–8.

Morrison, A. M., White, R. P. and Van Velsor, E. (1987) 'Executive women: substance plus style', *Psychology Today* 21 (8): 18–26.

Mumby, D. K. and Putnam, L. L. (1992) 'The politics of emotion: a feminist reading of bounded rationality', *Academy of Management Review* 17 (3): 465–86.

Nieva, V. F. and Gutek, B. A. (1981) *'Women and Work: A Psychological Perspective*, New York, Praeger.

O'Leary, V. E. (1987) 'Secretarial students' perceptions of women and men bosses', unpublished data, Boston University.

O'Leary, V. E. (1988) 'Women's relationships with women in the workplace', B. A. Gutek, L. Larwood and A. Stromberg (eds) *Women and Work: An Annual Review* 3: 189–213, Beverly Hills, CA, Sage.

O'Leary, V. E. and Donoghue, J. M. (1978) 'Latitudes of masculinity: reactions to sex-role deviance in men', *Journal of Social Issues* 34 (1): 17–28.

O'Leary, V. E. and Hansen, R. D. (1985) 'Sex as an attributional fact', T. Sonderegger (ed.) *Nebraska Symposium on Motivation*, Lincoln, NE, University of Nebraska Press.

O'Leary, V. E. and Ickovics, J. R. (1987) *Who Wants a Woman Boss? Only Those Who Have One*, Washington, DC, George Washington University (ERIC Document Reproduction Service no. ED 288174).

O'Leary, V. E. and Ickovics, J. R. (1990) 'Women supporting women: secretaries and their bosses', H. Grossman and N. L. Chester (eds) *The*

*Experience and Meaning of Work in Women's Lives* 35–56, Hillsdale, NJ, Lawrence Erlbaum Associates.

O'Leary, V. E. and Johnson, J. L. (1991) 'Steep ladder, lonely climb', *Women in Management, Review and Abstracts* 6 (5): 10–16.

Pierce, J. L. and Dunham, R. B. (1978) 'An empirical demonstration of the convergence of common macro- and micro-organization measures', *Academy of Management Journal* 21: 410–8.

Rosener, J. B. (1990) 'Ways women lead', *Harvard Business Review* 68: 119–25.

Schein, V. E. (1973) 'The relationship between sex role stereotypes and requisite management characteristics', *Journal of Applied Psychology* 57 (2): 95–100.

Schein, V. E. (1975) 'Relationships between sex role stereotypes and management characteristics among female managers', *Journal of Applied Psychology* 60 (3): 340–4.

Slade, M. (1984) 'Relationships: women and secretaries', *New York Times*, 15 October, 15.

Stratham, A. (1985) *The Gender Role Revisited: Differences in the Management Styles of Women and Men*, unpublished manuscript, University of Wisconsin, Parkside, WI.

Staines, G., Travis, C. and Jayerante, T. E. (1973) 'The queen bee syndrome', *Psychology Today* 7 (8): 55–60.

Sugawara, S. (1991) 'Firms holding back women, minorities'. *Washington Post*, 9 August, 1.

Sutton, S. D. and Moore, K. K. (1985) 'Probing opinions: executive women – 20 years later', *Harvard Business Review* 85 (5): 42–66.

US Department of Commerce (1991) *Statistical Abstract of the U.S.: 1991*, 111th edn, Washington, DC, Author.

US Department of Labor (1991) *Employment and Earnings*, 38, Bureau of Labor Statistics, Washington, DC, Author.

# Chapter 5

# Women managing in Turkey

*Alev Ergenc Katrinli and Ömür Timurcanday Özmen*

According to studies there are now more women in western countries taking a role in paid work (Davidson 1987; Davidson and Cooper 1992; HMSO 1991). And apparently there is a slight increase in the number of women in management compared to 1971 (Hansard Society Commission 1990). These changes may be the result of legislation and changing economic and social conditions, but the progress for women is slow and the ratio of women in managerial positions compared to the total female work-force is still small (Hansard Society Commission 1990; Hirsh and Jackson 1989).

The reason for the slow progress is most commonly explained by the different family roles that women play, with most women taking some time off their careers for child-bearing or childcare. But we observe that women in management are in a tiring struggle because of persisting prejudice. Some studies suggest that women are more obedient and accepting of service or subordinate positions. It has also been suggested that they are not able to maintain a leadership role or make logical decisions and that their subordinate male workers do not like to take orders from them (Dobbins and Platz 1986; Nelson and Quick 1985; Rosen and Jerdee 1973).

However, what is apparent is that women managers are now an established part of our work culture, our organizational relationships, and our managerial structures. But research is needed to understand more about the experiences of men and women in management to allay prejudice and develop better working relationships. This information is particularly necessary in Turkey where little work on women in management has been carried out. With this omission we have had to rely on research carried out in other national cultures to try to understand Turkish women managers' work.

This paper gives an account of a study we carried out which attempted to begin to address this omission by studying the issues which trouble Turkish senior women managers.

## OUR INTERVIEWEES

In order to discover some answers we began a series of research projects to examine different women managers' experience of work in Turkish society. Our study began in 1991 with a six months' pilot project in which thirty-one senior women managers from different organizations in Izmir were interviewed. Since then our work has continued so that we have now interviewed some sixty women but this paper represents the results of our first stage.

We obtained our sample by personal contacts with those we knew in companies which employed senior women managers. We attempted to include women from both the public and private sectors and we also included some who owned their own businesses. Our sample was made up as follows: public sector fourteen women; private sector fourteen women; and three who owned their own companies. We also wanted the sample to include women from different sectors of work and our thirty-one managers included women from the following areas: administration; technical work; health education; law; finance; security; public relations; the arts.

## THE METHOD

In order to obtain an understanding of the experiences and attitudes of the women managers we decided to interview them. We created an initial list of twenty-seven issues or items of interest. This was developed from our own research interests together with suggestions obtained from discussions with women managers. In creating this list we recognized our influence as researchers and therefore we were aware that these issues were our own contribution to the research, as legitimate as any of the comments of our interviewees and equally open to contradiction or dismissal.

Each interview lasted up to three hours. Although we had originally expected to take one and a half hours we discovered that the managers were pleased and interested to talk to us. They appeared to want to discuss the issues they faced in their lives and we found that interviews lasted longer than originally planned.

As two women researchers we wanted to work together and while one of us asked the questions the other wrote down answers. We had intended to tape-record the interviews, but during the initial interviews we discovered that some of the managers were resistant to the use of such a mechanical instrument so we decided to take notes ourselves instead.

The interviews were semi-structured in that we allowed the women to talk of their work generally and we interrupted them occasionally with some of our questions in order to address specific issues. All of the women appeared anxious to please us and we found the experience very rewarding.

## THE ANALYSIS

We have analysed the results of this first study under five headings in order to try to create a picture of the issues affecting Turkish senior women managers. We have included the number of respondents with different responses or 'attitudes', not claiming statistical significance in this study, but to give the flavour and strength of different types of response.

We begin by giving an account of how the interviewees had achieved their current job together with issues of promotion and factors affecting success. This is followed by a demographic break-down of our interviewees. The third section addresses difficulties which they described themselves as facing. Then we recount some reflections on their attitude to their emotions at work and finally we report on their interpretation of how their male colleagues feel about women managers.

## THEIR PRESENT POSITIONS

We were interested to know where the women had worked before achieving their present senior management positions. Of the total thirty-one women, eighteen said that they had moved to their present position from a level below in the same organization. Only five said that they had moved from a different department and another five said they had moved from a different organization. The remaining three had their own companies and did not address this question.

When we asked how they had managed to reach such senior positions, over half of the women (and this included all the women owners) said that this was due to their own hard work. However, eight said that their bosses were instrumental in their promotion to their current position and three gave the credit to relatives.

All the women said that male workers were preferred for promotion to senior positions and therefore women had to work harder and had to 'push' to succeed to the positions they desired. This corresponds to the findings of Dogan and Budak (1981). Although the number of female workers is increasing, male workers are still being preferred to female workers. The apparent reason for this is still that women's efficiency is thought to be restricted by the number of days they have off work, particularly with respect to the periods before and after childbirth.

Given the response to this question of responsibility for success, we asked the managers for the specific factors involved in their success. The most cited answer was 'hard work' (eight respondents). The second most common answer was 'being good at my job' (five respondents) and the third highest answers (both cited by four respondents) were 'being tolerant and practical' and 'not making mistakes'. They explained that not making mistakes was very important because women's errors are conspicuous and therefore not tolerated, whereas men's mistakes were not. One other factor given by three managers was that they needed to be liked by subordinates.

We then asked whether the factors which they had given us would be the same for senior male managers. Over half (sixteen) of our respondents said there was no difference. However, eight women said that women's feeling of responsibility is higher than their male colleagues. Four said that women are more optimistic and three said that women respect themselves more.

According to Dobbins and Platz (1986), results of research on the characteristics of managerial women are contradictory, but we in Turkey are led to understand that American women suppress their feminine selves in order to be successful, whereas European women attempt to express their femininity. There is obviously an opportunity for much more cross-cultural work on women in management which we hope will be taken up.

We then focused on some of the demographic characteristics of our sample. Over half (sixteen of the thirty-one) were married. Seven were single and another seven were divorced. The single women talked of the fear that marriage would affect the success of their careers. They felt that marriage would decrease their effectiveness because they would have to take care of their homes, husbands and children. They felt they would become tired and would not have the energy to work hard at work.

Some of the married women talked of the conflicts they had in their lives. They were bosses and in control at work, but not within their homes.

Almost all of our sample (twenty-nine of the thirty-one) had university degrees. Twenty-four of our sample were asked whether they had children. On reflection we now recognize the bias within this question that only the married or divorced women were asked. Of these women almost all twenty-two of the twenty-four had children with twelve of them having more than one child.

## DIFFICULTIES WOMEN FACE

In this section we asked women to talk about the difficulties they faced both in terms of promotion and in dealing with their current work. Fourteen of the thirty-one said that the most serious difficulty they faced in dealing with their jobs was the reluctance of male workers to work with female managers. Some jobs, they said, were treated as suitable only for men, so that women were not accepted for such jobs. They said that they believed that females were more 'human oriented' in nature than males and therefore would not be suitable for the previously-referred-to 'male' type positions. Management, they said, was seen as a job most suitable for males.

The second difficulty they mentioned was to do with business travel and meals in hotels, and so on. They explained that long distance business travel and business meals were not acceptable for women in their society.

Some of the women expressed difficulty with traditional attitudes towards women's work in the home and they said that the majority of the responsibility for work in the home was still the women's.

However, in spite of the above, ten women interviewed said that they faced no problems in their work, nor in their promotional prospects.

When we asked about the women's perception of male attitudes to women managers the results were similarly confusing. We asked first of all about the women's view of whether men were willing to work with female managers and ten women said that their male colleagues disliked working with female managers. According to these women, management is thought of as a male job and only men would have the appropriate leadership qualities. Because males do not think that women have such qualities they do not want to work with women.

When we asked whether they thought males would *employ* female workers, eleven women said they thought that males would employ females but only up to a certain level and then they would hinder their promotion. And five of the women interviewed said that hindrance of women's careers was 'normal' because of the days that women have to take off work. However, none of our respondents gave an opinion which matched with the findings of Ezell *et al.* (1980) and Chusmir and Durand (1987) whose statistics showed that there is a positive correlation between the prestige of position and reduction in the number of days off for women managers.

## EMOTIONALITY

In order to press our respondents to explain more about their view of women's characteristics *vis-à-vis* men we asked whether they believed women were more or less emotional than men. Again about half of the sample said that women were not more emotional. Seven of them appeared to be evaluating our question and said that women are more emotional but that they did not use such emotionality as an advantage. They went so far as to suggest that such emotionality was a strength in that it helped them in their relationships with their subordinates and helped them to reach decisions on time. This obviously leaves a great deal more to be explored about the use of our interpretation of 'emotionality' so we asked a more explicit question about women's tears.

There was a strong reaction to our question that women may use tears as a 'weapon'. Twenty-five of the sample said that this was absolutely not necessary and should not be used in such a way. However, six women pointed out that tears should simply be perceived as a way of obtaining relief and need not be interpreted as shameful or embarrassing.

## WHAT WOMEN THINK MEN THINK OF WOMEN

Our final section asked the women for their reaction to two statements which we posed and to a situation we described. First of all we asked them to react to the sentence 'Don't expect more, she is only a woman'.

Thirteen of our sample said that this is an expression which men used. Ten said that they had never encountered the sentence. Others reacted in a variety of ways from 'It is a shame' to 'It isn't true'. And one respondent reacted angrily saying that she would cause trouble if she heard it said.

We then asked the women to respond to the sentence 'Women think like men'. The reaction to this statement broke the respondents down into three groups. Eleven responded strongly saying that they did not want to be compared with the opposite sex. They explained that women should only be evaluated as women and men compared with men. It was inappropriate to compare across the genders in this way. Ten seemed unaffected and said they would not react in any way and the remaining ten varied between saying that it was possible and that it was 'a pleasant fact'.

We then asked a question to try to find out more about current practices or attitude to such traditional male behaviours as paying for lunch or carrying bags for women. Half the group said they would not permit such practices. Ten said they would and the remaining six said that they would take their cues from the males or in terms of meals that the person making the invitation should pay.

## OUR EVALUATION

From our review of the information we were given in this first phase we have created a generalized picture of a senior woman manager in Turkey. This woman would have worked hard and achieved her position on this basis, by her own efforts. She would have had to be self-consciously hard-working, pragmatic and fastidious. She would have a university qualification. Such a woman might say that there are no hindrances to her achieving success.

However, this woman would also say that she would have to show more effort and not allow herself to make any mistakes, for her mistakes would be 'seen'. She would have to be able to face a large amount of ambivalence from her male colleagues, some might be openly critical, particularly of her ability to lead. She would have to be particularly persistent and 'pushy' if she wished to achieve a very senior position although she might feel herself being encouraged by her boss to a middle management position.

Such a woman would say that there were differences in the qualities of men and women in work and that women had qualities which made them better managers. For example, any stereotypical sensitivity which a woman demonstrated would probably enable her to be a better manager of people and it would also allow her to make better decisions.

If this generalized woman were married, she would find herself carrying out most of the family duties: childcaring, shopping, household management. Probably she would allow her husband to make the management decisions for the family unit.

If she were as yet unmarried she would view marriage with great hesitation, recognizing that it could affect her position at work. She would see her married female colleagues as being over-worked, tired and stressed.

## CONCLUSIONS

This pilot study has raised a number of issues for us as researchers and as women in the workplace.

We discovered from our study that in spite of the apparent discrepancies and prejudice which was reported by approximately half of the women interviewed, there are positive attitudes to women's development in senior levels of management. The effect of education and training has obviously been influential in allowing women to use their talents in the work-force.

Since the birth-rate has been decreasing women will be less expected to take the traditional family role of the past and will be able to devote themselves to their careers if they wish.

We also discovered that many organizations are supporting women's careers by establishing crèches, schools, care for the aged and health services. We have been made more aware of the 'man-made' nature of these women's lives. Women work in organizations which have been developed under the domination of men's culture and values, so the systems and structures within these organizations replicate men's 'natural' patterns.

From our discussions with these managers we believe women

see male managers as 'insiders' – as a society made up of members who understand each other, their structures and their principles. They share common wants and dreams. They like similar types of training, playing and learning. It is going to be difficult for women to enter this 'natural system'. Women will have to find a way of developing their expectations and experiences so that they do not remain on the outside, with their contributions wasted.

But an overriding finding was that our respondents showed quite glaring differences in attitude toward issues which trouble women in their daily lives. From this it is clear that there is no one way of being a woman manager in an organization. But each woman will have to deal with significant conflicts. It may be the conflict between home and work, between their self-image as a leader or a follower (at home), or conflicts about the interpretation of traditional ways of accepting politeness from male colleagues. Each woman, it appears to us, has to create her own way of becoming an organizational insider, some at the cost of a loving relationship within a family.

## REFERENCES

Chusmir, L. H. and Durand, D. E. (1987) 'The female factor', *Training and Development Journal* 41 (8).

Davidson, M. J. (1987) 'Women and employment', P. Warr (ed.) *Psychology at Work* London: Penguin.

Davidson, M. J. and Cooper, C. L. (1992) *Shattering the Glass Ceiling: The Woman Manager*, London: Paul Chapman Publishing.

Dobbins, G. H. and Platz, S. J. (1986) 'Sex differences in leadership: how real are they?', *Academy of Management Review* 11.

Dogan, H. Z. and Budak, G. (1981) *Calisan Kadinlarin Sorunlari ile ilgili Bir Inceleme*, unpublished working paper.

Ezell, H. F., Odavahn, C. A. and Sherman, D. J. (1980) 'Being supervised by a woman: does it make a difference?' paper presented at 40th Annual Meeting of the Academy of Management, Detroit, Michigan.

Hansard Society Commission (1990) *Women at the Top*, London, Hansard Society.

Hirsh, W. and Jackson, C. (1989) *Women Into Management – Issues Influencing the Entry of Women Into Managerial Jobs*, paper no. 158, University of Sussex, Institute of Manpower Studies.

HMSO (1991) *Social Trends*, London: HMSO.

Lawless, D. J. (1979) *Organizational Behavior: The Psychology of Effective Management*, Englewood Cliffs, NJ: Prentice Hall.

Nelson, D. L. and Quick, J. C. (1985) 'Professional women: are distress and disease inevitable?', *Academy of Management Review* 10: 206–18.

Rosen, B. and Jerdee, T. H. (1973) 'The influence of sex role stereotypes on evaluations of male and female supervisory behavior', *Journal of Applied Psychology* 57.

# Chapter 6

# Managing emotion

*Elaine Swan*

A 1970 landmark study, known in the field as Broverman and Broverman, reported that 'Cries very easily' was rated by a group of professional psychologists as a highly-feminine trait. 'Very emotional', 'Very excitable in a minor crisis', and 'Feelings easily hurt' were additional characteristics on the feminity scale. So were 'Very easily influenced', 'Very subjective', 'Unable to separate feelings from ideas', 'Very illogical' and 'Very sneaky'. As might be expected, masculinity was defined by opposing sturdier values: 'Very direct', 'Very logical', 'Can make decisions easily', 'Never cries'. The importance of Broverman and Broverman was . . . in the authors' observation that stereotypic femininity was a grossly-negative assessment of the female sex and, furthermore, ran counter to clinical descriptions of maturity and mental health

(Brownmiller 1986: 161).

At the end of my formal training to become a supervisor in a retail organization, the main criticism of my behaviour from the training officer was 'Elaine must learn to curb her feelings'. A few years later I was training management trainees in assertiveness in which one of the main tenets is 'You have the right to express your true feelings'. This reflects the paradoxical regard with which we hold emotion in society. To paraphrase Douglas (1966), emotion is 'matter out of place', it is to be controlled, suppressed, and managed, and emotion is the touchstone of our true selves, to be valued and expressed.

In most texts on organizations, the realm of emotion is unexplored. Writers reflect and reproduce a dominant view that emotion is to be kept out of sight in the organizational world. This partial view creates ways of understanding organizations, influences management practices and delineates experiences for organizational workers. It feeds into, and out of, society's view of what the organizational world is like, and should be like.

Emotion is out of place in the rational organization, and in the rational organization of texts on organizations. The management of recruitment interviews, performance appraisal, and disciplinary procedures requires skills of rationality, objectivity and logic, not emotion. Emotion is to be expected in the less powerful such as interviewees and appraisees but the competent manager must herself remain unemotional. (The idea of emotion afflicting those who are 'inferior' is a historical inheritance and has in the past embraced women, children and slaves, as I shall discuss later.)

Where human relations psychology has raised the profile of emotion in theories on motivation, counselling or assertiveness, it has been as a means of pursuing a wider instrumentality: let your workers get things off their chests and then they will perform their tasks better; get things off your chest and you'll get what you want. Typically, emotion is to be managed, kept out of the public and kept in private, either behind the closed doors of offices or toilets or best of all, left at home, where it won't interfere with work.

The corporate management of emotion is represented by the management practices it endorses, and by those emotions it will acknowledge and encourage through public communications and rituals: happiness and praise for sales targets beaten; anger and disappointment at bad customer relations or industrial action.

What I want to do in this chapter is to bring emotion into the limelight by looking at the interrelationship between reason, emotion, gender and management. To do this, I summarize the historical associations between women and emotion, and men and reason. I follow this with a discussion of key theories on emotion and conclude with an exploration of the social construction of emotion and the implications for women in management.

I want to do this without recourse to reifying the concepts of emotion and women as natural, singular, universal entities. Traditionally, feminist theory has sought to differentiate between sex and gender; a person's sex being the anatomical and hormonal make-up that distinguishes the female from the male; and gender, the socially-constructed attributes and behaviours that are imposed on the sex differentiations. The terms 'female' and 'male' are used to denote the biological categories determined by bodily differences: 'women' and 'men' refer to the socially-constructed properties assigned to the female and male; 'femininity' and 'masculinity' are terms to describe gender norms, clusters of character traits which exemplify a 'proper', 'good' woman or man (Haslanger 1993). In this schema, different emotional dispositions for women and men could be attributed to anatomical differences (males are more aggressive because they have more of the hormone testosterone) or to culturally-defined role expectations (anger is not very feminine).

More recent debates have produced the argument that taken-for-granted 'naturalisms' such as biology and the body should also be seen as social products. This means we can challenge the 'natural' inevitability of bodily processes, and recognize that what is perceived to be important or unimportant in biology or medicine is culturally defined. An example is the current debate on whether pre-menstrual syndrome exists. The medical fraternity has declared recently that it does not. Many women are using the media to assert that, in their experience, it does.

If we destabilize the category of sex differentiation as socially constructed, the category of 'woman' has no stable essence and therefore to talk of a monolithic 'woman's point of view' or 'women's experience' as a singular, meaningful category reproduces the idea that there is an essential, ineluctable difference between women and men, and that this overrides any differences between women of different races, classes or sexualities. This does not mean that there can be no political agenda for women, but that it must take account of multiple and conflicting subject positions with which women identify.

Although the concept of woman has been under considerable scrutiny, the concept of emotion as an asocial, natural, singular phenomenon remains largely intact. It is seen as an individuated entity which is located internally and can be expressed through language or bodily expressions. I will explore how, like sex and gender, emotion is socially constructed, but more of this later. The danger in discussing emotion and women is that it reproduces and perpetuates a tradition which couples emotion with women in opposition to reason and men. The consequence is that the former is denigrated in contrast with the latter, as is prevalent in male-stream scientific discourse. Conversely, the connections between emotion and women are revalued in opposition to reason and men. Reason is seen as a masculine way of thinking and therefore to be shunned by women. The feminine attribute of emotion should be appreciated instead. This reinforces the traditional stereotype of the characteristic features and capacities of women.

At the same time as focusing on the gendering of emotion, I want to prise open the elision of women with the emotional domain, and men with the rational. To this end, I begin with a summary of competing and shifting associations between gender and emotion.

## THE EMOTIONAL FEMALE

In their exploration of spatial metaphors that we use to represent the world, Lakoff and Johnson write:

> *Rational is up: Emotional is down*
> The discussion fell to the emotional level, but I raised it back up to the rational plane. We put our feelings aside and had a high level intellectual discussion of the matter. He couldn't rise above his emotions.
>
> In our culture, people view themselves as being in control over animals, plants, and their physical environment, and it is their unique ability to reason that places human beings above other animals and gives them control. CONTROL IS UP thus provides basis for MAN IS UP and therefore for RATIONAL IS UP.
>
> (Lakoff and Johnson 1980: 17)

This quotation serves to highlight how much of western knowledge is structured in terms of polar opposites: man/woman: culture/nature: reason/emotion. Within this structure, the opposed terms are not equally valued and one term will always occupy a privileged position over the other. Different discourses privilege either the former or the latter term. By discourse, I am referring to the statements spoken, heard, written and read which produce and constitute our experience and our realities, and reproduce social structures. Thus, in some discourses, man; culture and reason, become inextricably linked and counterposed to woman; nature and emotion.

Since Plato, there has been a historical antagonism between reason and the passions, and the mind and the body. The word 'emotion' came into use during the seventeenth century and took the place of passion as subordinate to reason. It was particularly during the eighteenth and nineteenth centuries, in the period known as the Englightenment, that the valorization of reason and mind over emotion and the body rigidified. Reason became the privileged knowledge for 'mastering' the world, and particularly science, the means of dominating nature and its resources for men's designs. Together reason and science would facilitate what an influential male minority defined as social progress. The ability to reason with the mind was seen as evidence of man's 'humanity' and superiority over animals. Emotion and desire were vestiges of man's animality and threats from the inferior body to the supremacy of the mind and the progress of reason.

Within this context Jordanova (1980) has traced the association of woman with nature in the intellectual interests of an influential male elite of scientists and doctors. She writes that through their scientific writings the notion of women as natural had both positive and negative connotations – positive in their capacity to give life, in their natural morality and as repositories of nature's laws exemplified in the menstrual cycle; negative in their lack of reason, and therefore more easily dominated by extreme emotion, and more likely to be dangerous and to disrupt the order of reason.

During the Enlightenment, emotion and the body, as exemplars of nature, became demoted as inferior to reason and the mind, and as with nature to be controlled by the superiority of reason and the mind. Women were seen as closer to nature, more susceptible to the vagaries of their bodies and emotions and, as such, needing to be controlled by men and their rational supremacy. (Tellingly, Francis Bacon, the eighteenth century scientist, used metaphors of nature as a chaste bride to be wooed by male science – Haslanger 1993.)

There was a counter-rational discourse towards the end of the eighteenth century with the emergence of what we now refer to as the Romantic Movement in literature and philosophy. This celebrated both emotion and nature, but still held it in opposition to reason, and it had little impact on the increasingly powerful scientific and medical discourses and practices.

These two strands leave us today with a legacy of two competing discourses on emotion: emotion as capricious, disruptive and dangerous witnessed still in orthodox scientific discourse, contrasted with emotion as the touchstone of humanity and authentic selfhood evidenced in representations of artists and the theories of humanistic psychology.

The association of woman/nature/emotion is still a contradictory set of representations. On the one hand, 'the emotional female' is more sensitive, empathetic, and good at dealing with other people's emotions and therefore suitable for work in the private domain of the home, or in the public domain of the caring professions. On the other hand, 'the emotional female' is more unpredictable, irrational and susceptible to uncontrollable emotional outbursts both in the private and public arenas. Lutz (1990) suggests current biomedical research still feeds from and into this model by focusing on wombs, female hormones and menstruation and imbuing them with the capacity to generate natural emotional dispositions for women. Comments made within the last decade that women should not be allowed into the boardroom because of their raging hormones (Birke 1986) gain force from supposed scientific facts of women's natural emotional disposition.

In an attempt to redress the power imbalance between women and men, women have tried to appropriate 'the emotional female' and to celebrate emotion as an asset in a variety of ways. For some, the 'natural' emotional skills of women caused by their biological sex are counterposed to the 'natural' aggression and unemotionality of men. The emotional female is possessed of 'natural' feminine emotions which makes her more inclined and able to express feelings, better at establishing interpersonal relationships and more caring and empathetic than men in private and public domains.

Where femininity is viewed as socially-learned and mediated roles, the emotional female remains intact as a positive role model for women because emotion itself becomes romanticized and associated with nature and natural, and as such, represents the unsocialized, true self prior to gender socialization. Emotion usurps reason as the touchstone of 'humanity'. This model again stems from the interplay between the dichotomies of emotion/reason and nature/culture in which the former terms of each pair is privileged. Although Strathern (1980) has demonstrated that there are other juxtapositions of man/woman and culture and nature, in which man is associated with nature and woman with culture, particularly in respect of 'male' sexuality with its natural drives and irrepressibility and woman as civilizer, the motif of woman/nature/emotion is dominant.

As a management trainer and developer, I am exploring the relationships between emotion and management, and their implications for women managers, but through an orientation that destabilizes the man/culture/reason versus women/nature/emotion categorizations, and I want to denaturalize other binary oppositions such as outer/inner; public/private; authentic/inauthentic; mind/body which form part of how we theorize emotion. By denaturalize, I mean to highlight that certain concepts such as the body are not naturally given and determined rather than created by literally man-made knowledge. Our understanding and experience of our bodies cannot be separated from our own historical and cultural contexts. What qualifies as 'nature' and what nature means varies throughout historical time and social spaces. Once we problematize the viability of these constructions, we can begin to question and challenge the social practices that radiate from them, and address the very real power imbalances in society.

## THEORIES ON EMOTION

Emotion has been theorized within a variety of academic disciplines: biology, psychology, philosophy, and to a lesser extent, sociology. Although these vary in focus and methodology, the concept of emotion remains largely constant. Emotion is represented as an internal individualized phenomenon, experienced physiologically, manifested and communicated through an array of linguistic and paralinguistic expressions.

The social constructionist approach is the one that departs from this model. The fundamental difference between this and the orthodox model of emotion rests upon the extent to which aspects of emotion are seen to be mediated by socio-cultural norms. I will concentrate on the predominant biological, psychological and social-constructionist models.

Most biological models centre on a model of socially-unmediated emotion, in which emotion originates from a human's physiological make-up, seen as universal across history and culture, and manifested in certain culturally-modified emotional expressions. Psychological models of emotion retain the notion of the biological basis of emotion, and increase the level of socially-mediated dimensions of emotion by focusing on the mental processes involved. In this model, emotion inheres in socially-learned mental skills of cognition and appraisal, that is, understanding, assessing and responding to emotion-invoking situations; and socially-learned skills of expression and communication. Essentially, however, emotion is still held to be significantly embodied, both mentally and physiologically, and therefore largely natural.

The problem in both these models is the lack of emphasis on the intersubjective nature of emotion and the importance of language in constructing how we represent emotion and give it meaning and significance. These models do not take account of quite different concepts of emotion that have been constructed historically or cross-culturally.

Conversely, a social constructionist model of emotion does. Harré and Finlay-Jones (1986) outline a description of a medieval emotion called 'accidie' which was boredom, dejection or even disgust in fulfilling one's religious duty which they claim is obsolete now. Cross-culturally, there is a huge variation in the way different societies express, understand and differentiate emotions. In Japan, there is an emotion called 'amae' which means 'to indulge in another's kindness', it is a 'sense of helplessness and the desire to be loved' (Morsbach and Tyler 1986).

Abu-Lughod (1990) demonstrates how the question 'How do you feel?' is meaningless within the bedouin community in which she lived. Many other examples are explored by Heelas (1986) and Lutz (1986) which show how historically and culturally bound our understanding and experience of emotion is. Within a culture, emotions are also distributed according to gender, age and occupation. Armon-Jones (1986) describes the specific emotional experience children in our culture have structured for them which they 'mature' out of, and Crespo (1986) argues that there are specific emotions for police, priests and soldiers.

For the social constructionist, emotion is a social encounter. It is not simply the expression of emotion, and the mental skills of emotion which are socio-culturally informed, emotion itself gets its meaning and significance from the social realm. Social constructionists do not deny the physiological aspect to emotion but view it as largely irrelevant in our experience of emotion. They view our subjective experience of emotion as one which has been framed in and by language and which, as such, is a product of our historical and cultural specificity.

Lutz and Abu-Lughod (1990) differentiate between two types of discourse which construct our understanding and experience of emotion: 'discourses on emotion' which they define as local theories on emotion and 'emotional discourses' which are situated uses of emotional expressions and utterances. Both types of discourse create and reproduce our knowledges of emotion, the meanings inhering in emotion and our experience of emotion. In a very real sense (sic) emotion exists in language. So for Lutz and Abu-Lughod, 'emotion talk is in, and about social life rather than as veridically referential to some internal state' (1990: 11). Discourses on emotion and emotional discourses do not simply mirror an external or internally embodied reality, but have pragmatic effects. Language does not unproblematically describe or report, it is performative and, as such, language does things. As an example of the constructive nature of emotional discourse, Harre (1986: 25) writes, 'In avowing or expressing my thought or feelings, I am not describing how I feel, but am showing it'.

Emotional discourse is doing more than expressing an ontologically prior emotion, it is displaying an individual's commitment, not only to the local rules for framing emotion but also, as Armon-Jones (1986) identifies, to the cultural values exemplified in a particular situation. Emotional discourse and paralinguistic responses are deemed not only to be a manifestation of an understanding of shared expectations of appropriate emotion responses in a given situation, but as a prescribed feature which ought to be present to demonstrate a person's commitment to the local moral order.

Emotional discourse and discourse on emotion then construct and prescribe emotion in such ways as to sustain and endorse religious, moral and political beliefs, and the interests and values of a local community.

## EMOTION AND MANAGEMENT

The traditional model of organizations as rational, instrumental and technical gives us a starting point for investigating how the emotional life of workers is constructed. Not succumbing to romanticized notions of emotion as the source of a pre-social self or lamenting the wholesale commercialization of human feeling, I suggest that emotion in organizations has been excluded in representations of organizations. Given my earlier summary of the historical antagonism between reason and emotion, it is not surprising that, within constructions of organizations as models of rationality, emotion should be out of the frame. Emotion symbolizes disorder and therefore is kept beyond the boundary which organizes order out of disorder. These representations inform, and are informed by, organizational practices and play an influential role in producing the behaviour and self-understanding of individuals at work (what Hollway (1992) calls 'worker subjectivities'). As we have seen, these practices will impact on emotional discourse, and discourses on emotion, including rules for emotion display, obligations and appraisal in the organizational world. At the same time, these are legitimated by wider socio-cultural conventions.

The representation of reason as order and emotion as disorder is a symbolic construction which has real effects for people working within organizations. This is evident in research I carried out using five managers' accounts of emotion in a retail organization. The research was based on interviews with three women managers, and two men, and I focus my discussion on a dominant motif in the participants' accounts which Lutz (1990) calls the 'rhetoric of control': talk on controlling emotion. This reveals much about the local moral order of the organization and how it constructs emotion. It also reveals alternative constructions of emotion which subvert this but remain constant within society's discourse on emotion.

The concept of emotion as amenable and necessary to control rests upon a number of presuppositions about the location of emotion, the power of emotion and the relationships between self, emotion and moral responsibility.

## Location of emotion

As several theorists have noted (Gergen 1989; Sarbin 1986; Appadurai 1990) we represent what we understand to be our selves, thoughts, beliefs and emotions in terms of bodily interiority. It has long been traditional in western discourse of the self to view the body as a container in which our thoughts and emotions are anchored. We have an extended lexicon for 'describing' an internal topography, an inner space enclosed by the body but available for introspection at will. Foucault (1979) underscored the historical contingency of this model of interiority and internalization, and Lutz (1986) and Heelas (1986) have revealed the cultural specificity of this model in their studies of alternative models of the self and emotion. Typically, in our culture, emotion is said to be located in the body and its presence indicated by a range of physical happenings. For example, two of the managers interviewed explained:

I think when I'm angry, it's all very physical. Erm, it's all sorts of things that you're not directly aware of but together they kind of create that feeling of being angry. Like you know, you feel hot, your ears burn, your pulse is going really fast.

(Lisa)

It's right here in my diaphragm. Many of my feelings that are not nice are. They are very physical. They're there. It's the first sign that I've got them that they are there.

(Amy)

These examples should be seen as fulfilments of cultural expectations of emotional discourse and not unmediated descriptions of the bodily aspect of emotion. Even if we accept current research on the bodily aspects of emotion, the physiological processes documented are insufficiently differentiated to account for the range of emotions linguistically-available in emotional discourse. In addition, all talk constructs versions of reality from already existing linguistic resources and these must be coherent and legitimate in the context of the talk. Language is used for a variety of functions in a particular context and the participant may be conscious, or unconscious of the effects created by their talk.

The examples above reproduce the dominant cultural model of emotion in which we construct it in terms of physiological phenomena and interiority, and achieve results for the speaker. Self-elevation, demonstrating commitment and justification are some of the results evident in the managers' accounts.

The idea that emotion is internal and embodied rests upon binary oppositions of inner and outer, public and private and 'make sense only with reference to a mediating boundary that strives for stability' (Butler 1990). The mediating boundary may be the apparent surface of the body which we experience as constraining emotions under control, or the markers of public organizational spaces such as doors, offices and uniforms. The embodiment of emotion reproduces the idea that emotion is natural and the property of individuals. It pushes the responsibility upon the individual to check and discipline their behaviour to civilize any disruptive emotional impulses. The seat of reason, the mind, is sovereign over the body, the repository of emotion. At the same time, by describing emotion as natural, it also provides the individual with a justification for those situations when emotion cannot be managed. The rhetoric of control is to talk about limiting or putting boundaries around emotion, to restrain emotion to an acceptable level, to keep it inside from getting outside, to keep it private and out of the public domain.

## Power of emotion

The control of emotion is only consistent within a construction of emotion as something which warrants control: emotion as dangerous and powerful. An alternative discourse which endorses 'uncontrolled' emotion (as in certain counselling or training techniques from humanistic psychology or schools of art) also views emotion as dangerous and powerful. In this case, if emotion is repressed, it can cause disorder in the private space of the inner mind, or body, or in the public spaces of outer behaviour. The notion of 'uncontrolled' emotion is predicated on controlled emotion and oppositions of authentic/inauthentic emotion. In a sense, 'uncontrolled emotion' is as controlled as 'controlled emotion'. It is defined and mediated by cultural values and obligations. The authentic/inauthentic dualism is inextricably bound to views of nature and culture in which nature is privileged, and authentic emotion is unmediated and natural.

Both discourses extend the metaphor of the body as container into a hydraulic container, a body susceptible to the dynamics of emotion. More boundaries are set up about the limits and volume of emotion. Its power increases when it is in excess, or is intense. In the discourse which exhorts control of emotion, this natural power enables emotion to escape the boundary of the body and the control of the individual. Emotions are represented as building up, welling up, and will out, and express themselves in spite of attempts to control them. Individuals can use this model of emotion to absolve themselves or others of blame or responsibility for particular emotion responses such as anger or grief and yet still appear committed to the values of the local community. To lose control in particular situations is what an individual should do to remain in accordance with the local moral order. For it is the local moral order which constructs the discourse on emotion and the subsequent rules for emotion talk and display. In the managers' accounts, this model was only used to explain how other people lost control in public places. The example below is one manager's account of how individuals behave in management dismissals:

People do plead because it's all really coming from the heart, and you, one, me sits there, all that bare emotion very much in front. I should think more than a lot of people, I see bare, raw emotion in others.

(Michael)

Dismissal from a job is viewed as a situation in which it makes sense within emotional discourse to represent emotion as justifiably uncontrolled. It also allows Michael to juxtapose a contrasting representation of his controlled emotion:

The manager of the person concerned says 'I don't know how you managed to do that. It was all so pleasant, measured and cool'. Now I know I didn't necessarily feel that inside. I register the emotion and do control it or but again, almost for the other person's benefit as well. Probably the worst thing for them to see is the dismissing officer sat there shaking, crying and blubbing. What credibility does that give to one, and also the company?

This account is representative of how the managers accounted for themselves in terms of their control of emotion. Lutz's phrase the 'rhetoric of emotion' underscores one of the main functions it achieves for the speaker: it 'minimally elevates the social status of the person who claims the need or ability to self control emotions' (1990: 73). Typically, the managers, in line with orthodox representations of organizations, constructed versions of themselves as having emotion under control in public places.

### Self, emotion and responsibility

In order to show themselves as committed to the values of rational management, and at the same time construct themselves within the more positive model of emotion, the managers' rhetoric of control reproduced two dominant psychological models of the self: disposition self and humanistic self (Potter and Wetherell 1987). The disposition self is a model of the individual as composed of an essential disposition or temperament which determines and drives their behaviour. An individual is always true to his/her nature and his/her authentic self is revealed in his/her actions. Lisa talks below about her ex-manager whose position she assumed at the time of the interviews:

> She never thought before expressing any emotions. It kind of all came out and in a sense, it was all too honest, maybe to her detriment in the end because then she almost had a reputation for being emotional so that part of her make up was not business-like.

This model constructs emotion as a disposition over which an individual has no control. In this example it allows Lisa to justify her former boss's inappropriateness for the organization and, implicitly, to contrast her own suitability. In other examples it enables managers to associate themselves with the positive view of emotion and represent themselves as warm, sensitive and caring.

The humanistic self is a model of the individual comprised of a true self which lurks behind a variety of social selves, or roles. Lisa uses this to construct a work version of herself who practices self-control of emotion which conforms to the rational organization model of emotion. She is also able to represent her real self as someone who is emotional:

> I think I am an emotional person who tries not to be. And I think that's me at work, a person who is not emotional, or who has a very kind of limited range of emotions on a scale and maybe outside of work, I let myself be my real self.

By upholding themselves as individuals whose true selves are emotional but who control emotion in the public spaces of the organization, the managers align themselves with the view that certain emotion responses are appropriate to the business world. The reasons given sound like exhortations from training manuals and suggest that whilst seeing their true selves as emotional, they view their emotion self-control in work roles without irony or alienation, and consistent with good practice:

> I think I've learnt over the years to control my emotion, and not to take it out on other people because that isn't fair, and it's not good for forging good relationships in business.

(Helen)

At work if you're upset with somebody, you can't run around saying 'No'. We have to be mature about this. You have to be mature about it, clinical almost, and business like, behave in a business-like fashion. So you have to manage your emotions like figures on a page. It's a messy business not to be dealt with really.

(Paul)

Again we should not take these accounts necessarily as proof of how these managers behave. What these accounts demonstrate is that managers have chosen in this instance to endorse the dominant discourse of rational organizations and 'scientific' management. There are various constructions the managers could have chosen, but because the rational model is dominant and defines and creates professional management practice, it is difficult for the managers to represent themselves as good managers in any other way *vis-à-vis* emotion.

We have seen how managers talk about the control of emotion in public spaces, and consistent with the hydraulic model of emotion which represents emotion as something which can build up, they also construct private spaces in which it is legitimate to talk of expressing or purging emotion:

I couldn't hold it together. I couldn't maintain my demeanour, to the extent that I had to seek refuge in your office.

(Paul)

I tend to save it and then do something outside of work to get rid of it. I work out. I go to aerobics.

(Lisa)

And Michael talks below of the private space of his department away from 'outsiders':

There is a need for release and back to this thing that we do shitty things and that you've got to have a way of combating that. You express that or let it come out in another mode. We will all talk about the issues we've dealt with. Sometimes with relish, sometimes with concern, but vent it.

In constructing these private places, the managers are creating versions of reality in which emotion is cordoned off, marginalized, kept out of sight. An alternative version of emotion in organizations is to represent emotion as permeating all boundaries and leaking into all spaces. But this would represent disorder: disorder in current discourses on emotion in which emotion is something which is contained or expelled, not ever-present; disorder in the rational organization discourse in which reason and logic are different from and superior to emotion, and in which to use the rhetoric of control is to maintain the order and organization of the discourse.

To summarize, the rhetoric of control represents a view that emotion needs to be controlled, and it is the local rules and local moral order which regulates the emotions and emotion responses which are warrantable. Emotions have a regulatory function in society in ensuring the local values are endorsed, and certain behaviours sustained. The rhetoric of control demonstrates, not only that individuals recognize this, but that they are able to demonstrate their commitment to it. Emotions maintain their regulatory function outside of the rhetoric of control even when individuals talk of emotion coming out and being too powerful for control. This is because of the socio-culturally produced model of emotion which constructs emotion as natural. Certain situations are deemed legitimate for the representation of uncontrollable emotion and therefore to talk of giving in to emotion is to continue to demonstrate appropriate moral commitment to local values.

The representation of organizations as rational, and the development of psychology's worker subjectivity and management as a scientific and hence a rational set of practices, creates rules and conventions for emotional discourse, discourses on emotion and emotion responses. These herald from the prevalent view that emotion is not only opposite to reason, but disruptive of reason and its ends. At the same time, the managers endorse the romantic model of emotion in which emotion represents warmth, vitality and spontaneity. The managers' discourse on emotion then encompasses both the view that emotion needs to be controlled in the organization and conversely, the view that they value emotion.

## WOMEN MANAGERS AND EMOTION

And what happens to the 'emotional female' in the rational organization? Lutz (1990) notes that the incidence of the rhetoric of control was higher for the women she interviewed than for the men. She suggests that this replicates a widely-shared cultural view of the danger of women, and their emotionality. My analysis of the managers' accounts does not produce a higher incidence of the rhetoric in the women managers' talk, and this may be accounted for by the specific focus of emotion in organization I undertook. To construct a version of oneself as a professional business-person required both women and men to justify their self-control of emotion. How then does the heritage of the association of women and emotion juxtaposed to reason and men impact on women managers?

I think the answer is exemplified by the issue of crying brought up by the three women managers in the context of self-control of emotion. Crying is deemed to be a typical characteristic of femininity, a behaviour that 'normal' women manifest, and evidence that 'normal' women are sensitive, fragile and weaker than 'normal men'. Generally, women who cry are not blamed for their tears, although the tears may be seen as inappropriate or tedious. This is because they are represented in terms of the disposition self described earlier in which crying is a natural propensity over which the woman has no control. Crying that is viewed as an attempt by a woman to manipulate a situation is constructed from the humanistic model of the self. Her true self is not crying, the tears are inauthentic and unnatural, and she betrays herself as unfeminine. Unfeminine but not unwomanly, because as the Broverman quote in the introduction suggests, women are seen as sneaky.

Rationality, objectivity and logic are the properties of a type of exemplary masculinity (typically white and middle-class. Working-class men are represented in less rational terms) and, as the Broverman quote suggests, a sane, healthy individual. They are also the properties of an examplary professional manager. It is not surprising then that the women managers constructed versions of themselves in which they had their tears firmly under control:

> I never cry at work. It's to do with the sexual thing again you know that men don't and women do. I'm just being a 'girlie', if I do, you know, it's a 'girlie' thing to do.
>
> (Lisa)

To be a 'proper' manager requires that a woman reproduces an account of herself in terms of attributes which commonly represent a type of masculinity. This is not to say that men are rational, and women not. It is to show that the dominant model of professional management excludes the symbols of femininity. To distinguish between managers of different genders we talk of managers, and women managers. The concept man manager makes little sense. We can use the terms 'female' and 'male' managers, but this makes the sex of the manager visible and leaves the concept of manager as apparently ungendered, which it is not. The model of a professional manager manifests the stereotypic qualities of masculinity. A woman must disassociate herself from those features which define her femininity in other spheres. To construct a version of herself in such terms does not mean that a woman is denying her true feminine self. Or indeed that male managers do not also have to associate themselves with these exemplary masculine characteristics. The difference for women is that they have to reproduce a management self which is symbolized by the opposite of what they are supposed to be. The phrase 'woman manager' infects the meaning of the concept 'manager'. It suggests a different style of management which reproduces typical feminine skills of emotionality, intuition, caring and participation. Whether these skills are valued or denigrated is in a way irrelevant, because they do not conform to the construct of the professional manager. The women managers were aware that when they talked of controlling crying, or anger, that it was legitimate to do so in terms of male disapproval. They view the disapproval with some irony, but at the same time, reproduce a discourse which classifies men as the ones who define what is acceptable.

> I would never cry in front of my boss, because he would see it as a sign of weakness.
>
> (Helen)

> A lot of people you know, if a guy flies off the handle, gets angry in a meeting, or whatever, 'well, you know he's just a bit upset'. But if a women does that, what a lot of men think is 'she's a woman and they're all like that'.
>
> (Lisa)

What we don't know is whether the 'real' men cited in this talk agree with what the women say. We can say that in selecting the discourse in which male managers are arbiters of behaviour to justify their talked-about inhibitions, the women managers construct a version of themselves in which they control their true selves to meet the demands of men in management. The trouble is not that this is true, or untrue, but that it is difficult to imagine men constructing themselves in the same way in respect of women managers. Women managers cannot be represented by male managers as the ones who define what they as male managers can do. The local moral order which constructs the rules for emotion responses in organizations is dominated by white men. They dominate both the theorizing on organizations, and the management of organizations. Masculine attributes symbolize good management. Feminine attributes may symbolize good female management but not good management *per se*. Women managers, like emotion, are marginalized, put behind the boundaries of the construct 'female management' and kept controlled within the spaces of specialized 'female' roles and lower ranks. Women managers who cross these boundaries are 'matter out of place'.

Women cannot challenge these symbolic representations by celebrating feminine styles of management because this widens the divide between the rational male and emotional female. There are representations in which women can be said to think in the traditional ways associated with rationality, and men can be said to express or repress emotion. Rationality and emotion, women and men, management and organizations are all social constructions. Because they are socially constructed does not mean that we can ignore the material effects this has on dominant representations of women, and our experience of these effects. Emotional competence is viewed typically as a feminine competence. Management competence is viewed as an ungendered competence, and yet we have seen how it is constructed in terms of typical masculine competences. Rather than seeing emotion as a natural female disposition, or a socially-constructed reality which any woman, or group of women can change, we should as women and managers be looking to the gendered nature of power relations. It is here that we can begin to analyse who produces the knowledge which constitutes particular representations, and realities of organizations, emotion and management. In the past it has been white, middle-class, homophobic men who, to the exclusion of all women, have devised the symbolic structures which define what is legitimate. Womanhood is not a universal, singular set of identities and experiences, and neither is 'good' management.

## REFERENCES

Abu-Lughod, L. (1990) 'Shifting politics in bedouin love poetry', in C. Lutz and L. Abu-Lughod (eds) *Language and the Politics of Emotion*, Cambridge: Cambridge University Press.

Appadurai, A. (1990) 'Topographies of the self: praise and emotion in Hindu India', in C. Lutz and L. Abu-Lughod (eds) *Language and the Politics of Emotion*, Cambridge Cambridge University Press.

Armon-Jones, C. (1986) 'The social functions of emotion', in R. Harré (ed.) *The Social Construction of Emotion*, Oxford: Blackwell.

Birke, L. (1986) *Women, Feminism and Biology*, Cambridge: Polity Press.

Brownmiller, S. (1986) *Femininity*, London: Paladin Books.

Butler, J. (1990) *Gender Trouble*, London: Routledge.

Crespo, E. (1986) 'A regional variation: emotions in Spain', in R. Harré (ed.) *The Social Construction of Emotion*, Oxford: Blackwell.

Douglas, M. (1966) *Purity and Danger*, London: Routledge.

Foucault, M. (1979). *Discipline and Punish*, Harmondsworth: Penguin.

Gergen, K. (1989) 'Warranting voice and the elaboration of the self', in J. Shotter and K. Gergen (eds) *Texts of Identity* London: Sage.

Harré, R. (ed.) (1986) *The Social Construction of Emotion*, Oxford: Blackwell.

Harré, R. and Finlay-Jones, R. (1986) 'Emotion talk across times', in R. Harré (ed.) *The Social Construction of Emotion*, Oxford: Blackwell.

Haslanger, S. (1993) 'On being objective and being objectified', in L. Antony and C. Witt (1993) *A Mind of One's Own*, Boulder, Colo.: Westview Press.

Heelas, P. (1986) 'Emotion talk across cultures', in R. Harré (ed.) *The Social Construction of Emotion*, Oxford: Blackwell.

Hollway, W. (1992) *Work Psychology and Organisational Behaviour*, London: Sage.

Jordanova, L. (1980) 'Natural facts: a historical perspective', in C. MacCormack and H. Strathern (ed.) *Nature, Culture and Gender*, Cambridge: Cambridge University Press.

Lakoff, G. and Johnson, M. (1980) *Metaphors We Live By*, Chicago: University of Chicago Press.

Lutz, C. (1986) 'The domain of emotion words on Ifaluk', in R. Harré (ed.) *The Social Construction of Emotion*, Oxford: Blackwell.

Lutz, C. (1990) 'Engendered emotion: gender, power, and the rhetoric of emotional control in American discourse', in C. Lutz and L. Abu-Lughod (eds) *Language and the Politics of Emotion*, Cambridge: Cambridge University Press.

Lutz, C. and Abu-Lughod, L. (eds) (1990) *Language and the Politics of Emotion*, Cambridge: Cambridge University Press.

Morsbach, H. and Tyler, W. J. (1986) 'A Japanese emotion: amae', in R. Harré (ed.) *The Social Construction of Emotion*, Oxford: Blackwell.

Potter, J. and Wetherell, M. (1987) *Discourse and Social Psychology*, London: Sage.

Sarbin, T. (1986) 'Emotion and act: roles and rhetoric', in R. Harré (ed.) *The Social Construction of Emotion*, Oxford: Blackwell.

Strathern, M. (1980) 'No nature, no culture: the Hagen case', in C. MacCormack and M. Strathern, *Nature, Culture and Gender*, Cambridge: Cambridge University Press.

## Chapter 7

# Power, continuity and change: decoding black and white women managers' experience in local government

*Linda Martin*

## INTRODUCTION

Black and white women entered senior management positions in British local government in the last decade, mainly as a consequence of changes in legislation; the introduction of equal opportunity policies; socialist experiments in local government at the time; and black people and women's campaigns for more relevant public services. Nevertheless, women, and particularly black women, remain significantly underrepresented in the most senior grades, and tend to be located in service-oriented rather than policy-making posts (Button 1984). Local government remains dominated (in the sense of who holds most senior jobs) by white middle-class men.

In parallel, black and white women managers' experience and sense-making, and particularly their role in developing effective management practices and implementing equality strategies in local government, is absent from most theorizing of local government, organization and management, or management training. Where it is included (for example Kanter 1977; Marshall 1984; Mills 1989; Sheppard 1989), theorizing of women managers often excludes black women's experience, and tends towards essentialist arguments. (That is to say, the supposed essential nature of women and men is proposed as binary oppositions of identity characteristics and preferences (Gunew 1990); and women's experience is presented as if uniform, conflating differences of race, class and sexual orientation).

The purpose of this chapter is to describe and decode black and white women managers' organizational experience and strategic interventions in local government. It argues that this experience reveals institutionalized racism and sexism in organization as both discourse and practices; that organizational racism and sexism are embedded by management thinking and behaviour, and reinforced by management and organization theory.

The chapter considers four main themes:

1 black and white women managers' individual power to act;
2 'race' and gender power relations as characteristics of organization and management discourse and practices;
3 continuity and change in the power relations of organization;
4 the relationship between theory and practice.

I want to suggest that

- there are within and outside organizations, diverse, interactive and competing knowledges and discourses about organization, management and women managers. Such discourses are constitutive of 'regimes of truth' (Foucault 1980) about organization, which reflect and reinforce relations of dominance in terms of gender, race and class.
- black and white women managers both assert their different meanings through their practice, and work towards shared meanings. However, their attempts to achieve shared organizational meanings about race and gender inequality are mainly resisted and repudiated. Transactions about meanings reveal the ways in which race and gender power relations are embedded in and by individual, group and organizational practice (Collins 1990; Martin 1990; Vince 1991), and demonstrate that within those power relations there is both continuity and change.
- black and white women managers as agents of change attempt to adopt a strategic approach to both coping and intervention. A key element of this strategy is to decode organizational events and interpersonal transactions as competing organizational knowledges and discourses; and to choose whether and when to render the competition visible.

I have reached my analysis and conclusions by decoding specific episodes and transactions from black and white women managers' experience in dialogue with them, in groups, or individually, between 1989 and 1991, mainly contacted and interviewed during my MSc dissertation work. My analytic framework is of necessity cross-disciplinary and eclectic; it draws on recent organization, management and local government theory (for example, Stewart

1986, 1988; Stoker 1991; Marshall 1984; Hearn *et al*. 1989; Morgan 1986; Reed and Hughes 1992); on black and white feminist and post-structuralist theory, and theory of the state, local state intervention, and politics of interpretation and empowerment (for example, Fraser 1989; Collins 1990; Hernes 1988; hooks 1989, 1991; Watson 1990); on anti-racist theory of the local state in Britain (Ball and Solomos 1990; Ben-Tovim *et al*. 1986); and on post-structuralist and critical theory of power (Foucault 1980; Lukes 1974; Clegg 1989).

My purpose is to make notions of local government organization and management that are evident to black and white women managers working for change and equality more widely visible, so that management and organization theory, and management training can be influenced; and so that public sector management and organization practice can address the negative aspects of black people's and white women's experience as managers, as workers, and users of services.

The chapter is in two sections:

1 Decoding black and white women managers' experience.
2 Continuity and change in organizational 'race' and gender power relations.

*Note*: 'Race' appears throughout in inverted commas, in keeping with practice which acknowledges the contested nature of the term in the context of processes of racialization (Husband 1987).

## DECODING BLACK AND WHITE WOMEN MANAGERS' EXPERIENCE

### Context: individual power to act

Local government has been a focus for the intervention of black and white women for a range of reasons related to discrimination in employment, access to services, and the availability, kind and quality of public services. Policy and management in local government have frequently reinforced inequalities of 'race' and gender within local government organization and in its relations with users of services (Ben-Tovim *et al*. 1986; Martin and Gaster 1993). The situation is not static, however. British local government organizations and management practices are subject to both continuity and change in 'race' and gender power relations, and in their effectiveness in delivering 'race' and gender equality. The entry of black and white women managers into senior management positions has coincided with considerable activity to promote 'race' and gender equality in the local state, its services and its spheres of influence (Button 1984; Stone 1988).

Black women and white women managers' experience has demonstrated differences in their experience of power and powerlessness in local government. They exhibited similarities and differences in relation to their focus on equality strategy. All the women in my study described a bias for action, and for equal opportunities to be an important and central area of management practice. All the women focused on changing practices not people as their strategy for equality. They varied in their understanding of equal opportunities practice, in their strategy, expectations, and prioritization of 'race' and gender equality.

The conditions influencing these variations seemed to include:

- being part of a mixed team which included black and white women and men, compared with being the only black, or female or black woman manager;
- being in a department with a high profile on equal opportunities, as opposed to a department where this was new or felt to be 'lip-service';
- perceiving alliances and collaborating actively in the community with women and/ or black people and organizations, as opposed to limiting their focus to established public figures and mainstream organizations;
- having an orientation towards learning, development, and personal reflexivity alongside action;
- having expectations of equal opportunities as implementation through changed practices and positive action, as opposed to understanding equal opportunities as intentions;
- understanding the dynamics of 'race' as well as gender power relations in organizations;
- considering the politics and psychology of managing change, as processes involving both power and unconscious behaviour.

Major reported factors affecting a woman's experience of, and approach to, organization and management were:

- her consciousness of herself as an agent of change;
- her critical awareness of the power relations affecting her as black or white and a woman, and in some cases, coming from a working-class background.

Women with a clear sense of themselves as agents of change for equality in organizations tended to be innovative, enabling, collaborative and accountable managers. They tended also to be developing an empowered sense of self, derived from consciously-constructed positive identities and from their involvement in collective or community action. What this meant for women was that they had recovered a sense of their personal authority by engaging in self-definition, self-determination and self-actualization (Collins 1990), and by facilitating others in these processes within and outside the organization, as an integral aspect of their management role, and of their strategies for equality. This process of 'politicised self-recovery' (hooks 1989) supported the women's individual power to act in organizational contexts which were covertly and overtly hostile to their empowered sense of self-identity and mode of self-presentation.

Moreover, this process and its effects on individual women meant that positive identities of black and white women managers were also affirmed at the level of organizational meaning. This happened when organizational and management discourses which objectify and constrain black and white women in organizations surfaced in relation to the women's presence, or were consciously surfaced by the women, through their discourse and practices. By making apparent a perspective that their (and all) 'knowledges' were partial, and situated in relation to identities, two important aspects of organizational discourse and knowledges were made visible:

1 That knowledges and discourses about black and white women managers and hence about 'race' and gender are in dynamic engagement, either competing, or collaborating towards shared meanings.
2 That some partial, located knowledges (white men's and women's), including organizational research, are privileged over others in gendered, racially-stratified and class-structured ways, to dominate interpretations of power relations (as relations of dominance and subjection); organization (as static, monolithic, hierarchical, bureaucratic; as race and gender neutral, and

as structure); management (as rational control, fair, asexual, apolitical, white, male and right); and black and female identity (as the repository of otherness, difference, inferiority, emotion, sexuality, race, gender and class). Such institutionalized interpretations (Fraser 1989) constitute a regime of truth (Foucault 1980) in organizations which black and white women managers have to engage with, because women's identities and power to act are invoked, penetrated or subjugated by it. When engagement takes the form of conscious intervention, then black and white women managers have been able to affirm their 'interpretations'; sustain a self-defined identity and the power to act as managers; and, because their position is marginal (hooks 1990), make visible the existence and contest the workings of the regime.

### Institutionalized discourse about difference

Institutionalized interpretations about management as a white and male job are achieved in two main ways. First, through denial or silence about institutionalized norms; and second, through discourse which proliferates in organizations about supposed black and or female identity, behaviour, characteristics and needs, to define 'difference'. Specifically, there is talk about black people and women as the supposed repository of difference (Pringle 1989), and therefore of, for example, race, gender, emotion and sexuality. Consequences include negative or stereotyped interpretations of black people and women's behaviour in organizations. What is obscured is that organizational norms are being asserted through the exercising of power to define, and that some definitions are simultaneously legitimized by, and institutionalized as, the regime. In the context of the institutionalized definition or paradigm of manager as white and male and middle class, black and white women are highly visible as 'other'. They are therefore rendered 'contraparadigmatic' (ibid.), and presumed to be intrinsically in deficit as managers.

Such discourse serves to justify black and white women's continuing exclusion from jobs, or from credibility in management discourse. Women in my study experienced the double bind that as managers they were defined as essentially unfeminine since they were managers, or not proper managers since they were black and/ or women.

When black and white women entered management posts, 'race' and gender talk was produced around those women and all that they undertook: their difference and otherness from the institutionalized notion of the norm was continually commented on. Focusing on them seemed to conceal that these notions were institutionalized in the organizational discourse, and to mask that the deep structures of management thought, language and day-to-day practices are racist and heterosexist, and that women have to take up positions in relation to those discourses and practices whether they want to or not in order to undertake management.

For example, women spoke of the credit for their appointment being ascribed to the positive equality policies of the organization, or to the enlightened approach of white and male senior managers. Since no mention was made of the woman's skills, expertise or experience, her blackness, her femaleness, and her otherness from the supposed norm of manager were covertly highlighted. By implication, she was deskilled and depowered; the managerial skills of the white and male manager asserted; the power relations of race and gender confirmed; her place as the subject in discourse decentred. She became the object of (racist and sexist) knowledge. Her 'difference' was reaffirmed, and legitimated as the subject of open, racist and sexist attention.

Once in post, a woman manager was highly visible; as a black woman, an 'out' lesbian, or a woman with a disability, particularly so. Rather than this serving to indicate the organizational biases in favour of other groups, the focus of attention was the woman's difference, and by implication, if not explicitly, her lack. Several women referred to having to continually re-establish their power of role as managers, in each interaction and context. Unlike white and male managers' role power, it never became given over time.

There frequently developed a discourse of 'cultural exotica' about the woman manager, especially for black women; manifesting as a tendency to view as exceptional relatively ordinary achievements or errors. This serves to defend traditional forms of interpretation in the following ways: first it reinforces the notion that women and black people are unusual or in deficit in management positions; second, it suggests that management jobs are the province of the exceptional (for women and black people) few. Third, it reinforces the dominance of white male managers, about whom such remarks are not made. The power relations are asserted and concealed at the same point since the remarks masquerade as praise.

Decoded, they reveal the prejudice of the speaker. That this is not immediately evident, demonstrates that power relations are involved.

These notions of black and white women's difference were repeatedly reinforced by interpersonal transactions inside and outside the organization. For example, every woman I talked to had been assumed to be the committee clerk when attending a committee meeting, especially if she had been the only woman present. Alternatively, but none the less reinforcing of her 'contraparadigmatic' status, if she was the only woman, and especially the only black woman, manager, she discovered she was expected at meetings, as 'the' black/woman manager; people had heard about her before meeting her, and welcomed her with open curiosity (statements, repeated glances, exaggerated smiling).

The false assumption was frequently made that women were likely to or had used heterosexual sex to their organizational advantage. However, as both men and women know, women (managers) are much less likely to initiate sexual contact at work than men, and much more likely to experience harassment or abuse (Stanley and Wise 1983). Sexual harassment, joking, abuse and sexualized references are routine ways for men to exercise authority towards women in organizations. Where a woman was perceived to be powerful or skilful as a manager, her socially subordinate status as a woman or as a black person was invoked by white men and women to depower her. Simultaneously, therefore, white and male power, gender relations of dominance, and/ or racist convictions of rights of access to black women were covertly asserted by behaviour and language.

Along with more overt exercising of power and harassment, this was the context for a woman manager's interpretations, actions, and the dynamics which her interventions had to address, in order to be an agent of change. She therefore needed:

- recognition that these are the dynamics and processes of power in organizations;
- awareness that the context constructs and is likely to continually perceive her in racially-structured and/or gendered ways;

- the support and ability to recover again and again an empowered consciousness of her subjective experience, self-definition and personal power to act;
- a strategic approach to her own behaviour and intervention which is both self-protecting, and engages with disciplinary, group and personal power. She has entered a hostile environment, but one where paradoxically, her marginal position can foster her creativity and self-empowerment, as well as her frustration and oppression (hooks 1990).

There were differences in the ways black women and white women were perceived and constructed as managers within the organization. Hence black women in my study were involved in specific struggles for inclusion in the category 'manager' which depended on the power relations of 'race' rather than gender. Decoding their experience revealed that black women managers were without exception defined as black and female before being defined as managers, by the language, actions and practices of white male and some white female managers.

For example, a black woman manager attended, with white male colleagues, a meeting with members of black communities. The white and male managers walked away from her together, and formed an inward-facing, closed circle around the coffee table. It was assumed by them (but not by the people, nor by herself), that she had immediate acceptance by the black people present, and automatic membership of what was presumed to be a black group. Decoding this transaction shows that, at a number of levels, she (and the other black people present) is being defined by white and male managers primarily as black, and a member of an undifferentiated group, representing a similarly undifferentiated community, characterized by 'blackness' or 'race'. At the same time she is 'defined out' (Lukes 1974) of the group 'manager', or membership of the professional community. Further, the transaction serves to deskill her, by collapsing into one visible aspect of her identity the interpersonal and community development skills she has to employ as a local authority manager and middle-class professional in negotiating with local people.

She is potentially 'silenced'; no shared space is assumed for her to define or negotiate the experience and its meanings on her terms. The right to define and control the situation is wholly appropriated by the white and male officers, arguably also masking their anxiety and defensiveness in the face of what they assume (and fear) to be black collectivity. These meanings and complexities of process are masked by, and in turn, mask, the power and assumed right of the white and male group to define their interpretations as the way things are through focusing attention on the black woman manager and other black people present. The fact that they are a (white and male) group, and operate as such in their own perceived interests, is projected on to the black people present. Mobilization of bias (Lukes 1984) as the power to act in the interest of white and male and professional collectivity (Vince 1991) is paradoxically concealed and affirmed at the same time.

Confronting and challenging this kind of behaviour, as the woman in question did, constitutes extra (frustrating, enraging and exhausting) work for black and white women managers, and gets in the way of collaborative organizational development, equal opportunities, management effectiveness and positive human relations.

Black women managers recognized that although any difficulty and unreasonable behaviour was constructed as if theirs, it was the perceptions, practices and resistance (to taking responsibility for their behaviour and its consequences) of others that needed to be addressed. Black women continually had to deal with other people's difficulties in seeing them in other than racially-constructed and gendered ways.

White women managers, on the other hand, were sometimes included in the category of manager by /with white male managers, in ways that black women managers were not. Nevertheless, this usually occurred in order to detach the woman manager from solidarity with other women in the organization. So, for example, a white woman manager spoke of how her white, male senior officer presumed her loyalty to management in opposition to women workers' demands, despite having previously agreed to her involvement in women workers' groups as part of a gender equality strategy. It was clear that the white male manager had no notion of the woman manager's need to negotiate her position both in relation to women workers and to senior management, since she experienced herself as having loyalties to, and differences from, both. It is also clear that at some level – in this case I would argue specifically through shared white identity, since he overlooked her subordinate gender position – he included her in the definition of manager. Such inclusion was interpreted by some white women, with the power to generalize from their white experience, to conclude that the main organizational barriers to women were overcome.

## Implications of institutionalized discourses

There are significant exclusionary effects arising from gendered and racially-structured discourses about difference in relation to management in local government. These are that women especially black women,

1 are discriminated against in access to management jobs;
2 are continually constructed as in deficit in relation to holding management positions;
3 are in the position of having to continually affirm or seek reinforcement for their role and status as managers, since it is never taken for granted;
4 can sustain physical and psychological stress and damage, not only from the risk of overt sexual and racial harassment, but from the work of engaging within and against discourses and practices that are covert, unconscious or denied, attack their identity, and undermine their professional practice, while calling for leadership to assist managers, staff and users in resolving these very issues.

Nevertheless, the black and white women managers I talked to adopted a strategic approach to these potential problems. They resisted discourse and practices about difference residing essentially in binary oppositions of black and white, or male and female. Their approach was to decode interactions, events and discourse as differences in power and powerlessness. Consequently, they transformed conflicts over definitions of identity into opportunities to reveal competing, institutionalized meanings and biased organizational practices. They operated in ways which demonstrated how the 'race', sexuality and gender of organization and management are contested, and simultaneously produced as power relations. In other words, they recognized the relationship between organizational power relations, management behaviour and institutionalized processes, and they consequently assumed the potential for change.

In view of black and white women's strategic relocation of

conflict in this way, it seems important to question the value, for black and white women managers, of those theories of organization, management and women managers which propose fixed, essential difference residing in female and male identity.

## Theorizing for change

Some theories of gender in organization and management have suggested that dominance and subjection are integral and essential aspects of male and female identity respectively, and imply fixed and inevitably polarized gender power relations. They tend to construct women and men in terms of fundamental and unchanging binary oppositions that encourage thinking in terms of continuing division, and marginalize racism and other forms of discrimination and oppression affecting women differently (Carby 1986). They reinforce institutionalized notions of organizations as fixed and monolithic structures, and obscure the dynamic nature of processes producing the 'race', gender and class power relations of organization. By not differentiating continuity and change in gendered power relations, they deny the possibility of women managers' active engagement in those processes as agents of change. Such approaches therefore are unhelpful in conceptualizing and implementing strategies for change.

Central to essentialist theories of gender and organizations have been notions, for example, of 'male organizational culture' and 'women's management style'. As ways of thinking about change towards equality and change agency in organizations, these are limited concepts, especially in terms of the analysis of power. The model of power implied is fixed and linear; the dynamic processes by which power is enacted and produced are obscured; the operations and intersections of 'race' with gender oppression, and therefore the specificity of black and white women's different experiences of sexism, of black women's experience of racism, and of white women's oppressor role, are missing. As fixed oppositional notions, they offer women only polarized options to address the gender power relations of organization – assimilation or fight – and fail to address the options for men. They omit or conceal the necessity for the racism of organizations to be addressed as a priority for the appropriate advancement of some women, and the ways in which privileging gender discourse can be used to avoid addressing race equality. Such notions, therefore, may themselves contribute to discourses which are disempowering for women.

For example, it is claimed that it is the masculine culture and style of organizations that acts as a barrier to women's progress within and into management (Mills 1989). Such an assertion serves only to perpetuate the mystification of management, men's ownership of it, and takes as self-evident that women want management on the same terms. The dynamic and interactive character of power relations in organizations as struggles over meanings and practices is denied. It is an unhelpful and inadequate conceptualization for two reasons: first, the implication that male organizational culture is static, fixed, and monolithic; and second, the failure to represent the active roles of male and female managers in power struggles to resist and create change. I shall say more about both of these below.

### 'Male organizational culture'

'Male organizational culture' is neither static, nor a given of organizations, but a product of dynamic, interactive homosocial and sexist discourses and practices that produce institutionalized organizational meanings. Conversely, organizational 'race' and gender power relations are not fixed in pre-existing white and male-dominated culture (Hearn *et al.* 1989; Watson 1990; Reed and Hughes 1992). Rather the power relations are produced and contested by the gendered nature of discourses and practices of organization and management, which in turn create 'organization' as sites and arenas constitutive of, as well as reproducing, political, economic and social power relations.

Rather than the disembodied, dehumanized, and non-accountable notion of 'male organizational culture', we need to think about the active engagement in behaviour, and transactions between persons and groups as processes constitutive of organizational power relations. It is primarily white and male denial that such power issues exist; avoidance of responsibility for dominating behaviour; and covert and overt exercising of power to resist change and maintain control of women and black people, that reproduce the regime and constitute the continuing barriers to black and white women within organizations. Power, denial and avoidance (Watson 1990; Vince 1991) are exercised through day-to-day management practices and transactions.

In this study it was clear that it was not (white and) male culture that was the barrier to women. On the contrary, women being as it were participant observers, were in a unique position to 'know' male culture, its conscious and unconscious effects; to learn the character of organizational politics, blocks and barriers, and to be strategic in dealing with them; and to evaluate white and male management practice. Women stated that they had learned much about how and how not to do management, and how to prosper in a hostile environment, from their observation and experience within 'male organizational culture' in a range of public and private settings.

Black and white women had developed a critical consciousness about organizational practices, and saw themselves and the organization in continuous and interactive dynamics of change that were frustrating, but also potentially creative. They tended to construct their own organizational experiences, including negative or distressing experiences, as opportunities for learning; and their approach to managing change included working towards a 'learning organization'. However, what constrained women was the necessity to continuously address or engage with the exercising of male power.

This took the form for instance of men's assumed right to define and decide; refusal to negotiate interactions and collaborative action, and persistence in competing over or defending meanings, rather than creating opportunities to negotiate shared meanings; behaving as if in various ways women were in need of white and male solutions and consequently representing women as in deficit, childlike, dependent, sexualized, inferior; assuming that racist and sexist ignorance was organizational ignorance.

It seemed, however, that 'male organizational culture' was likely to be a block and a constraint for men, since they seemed to be frequently constrained by fixed and inflexible modes of thinking and operating, and acted as if male managers and a white and men's organization was a fixed and essential good, which needed to be defended from the presence and interventions of black and white women.

Thus from the experience of black and white women managers it appears more accurate to conclude that it is the notion of white and male culture which restricts men, and the exercising of white and male power which restricts women. It therefore follows that equality strategies within organizations need fundamentally to address power and how it is exercised, by changing management practices and behaviour; and by developing open and flexible structures for power sharing. This, for black and white women managers, was the meaning and purpose of equal opportunity.

### 'Women's management style'

The notion of 'women's management style' has been proposed as a by-product of, or antidote to, 'male organizational culture', but this notion also suffers from the limitations of essentialism and inadequate power analysis (for example, Sheppard 1989). The concept is underpinned by notions of women's and men's essential difference, and has influenced not only analysis, but also much training targeted at women managers.

Supporting the idea of women's management style is the characterization of women managers as in conflict over aspects of identity where a predilection for relating represents the main characteristic of a woman's supposed authentic self. Relatedness or caring, it is argued, is consequently both the cause of her problems in male-dominated organizations, and the hope for transformation of organizational life. This a problematic analysis and a potential trap for women, since it sustains the binary oppositions that constrict theory, practice, and personal and collective empowerment.

First, the notion of 'women's style of management' is stereo-typed, and denies to both women and men the ability to exercise certain characteristics. Arguably, all human beings experience internal conflict over aspects of identity. Caring, relatedness and concern for relationship are neither essential female characteristics, nor unavailable to men. Nor are they necessarily and in all contexts a priority choice of strategy for women. Where they are, it may equally be argued that it is a covert form of power-seeking, an attempt at control or manipulation, taking the form of an organizational, negative 'mother' role (Pringle 1989).

The notion of a 'woman's management style' implies universality, and is therefore itself exclusionary: what of the woman who operates primarily as an agent of change, or with ambition, or who covertly and overtly seeks power and control? Is this to be defined as adopting a 'male' style and excluded from a notion of 'superior' female identity? Is it to be assumed that she lacks an authentic female self? What of women who want to establish boundaries and limits for their caring and availability to others, in their own interests?

Claims that organizations need 'women's management style' to transform and humanize organizations, are alienating in apparently seeking to monopolize all loving behaviour and human values on the female side. As a strategy, it is both stereotyped and at best double-edged for women, in reinforcing that women should take this responsibility. As a notion it reinforces dominant discourse and constrains women's possibilities in practice.

Black and white women managers in my study demonstrated a range and flexibility in their approaches, inclusive of a full range of emotional and professional styles and characteristics. Of particular interest in this context are Marshall's (1984) notions of communion (relatedness to self and others) and agency (the power to act in the world). I would argue that, rather than assuming one of these as the preferred female or male identity characteristics, a more complex, psychological and political model is needed than the stereotyped and essentialist version allows.

Thus, as internal, conflicting aspects of human personality, agency and communion are enacted in organizations as gendered and racially structured power relations between men and women. As internal conflicts they are acted out and projected in organizations, but in stereotyped ways, because both the characteristics and the conflicts are gendered and racially-structured as relations of dominance and subjection. Communion and agency are notions that are socially and politically constructed, in an organizational context as elsewhere.

From this perspective, an analysis of how agency and communion are constructed, mediated, rewarded and sanctioned differently in organizations, for women and men, would seem more useful both to black and white women managers; and to understanding the relationship between personal empowerment and continuity and change in organizational power relations. So, for example, agency has been ascribed to white male identity, and rewarded in white men, in organizational and public life. The notion of agency as a male characteristic has been significant in the process of producing discourses of 'public' and 'private' which underpin the sexual division of labour, including the masculinization of management (Stacey and Price 1981).

For women in public life, and in organizations, characteristics representative of communion are both rewarded and sanctioned.

On the one hand, communion and other characteristics like caring are ascribed to female identity, and represented as a barrier to women's management (agency) potential. On the other hand, women managers are steered into communion and caring arenas in the organization, for example, staff development rather than policy-making functions of management. In traditional organizational discourse and practice, women are expected to somehow humanize the organization (Davies and Rosser 1986; Showstack Sassoon 1987) by doing the emotional work to sustain relationships, with a caring approach that is assumed by some women as well as men to be a female attribute, rather than a learned human skill.

In attempts to validate women as managers, 'women's management style' is encouraged as an organizational necessity, while being represented as a barrier and a block to women's progress that needs to be addressed by assertiveness training for women. Women thus take on more and more emotional work, while also arguably occupying both the moral high ground and the traditional (double-edged) locus of female 'power', that is, to control the definition of authenticity and relatedness.

Decoding the effect of such constructions makes visible how women are deskilled as well as excluded from powerful arenas in the organization, when women's interpersonal or communion skills are collapsed into aspects of female identity. Where women present areas of skill representative of agency, these are often denied or denigrated by the reverse strategy: collapsing them into notions of identity by calling a woman's femininity/womanhood into question. Some women collude with men in this strategy to undermine highly visible, authoritative, agentic women; and some white women collude to undermine black women's agency.

Further, a common strategy of defensiveness in 'race' and gender equality issues, is to assign a woman's analysis and perspective to her visible and perceived-as-subordinate identity; to her femaleness, her blackness, her lesbianism, rather than to her skills or her identity as 'manager'. All the women I have interviewed were aware of this particular sanction and took steps to avoid it; primarily by attempting to locate all proposals for change within a professional/managerial discourse, and out of a personal identity discourse.

It can thus be seen how discourses of polarized and essentialist identity can serve to depoliticize the challenge to meanings and practices posed by black and white women's agency and intervention. Issues are 'defined out' (Lukes 1974) of 'race' and gender politics and the public arena, and into the private and the personal domain of identity. The idealistic celebrations of self proposed by 'women's management style', do not do justice to the political and psychological challenge of black and white women's organizational engagement. Women's strategy does need to include developing a conscious, empowered notion of self, but this is not derived from an inner authentic female, awaiting discovery or release.

Black and white women managers' reported concern for human values in organizations, networking, support and team-building can therefore as easily be seen in terms of enlightened self-interest, as in terms of the moral high ground that is claimed by the proponents of 'women's management style'. Black and white women needed support where their positive and flexible identities, agency and intervention were reinforced by others, to lighten the workload of creating and sustaining it for themselves.

Aspects of 'communion' could therefore be seen politically, related to the need for support and validation while working strategically in environments hostile not only to women's fulfilment, but also to their integrity as persons. As one black woman manager said, at the stage of reluctantly leaving her management job, 'Sometimes the cost is too high'. For another black woman and a white woman (working in a context where each was the only black and/or woman manager), working with a planned date to leave was part of their strategy to manage for achievable change, protect their integrity and health, and retain the energy to be effective in a new context. Working as an agent of change for organizational equality demands a political strategy that addresses different levels and processes of power, including those related to the self and the body.

Another black woman manager interviewed had a clear long- and short-term strategy for intervention, rooted in her awareness of herself as a black woman, and her knowledge that because of the racism and gender relations of the organization, she would need continually to deal with other people's difficulties in seeing her in other than racially-constructed and gendered ways. Based on this understanding, she was able to choose if, when and how to respond to specific situations in ways that did not compromise her as a black woman. This meant always acting strategically, and with a clear awareness of her personal and professional boundaries.

She could thus focus her change strategies where they would be most effective and let the rest go or adopt a longer-term approach.

To do this, black and white women managers developed a portfolio of styles to draw on within an overall approach to managing change which was strategic at three levels:

### A strategic engagement with the self

This included personal empowerment; clarity over personal boundaries; priority for her own health and well-being; the ability to learn from her experience through reflexivity about herself in her context; self-protection through awareness of, and decoding, the racially-structured and gendered identities that would be, and were, projected on to her; expectation that she would continually be dealing with other people's difficulties with her authority and power to act; conceptualizing self-protection as knowing when to be armoured, when to fight, when to be impervious, when to imagine a screen in front of her receiving other people's versions of her, when to engage openly with making conflicts and power struggles visible. Above all, knowing her personal limits and the limits of individual intervention.

### A strategic engagement with individual and group power and process

This included, for example, developing a critical consciousness of the ways in which others exercised their power individually and collectively in the interests of particular groups; the ability to decode interpersonal transactions and day-to-day practices as constitutive of 'race' and gender power relations in the organization; relocating discourse and practices as organizational, managerial and procedural, rather than personal and individual; modelling effective, enabling management; choosing when to challenge, compete, collaborate or work towards shared meanings and practices.

### A strategic engagement with the organization as an agent of change for equality

This included an awareness of institutionalized oppression and domination and their operations; understanding how organizational power is processual as well as structural; having a concept of local government organization as a diffuse, fragmented and interactive network, and consequently having a complex model of change; perceiving her management role as an enabler in a network with the ability to mobilize alliances and to work collaboratively; having a sense of purpose and commitment to staff and to users of services. Above all, she understands the relationships between the personal, the group and the institutional levels of power.

## CONTINUITY AND CHANGE IN ORGANIZATIONAL 'RACE' AND GENDER POWER RELATIONS

Black and white women managers, with an analysis of race and gender power relations and processes of change within local government organization, believed themselves to be actively engaged in challenging and changing the status quo as an integral element in their work. Those women spoke of notions of management where implementing equal opportunities, anti-racism and anti-sexism was central to effective management practice, in order to ensure equity and quality in service delivery, employment and promotion. Their aims involved:

1 Attempting to introduce change into organization, management practices and service delivery.
2 Attempting to introduce change into the meanings of organization, management and service delivery.

Black and white women managers' accounts of their interventions for equal opportunities testify to processes of continuity and change in the ways that power in organizations is exercised and resisted; and in the interactive nature of discursive and material struggles over 'race', gender and class.

### Continuity: implementing equal opportunities

Continuity is evident in the extent to which white and/or male power as institutionalized domination has been defended and maintained in organizations. This has frequently been achieved specifically through discourses which deny the importance of 'race' and gender power relations (Watson 1990), and of equality strategies as implementation.

Black and white women managers experienced both creativity

and immense frustration in local government, in managing power and equality. Many women managers, especially black women, were appointed with the explicit or assumed expectation that they would contribute to equal opportunities. Nevertheless, their knowledge, experience and skills to implement equality practices were continually, if often unintentionally, blocked by the lack of knowledge, understanding and skill, by the misinterpretation, and by the resistance, avoidance and defensiveness of primarily white and male managers.

Three significant issues were reported:

1 Enormous defensiveness was brought to bear on the notion of implementing equality, and the idea that changing existing management practices was necessary to that end. Because it hinges on the understanding that management practices and behaviour produce organizational power relations, and that equality strategies in public sector organizations are about sharing (managerial and professional) power, *doing* equality means doing things differently, starting to open contexts and forums to other 'knowledges' and clearing the way to act on them (for example, to define needs, plan services and allocate resources).

   Paradoxically, conflicts over implementation of equality strategy were hidden as deliberations about how to implement equality strategy. White and male managers were left frustrated with charges of 'lip-service', and the sense that nothing they did was good enough; black and white women were frustrated and exhausted by continually explaining and having misunderstood what they would rather be implementing. Struggles over meaning were denied, and the necessity to address differences and work towards shared meanings resisted.

2 Hidden within institutionalized interpretations by the power relations, but made visible by the interventions of black and some white women, was the fact that a power struggle was taking place between two competing discourses about equality. These were the institutionalized and the contesting interpretations of the meaning of 'implementing equal opportunities'. This difference can be summarized as the difference between understanding equality as future intention, and understanding equality as present action.

3 Where action on equality was concerned, some women managers were in the position of training all the time. Their knowledge and skills about equal opportunities as practised were not part of the organizational common sense; not accepted as knowledge in the organization. Women were thus continually in the position of having to explain, make out a case, research, demonstrate evidence for, what for them were the givens of how to do equality. At the same time, what they said about equality was continually constructed as the women's personal, black/female point of view, bias, or hobby-horse, by white and or male managers, whose notions were invisible as interpretations (white and/or male point of view; bias, hobby-horse), because they were institutionalized as organizational common sense. Interactions involving explanation and defensiveness served, intentionally or not, to defend the status quo, and to act as a barrier to change.

Black and white women active for equality were aware of ways to put into practice the basics for positive action, monitoring and accountability within all aspects of management practice. Most white or/and male managers constructed equality strategy as something that the organization needed to learn about, generalizing from their own position: a power contest between meanings is taking place at the interpersonal level. At the organizational level, this means they exercise their power to block. They thus unconsciously mobilize their bias as a group (Lukes 1974), institutionalizing their interpretations as the truth, and as organizational and managerial practices.

Black and white women's strategy included attempts to make clear that defensiveness over equality represented conflict about power over meanings. Black and white women managers who are active for equality can therefore be described as knowledge agents (Collins 1990), making interventions, not only about practices, but about the discourses that underpin them. Managers who were active for equality understood this, and were engaged in reviewing and reconstructing their thinking and practices. However, the persistence of institutionalized meanings and practices around equality in local government management represents continuity in the 'race' and gender power relations of organization.

## Continuity and white fraternity

In organizational terms, change and continuity in 'race' and gender equality can be represented by a shift from white and paternal to white and fraternal power (Pateman 1988; Watson 1990; Martin 1990). In turn, this is paralleled by a shift as local government restructures, from discourses of professionalism (the traditional, apolitical, public service ethic) to discourses of managerialism (competition, privatization, business efficiency and consumer-orientation). Power continues to be exercised in the interests of a white fraternity as collective responses to the perceived threat of the acquisition of (limited economic and personal) power by some black and white women. And, as has been shown, it is specifically through shared 'whiteness' that the white fraternity is able to co-opt some white women into its membership in order to redefine black demands (Ben-Tovim *et al.* 1986; Watson 1990) and limit 'race' equality programmes.

The notion of the regrouping of the power of a white fraternity is especially useful in thinking about continuity in local government power relations of 'race' and gender. Avoidance and defensiveness about equality strategy, and about the significance of 'race' and gender power in the organization, are practices by which change is resisted, and around which white and male managers regroup to mobilize white and male bias in the organization. Women in this study reported both a conviction that equality of opportunity was now a more accepted objective (especially in mixed managerial teams), and a frustration with the new terrain of conflicts over implementation. The terrain has shifted, but the contest remains.

Aitkenhead and Liff (1991) describe this paradox as a simple difference between two interpretations: equality as objective, and equality as outcomes. They explain, in terms of social identity theory, to-be-expected differences in social understanding, arising from different identities. Analysis of the limited success of equal opportunity policies is to an extent helped by the notion of different understandings of their meaning existing simultaneously in an organization, and preventing effective implementation. We have, however, already seen the limitations of notions of difference which do not focus on differences in powers. Difference in understandings/meanings does not adequately explain the tendency for conflicts over meanings, nor for meanings to be reformulated in ways which reaffirm the status quo in new terms. The power relations inscribed in conflicts between meanings and in social identities are omitted. It is the exercising of power within conflicts over different meanings about equality strategy that limits the success of equality policies, and ensures continuity in the racism and sexism of local state organization.

Thus in local government, discursive and material power is exercised and contested at the individual level in interpersonal transactions as management practices about needs-interpretation and identity. At the collective level, group or individual defensiveness or avoidance invokes the mobilization of group bias (Lukes 1974), so that discriminatory practices and processes of domination become institutionalized materially as disciplinary power, and discursively as the regime of truth (Foucault 1980; Vince 1991).

There is thus a necessity for managers to be aware of the interpersonal, institutional, economic and political processes which uphold race and gender domination, and to recognize the part that is played in these processes by their practice.

Far from being deniable aspects of the local state, continuity and change in 'race' and gender power relations *are* the state, since they are embedded in all its processes, practices and structures. It is for this reason that equality strategies are central and integral to effective management within state organizations.

In order to engage in struggles for change in this context, black and white women need individual power to act, and collective political power to deconstruct and oppose the disciplinary power of the regime.

As conscious agents of change, women's 'discursive strategies' *vis-à-vis* the state need to be diverse, and relevant to specific contexts. Some policies and practices reflect a patriarchal, others a capitalist and others a nationalist or/and imperialist state (Watson 1990; Williams 1989). Consequently, different central and local state policies may impact differently on different women as a consequence of the particular 'states' that may be in the foreground, and different forms of struggle may be required to bring about change.

### Change: emerging notions of organization and management

Most organization and management theory excludes black and white women managers' experience and consequently shows serious omissions. Where women's experience is included, it tends to be mainly white and middle-class women's experience, and women's agency is undertheorized. Where black people's experience of local government is included, there tends to be no focus on the specificity of black women's experience of racism, and of sexism in organization and management.

Theory can assist practice by making visible the ways in which organization is constructed and produced. By failing to conceptualize organization and management adequately, institutionalized means of interpretation of local government organization, management, and of race and gender power relations, are sustained. Discourse-oriented theory assists in demonstrating the symbolic and material diversity and dispersal of local government organization; and in decoding specific instances of organization and management practice as processes constitutive of nationality and citizenship; and 'race', gender and class power relations. The approach of this account, like the practice of the black and white women I spoke with, is to describe and deconstruct specific mechanisms, practices, transactions and behaviours through which power relations are produced, intersect, are perpetuated or contested in organizations. This acknowledges process, continuity and change, and the potential for strategy to create conditions for collaboration and alliance.

## Organization

The institutionalized notion of local government organization is of a 'race' and gender-neutral, static, bureaucratic and hierarchical structure, located in the town hall and its satellites. Struggles for equality are assumed to take place outside, or at the organizational boundaries, within 'local interest groups' (Stoker 1991) and communities. Because these groups' and communities' interests are assumed to be distinct from the interests of an undifferentiated (that is, 'race' and gender-neutral) 'public' or 'consumer', the notions of public, consumer, interest group and organization are themselves gendered (Sheppard 1989) and racially-structured notions (Ouseley 1984).

These ascribed meanings of organization and its supposed boundaries have been produced through both rational management and organization theory, and through institutionalized discourse and managerial practices in local government. Local government managers have traditionally acted as if organization were a monolithic, static and fixed structure, and as if management has an uncontestable right to interpretation and mediation of competing interests and needs. Thus discourses and practices which control and exclude different knowledges, powers and experience have been institutionalized.

For black and white women managers managing for equality, the conceptual boundaries of local government organization went beyond the institutionalized notion. Their symbolic construction of 'organization' included both a dispersed network, and the management practices necessary to mobilize and enable interaction between them. So, for example, networks might include the public, voluntary and private sectors, and most significantly for equality strategies, individuals, groups, organizations and communities (Ben-Tovim *et al.* 1986; Dahlerup 1986) on their own ground. Often, a manager's initiative was focused on creating contexts specifically to meet the self-defined needs of potential or excluded users and communities (for example, women with young children; young black people; people with disabilities among others). Such approaches have been necessary to develop provision which has been lacking from 'mainstream' service delivery, or to include knowledges lacking in the 'mainstream' organization.

Organization itself therefore, has been reconceptualized as fragmented, existing in diverse forms, sites, and arenas (Watson 1990), and this has been a 'given' in the experience of black and white women managers who are active for change. Some of these arenas have been created by black and white women managers themselves to assist and enable access to persons, communities and knowledges which are specifically excluded by institutionalized notions of the organization's structure and location, and by traditional management practices. Working through active, complex networks of organizations, across sector boundaries, is basic to quality and equality, through ensuring wide participation in service planning and delivery. In terms, therefore, of conceptualizing organization, and practicing management, some black and white women managers have developed approaches to organization which focus on process and practices rather than structures and roles; and on dispersal, fluidity and change, rather than static location.

The experience of black and white women managers indicates that 'race' and gender power relations are core organizing principles in the discursive and material production of organization in the public sector. Conversely, organization is a social context, comprising diverse arenas, sites, discourses and practices, which contribute to contested 'race' and gender power relations. Local government organization, and social power relations, are simultaneously produced discursively and materially at all those points of intersection and interaction between official institutionalized discourses and practices and the discourses and practices which contest them in terms of class, race and gender (Ben-Tovim *et al.* 1986; Fraser 1989; Watson 1990). As well as the 'race' and gender of organization, we are here considering the organization of 'race' and gender (Hearn *et al.* 1989).

Power is not therefore fixed and held in an essentialist way in local government organization. White and primarily male organizational and managerial domination, and black and female subordination are not fixed and unchanging structures outside specific times, contexts, meanings and practices. Black and white women managers' practice and experience testifies to dynamic processes, where managers can operate as change agents, individually and collectively, to enter into or create opportunities for collaboration or struggle over 'race', gender and class power relations, at the levels of discourse and practices.

Interactions over meanings and practices are the specific instances of the dynamics of 'race', gender and class power that produce and are produced by local government organization and management. The outcomes are both continuity and change in those power relations, and in material and symbolic forms of inequality.

Through their practices, black and white women managers make visible the subjugated meanings of organization and management as processes of power and change. Moreover, understanding organization and management in these ways is a prerequisite to imagining the practices necessary for equality in local government.

It is not simply the inclusion of 'race' and gender that makes a difference to theory and practice, but conceptualizing 'race' and gender power relations as interactive processes of continuity and change rather than static structures or cultures. Similarly, conceptualizing power as exercised through practices, rather than held or not held in a fixed and essentialist way by individuals or groups, assists in showing that change in the practices and behaviours that constitute exercising power is necessary and possible.

## Management practice

Management is central to organizational processes of power, and it is possible for managers to engage proactively with those processes as facilitators of change. Managers, moreover, have choices about where and how power conflicts are conducted, but not, despite their resistances, denial and avoidance, whether the conflicts take place. Black and white women and black men are engaged in conflicts about power relations as classes, as persons and as bodies. Black and white women and black men bear a disproportionate burden of the negative effects of conflicts over 'race' and gender power.

For black and white women managers in local government, wider options (for themselves, and for employees and users of services) were opened by their working strategically and self-reflectively as agents and enablers of change, in collaboration and alliance with local struggles for equality.

In so doing, a woman had to recognize the limitations for herself, her role, and local state equality/reform programmes, but did not need to doubt the place these have in the political process alongside other local and national equality strategies. Further, black and white women managers have brought a new rigour to the practice of local government management, by effectively managing change as change towards equality; by instituting empowering, accountable and consultative practices; by consequently extending the potential of the work-force and increasing the relevance and quality of services.

Such approaches underpin effectiveness and quality in a restructured local government, managing and evaluating mixed economies of provision. They also demonstrated in advance of post-modern organization theory and local government reorganization, a radical version of enabling and empowering management.

## Management training

This study suggests that it is important:

1  that management training and development addresses power as central to processes of organization and management;
2  that management training and development supports empowering management for equality, by addressing 'race', gender and class

relations in management practice, and the heterosexual and able-bodied dominance of organization;

3 that management training and development clarifies how training for women may contribute to sexist and racist assumptions.

Training for management, therefore, needs some analysis of the complexities of power in organizations. This has implications for curriculum, methodology, course organization and pedagogical practice in confronting 'race' and gender power relations in organizations, management practices and training groups. As some black and white women undertaking traditional MBA and DMS courses testified in my interviews, existing expertise in training institutions may be inadequate in these respects. The recruitment, promotion and organizational practices of the training institutions themselves may be the next arena of the struggles outlined here.

It is clear that training can have a role in addressing those aspects of inequality which are affected by managers' avoidance, defensiveness and exercising of power. To do so training will need to decode both its own, and management's practices of domination, in the light of especially black and white women's, and other excluded groups', experience of power and powerlessness in organizations. It will need to address group process and the psychodynamics of power relations, in the construction of self and other, in order to subvert the gaps between intention and action, between espoused values and behaviour. Along with management theory and management itself, it will need an active engagement to promote change for 'race' and gender equality in organization, and equal opportunities within management practice.

## REFERENCES

Aitkenhead, M. and Liff, S. (1991) 'The effectiveness of equal opportunity policies' in J. Firth-Cozens and M. A. West (eds) *Women at Work: Psychological and Organisational Perspectives*, Milton Keynes Open University.

Ball, W. and Solomos, J. (1990) *Race and Local Politics*, Basingstoke: Macmillan.

Ben-Tovim, G., Gabriel, J., Law, I. and Stredder, K. (1986) *The Local Politics of Race*, Basingstoke: Macmillan.

Button, S. (1984) *Women's Committees – A Study of Gender and Local Policy Formulation*, School for Advanced Urban Studies (SAUS) working paper 45.

Carby, H. V. (1986) 'White women listen! Black feminism and the boundaries of sisterhood', Centre for Contemporary Cultural Studies, *The Empire Strikes Back*, London: Hutchinson.

Clegg, S. R. (1989) *Frameworks of Power*, London: Sage.

Collins, P. H. (1990) *Black Feminist Thought: Knowledge, Consciousness and the Politics of Empowerment*, London: Unwin Hyman.

Dahlerup, D. (1986) *The New Women's Movement: Feminism and Political Power in Europe and the USA*, London: Sage.

Davies, C. and Rosser, J. (1986) *Processes of Discrimination. A Study of Women Working in the NHS*, Department of Health and Social Security.

Foucault , M. (1980) (trans. C. Gordon) *Power/Knowledge: Selected Interviews and Other Writings*, Brighton: Harvester.

Fraser, N. (1989) *Unruly Practices: Power, Discourse and Gender in Contemporary Social Theory*, Cambridge: Polity Press.

Freire, P. (1972) *Pedagogy of the Oppressed*, Harmondsworth: Penguin.

Gunew, S. (1990) *Feminist Knowledge: Critique and Construct*, London: Routledge.

Hearn, J., Sheppard, D. L., Tancred-Sheriff, P. and Burrell, G. (eds) (1989) *The Sexuality of Organisation*, London: Sage.

Hernes, H. (1988) 'The welfare state citizenship of Scandinavian women', in K. B. Jones and A. G. Jonasdottir, *The Political Interests of Gender*, London: Sage.

hooks, b. (1989) *Talking Back: Thinking Feminist Thinking Black*, Boston: Sheba.

hooks, b. (1991) *Yearning: Race Gender and Cultural Politics*, London: Turnaround.

Husband, C. (ed.) (1987) *Race in Britain: Continuity and Change*, London: Open University/Hutchinson.

Kanter, R. M. (1977) *Men and Women of the Corporation*, New York: Basic Books.

Lukes, S. (ed.) (1974) *Power*, London: Macmillan.

Marshall, J. (1984) *Women Managers: Travellers in a Male World*, Chichester: John Wiley.

Martin, L. (1990) *Feminist and Anti-Racist Critical Theory: The Local Government Experience of Black and White Women Managers*, dissertation, Bristol University.

Martin, L. and Gaster, L. (1993) 'Community care planning in Wolverhampton', R. Smith, L. Gaster, L. Harrison, L. Martin, R. Means and P. Thistlethwaite (eds) *Working Together for Better Community Care*, SAUS Publications, University of Bristol.

Mills, A. J. (1989) 'Gender, sexuality and organisation theory', in J. Hearn, D. L. Sheppard and P. Tancred-Sheriff (eds), *The Sexuality of Organisation*, London: Sage.

Morgan, G. (1986) *Images of Organisation*, London: Sage.

Ouseley, H. (1984) 'Local authority race initiatives', in M. Boddy and C. Fudge, *Local Socialism*, Basingstoke: Macmillan.

Pateman, C. (1988) *The Sexual Contract*, Cambridge: Polity Press.

Pringle, R. (1989) *Secretaries Talk: Sexuality, Power and Work*, London: Verso.

Reed, M. and Hughes, M. (1992) *Rethinking Organisation*, London: Sage.

Sheppard, D. L. (1989) 'Organisation and power: sexuality: the image and self image of women managers', in J. Hearn, D. L. Sheppard and P. Tancred-Smith (eds) *The Sexuality of Organisation*, London: Sage.

Showstack Sassoon, A. (ed.) (1987) *Women and the State*, London: Hutchinson.

Stacey, M. and Price, M. (1981) *Women, Power and Politics*, London: Tavistock.

Stanley, L. and Wise, S. (1983) *Breaking Out: Feminist Consciousness and Feminist Research*, London: Routledge & Kegan Paul.

Stewart, J. (1986) *The New Management of Local Government*, London: Allen & Unwin.

Stewart, J. (1988) *Understanding the Management of Local Government*, London, Luton: Longman/Local Government Training Board (LGTB).

Stoker, G. (1991) *The Politics of Local Government*, Basingstoke: Macmillan.

Stone, I. (1988) *Equal Opportunities in Local Authorities*, London: HMSO.

Vince, R. (1991) 'Management by avoidance: male power in local government', *Management Education and Development* 22(1); 50–9.

Watson, S. (ed.) (1990) *Playing the State: Australian Feminist Interventions*, London: Verso.

Williams, F. (1989) *Social Policy, A Critical Introduction*, Cambridge: Polity Press.

Chapter 8

# Motherhood and management

*Joanna Knight*

## INTRODUCTION

I recently became a mother and did not want to let this experience go by without exploring and trying to capture its meaning for me. This was the driving force which motivated me to research the impact of becoming a mother on women's lives, in the expectation that examining its meaning for other women would enable me to understand it better for myself.

I particularly wanted to focus on women who were managers (in the generally accepted sense of this term as indicative of a certain level of responsibility and authority) to see whether or how any learning from their experience of becoming a mother affected their work lives. I was interested in whether any learning derived from such an intensively personal experience was transferable and applicable to the work situation. I was also concerned that one of the reasons why there are so few women at the top of organizations might be due to difficulties (real or perceived) in combining these two roles of working and mothering.

I was conscious that I was very closely involved with the subject of my research. My objective was therefore to achieve 'a critical awareness of my own personal perspective, a knowing subjectivity' (Marshall 1984: 12).

## THE RESEARCH PROCESS

I decided to approach individual women with whom I was acquainted, who had recently become mothers, and who were attempting to combine this new role with their existing role as successful working women. All the women readily agreed to help me with my research, seeming to welcome the opportunity to discuss an issue which was of current importance in their lives. Maybe this willingness indicated some feelings of isolation and a desire to share their experiences, satisfactions and concerns with others who were in a similar position and who might, therefore, be expected to understand.

I wanted to study women from different organizations, to provide an indication of whether the issues were experienced by women generally, rather than women in a particular organization or industry. I focused this research on the private sector, first, because I have more knowledge and experience of this sector, and second, because the small size of the research sample suggested a relatively narrow focus of attention.

As the research interviews progressed, I became aware that a common theme was starting to emerge – women saw their future work lives as being largely outside organizations. I became concerned to test this trend by interviewing women outside of my direct acquaintance. This also gave me the opportunity to compare the experience of interviewing women whom I already knew, via my work as an independent consultant, with those with whom I had no prior relationship. I could then see whether there was any appreciable difference in the level and quality of the data gained.

In the end I interviewed a total of six women, four of whom were known to me previously. I decided on a relatively small research group for practical and philosophical reasons, but the final number was influenced by the data themselves – I stopped when I felt I had enough information to indicate certain trends and common experiences. I am also conscious that this work could be taken further.

It was important to me that these women fulfilled certain criteria. They were all educated to degree level and were already operating at middle or senior management levels within their organizations, so they might be expected to be successful (if any women are) at the most senior levels. They also came from different organizations fulfilling different functions, for example, rental, retail, public relations and medical products. They were women working in traditionally female environments – personnel and training and development – and two were in marketing and market research. They also represented a reasonably wide age spread (from 26 to 36) and were looking back at the birth of their first child from a range of time perspectives (between four months and three years). I hoped that these different perspectives would each bring their own value to the research, as it is possible to have different views on the same significant life change, depending on the passage of time in relation to the change (Griffin 1987). Hopefully, however, this restricted time-frame ensured that none of the women was so distanced from the event that they had lost touch with the experience of becoming a mother and what this meant to them.

I did not expect to arrive at some form of absolute truth, but rather to explore meanings which were 'attached very firmly to a person, and a time, and a place, and a system' (Rowan and Reason 1981: 136). To achieve this, I used a qualitative rather than a quantitative approach which is suited to examining 'the meaning people attribute to their experiences, how people perceive themselves and their worlds and how they communicate their understandings to others' (Boud and Griffin 1987: 9). It seemed to me self-evident that each woman was the 'expert' on her own situation and experience, and therefore well able to contribute actively to different stages of the research process, in a spirit of collaboration. As far as possible, the level of involvement in this research was left to each individual to determine, based on her interest in the research topic and the availability of her time and attention.

My research plan was a simple one. In my initial approach to other women I considered the information which they might want to know – basic data about what I wanted to explore and why; how I saw my role as researcher; the possibilities for their role; the fact that in-depth interviews were to provide the major source of information; that they were welcome to influence the nature and content of these interviews.

The interview was my main source of data, so I attempted to create an informal and relaxed atmosphere to encourage all the women, particularly those who didn't know me, to feel able to share their views on such a personal subject. I would be attempting to carry out 'depth interviews', where

> the interviewer is genuinely concerned with the interviewee as a person, going beyond the search for delimited information input. In turn, the interviewee sufficiently reciprocates this feeling, valuing the interviewer's motives and seeking to respond in appropriate depth.
>
> (Massarik 1981: 203)

The women themselves also took responsibility for helping to create this environment. I believe that the desired atmosphere was achieved – I look back on images of myself talking with women in their homes over a cup of coffee, in the park while eating a picnic under a shady tree, over lunch in an informal restaurant, and even the one interview conducted in an office took place over a glass of wine, taken from an office party!

In order to create this type of atmosphere, I believe that two factors were particularly important – first, the fact that I was also a mother and therefore likely to be facing similar issues and have some understanding of these women's situation; and second, the fact that all the women were keen to take part in this research and to have an opportunity to discuss these issues, despite suffering from what many writers (Falkenberg and Monachello 1989; Marshall 1984; Forrest 1989; Sekaran and Hall 1989) have called role overload.

While I was concerned that the interviews should have the feel of informal discussions, I had some particular topic areas which I wanted to cover. Although questions were not tightly formatted, nor asked in a particular sequence, leaving each woman free to influence the discussion differently, the following areas were covered in each interview:

- any impact that becoming a mother had on their lives, including their work lives;
- any learning they derived from this experience;
- their experience of returning to work;
- whether and how any learning they experienced was also applicable to the work situation;
- the main pressures and satisfactions of combining work with mothering;
- the role played by partners and employing organizations in helping them balance their professional with their domestic responsibilities;
- how they foresaw their working lives developing.

In addition, other information seen as relevant by individual women was also discussed. While the interview was in progress the conversation was recorded on a dictaphone, so that I remained free to observe each woman's facial expressions and body language in order that this additional data could help me in my interpretations. After trying to put the women at ease by explaining what I was intending to do I tried to take little part in the conversation, to avoid the possibility of influencing others by my own opinions, and adopted a facilitative role.

After the first interview I was highly encouraged by the quality and depth of the data which I had gained, and this continued to be my response after each interview. All these women were forthright in the expression of their views and the open sharing of very personal experiences. I felt highly conscious of the trust they had placed in me in doing so. This was my experience with those women whom I already knew and those whom I was meeting for the first time – it felt as though our common experience helped us develop empathy quickly.

## THE IMPACT OF BECOMING A MOTHER

I want first to examine the impact of becoming a mother on women's lives, particularly their working lives, because this seems to me to be the point from which the other issues flow. Although each woman whom I interviewed described the impact of becoming a mother differently, they all described it as a major life event entailing significant changes of different sorts for them.

One woman talked of feeling 'dominated' and 'taken over' by the demands which her baby made of her, and although initially she had enjoyed being immersed in the experience of motherhood, this feeling prompted her to return to work more quickly, in order to gain 'time for myself'. Work was perceived as a means of reasserting some important aspects of self. Another woman also felt the impact of this event very forcefully: 'In some ways I don't feel any different, really, at all . . . but then, on the other hand, I feel so fundamentally different . . . I am not the same person'. She went on to explain that the difference, for her, was not so much connected with the practicalities of looking after a baby, but with the emotional aspect of being a mother: 'It's not possible, in my view, I think, to have a baby and not feel a really fundamental emotional difference'. Other women commented on this overpowering love for their child too:

> There isn't anything I wouldn't do for her, and there would be no end to my anger if anybody hurt her. Every now and again I get glimpses of this huge pool of power, I suppose, which is tied up with her, with being a mother.

While not all women articulated their feelings directly in this way, it became apparent that this strength of feeling which becoming a mother engendered had a huge impact on the perspective with which these women viewed their lives: 'It makes you change your priorities in life. Now A. [her son] is the most important priority, that's the biggest impact'.

Another commented that 'my perspective on everything' changed, and that 'many things feel relatively unimportant now'. Some cited examples of what they would previously have considered to be major difficulties in life, such as being made redundant or losing £50,000 on a house, which they were now better able to cope with, due to this new-found perspective:

> I think its really just showed me that the most important thing in life is people, and that lots of other things really don't matter very much, so I think I'm better at handling problems both at work and at home.

Provided that their child was all right, the women seemed to be able to face problems or difficult situations with increased equanimity.

Linked to this change in perspective seemed to be some change (articulated directly by some women only) in what gave them their sense of identity. One woman described the process of this change when I asked her why she had been interested to help me in my research:

> I found it very interesting, having a baby, in terms of looking at me . . . its a great time in your life . . . its opened up a whole load of questions about you, how you see yourself, your role in life, where you're going . . . its quite interesting to sit down and talk with other people and question it.

For this particular woman, one result of this self-questioning process had been that: 'Work doesn't feel as important as it did before . . . I felt so important being a Mum . . . I don't have to get my feeling of importance from being a Director of a company'.

Another woman expressed similar feelings when talking abut her attitude to a recent redundancy, acknowledging that her feelings about this, prior to having her baby, would have been very different:

All of my identity was about my career, me as a professional woman, and a relatively successful professional woman . . . I still wanted to think of myself as a working woman . . . but [this was] far less important in terms of my own identity than it had been.

Becoming a mother and making decisions about whether/how to continue their careers had forced these women to consider what gave their lives real meaning, and therefore to rethink the fundamental source of their identity. In doing this, however, they did not appear to be denying the value of old sources of identity, but rather to be establishing a new balance, recognizing and valuing different aspects of themselves. This seems to support Joan Gallos's assertion (Gallos 1989) that, while men look to increased autonomy and distance from others as a means of strengthening their identity and achieving a satisfying life, women look to their attachments, relationships and responsibilities for their identity formation.

Certainly, the women whom I interviewed were all conscious of the fact that they had now got additional, important responsibilities in their lives. They considered these when planning how to use their time, both at home and at work. They were very aware that in making any work plans they needed to consider the likely impact on their child and childcare arrangements. One woman commented that 'planning takes on a whole new meaning'. Very often it seemed that, in their efforts to ensure that neither their child nor their work lost out in terms of their time and commitment, it was the woman herself who bore the brunt (albeit willingly) of this aspect of being a working mother:

It affects the way I plan and schedule the work, but I don't think it affects my attitude to work. I haven't let work fall back because of J. [her child]. Its other things that I've had to, not sacrifice, but just decided to change how I do them.

This was a price which they expected and were prepared to pay for the satisfactions of being a working mother.

## LEARNING ASSOCIATED WITH BECOMING A MOTHER

I thought that becoming a mother was such a major life event that it might be expected to yield useful learning for women (Antonis

1981). In addition, I was especially interested to find out what such learning (assuming it had taken place) might be about and whether any of it was applicable to the work situation.

The data showed that becoming a mother had triggered some important learning for women, perhaps resulting from the re-evaluation or highlighting of what was most important to them in their lives. For one woman this was highlighted in a particularly graphic way, when her daughter became seriously ill:

> That's when I began to re-evaluate what I was doing . . . It actually taught me that when it came down to it, between work and child there was no choice . . . the child would always come first.

As a result, she felt that she had gained a different perspective on work problems or difficult situations, which enabled her to handle them more effectively. Another woman supported this view when she commented that, despite additional time pressures from juggling new family and work responsibilities, she had been told that she seemed more relaxed! She connected this with the fact that motherhood had given her a new perspective on work. Another woman said:

> I find it much easier to take it in my stride because the perspective I've got is so much greater, so the problem becomes smaller . . . I think that's quite good, because when everyone else around you is panicking . . . you can be a bit calmer . . . and be the one who solves the problem.

Most women were very aware of the positive impact of this new perspective on their work lives. Even those who initially denied that their attitude to work had changed later went on to give examples of how things had, in fact, altered for them. For all, the fact that work was less important in their lives had paradoxically had a positive impact on their work performance.

As well as helping put problems into perspective, thereby increasing the likelihood of being able to resolve them, there were other perceived benefits from this new sense of what was really important. One woman talked of her increased willingness to take risks:

I'll tell you the change about me. I was less scared of taking a risk . . . I wasn't scared of anybody even though I was a bit less confident about myself . . . [I thought] 'I've had a baby, I've done that, I can do anything'.

Judi Marshall (Marshall 1984) has also noted how the fact that work is only one of several important life areas for women can give them some independence enabling them to take greater risks than their colleagues. Another woman talked of a more relaxed approach to her work, particularly in her dealings with senior managers, and felt that she was more effective as a consequence. This new-found attitude and inner confidence also enabled women to be more themselves at work. One talked about 'Letting my own personality come out in the workplace, rather than necessarily being the company machine'.

In addition, all the women mentioned the fact that their organization and planning skills (presumably not lacking in the first place or they wouldn't have achieved positions at middle/senior management levels) had been enhanced by their having to manage the practical difficulties and demands of combining work with mothering. One woman was typical when she described this increased emphasis on planning: 'I think further forward and plan further forward than I ever did before, and I've had to do it better. I can't afford for things to go wrong'.

This enhanced organizational ability enabled her to maintain her desired standards of work. If things were allowed to go wrong, then women perceived that either their children or their work credibility would suffer – neither of which they were prepared to let happen. Again, what might be perceived as a potentially difficult or negative aspect of combining these two major roles seemed to have been turned to advantage, so that a similar quality of work was achieved within a shorter time-frame.

Women also seemed to have experienced some significant changes described by one woman as the 'development of my personality', which were triggered by becoming a mother. This same woman went on to characterize herself prior to becoming a mother: 'By nature, I'm very impatient, don't suffer fools gladly, do what I want to do when I want to do it'. She then described what she saw as the changes to herself:

It's made me slow down . . . I think it softened me quite a lot . . . that's been the biggest benefit . . . people have said that to me . . . 'you're much less autocratic, try and see another's viewpoint' . . . I'm less of the perfectionist . . . it's probably made me more patient, less concerned about what others think.

It is interesting to note that she viewed this shift in her behaviour and feelings as entirely positive and that it had apparently brought beneficial results for her in her work, including a much-wanted promotion into a senior management position. Another woman reported a similar experience:

It was inferred that I'd become softer, that could be interpreted as not so aggressive or harsh . . . I'm sure it [motherhood] has . . . allowed some of the feeling side of me, my emotional side, to be stronger, to be allowed to be there, and to be OK.

This woman specifically mentioned that she felt that this softer side of herself had been denied full expression in the past, largely because of the fact that she was working within a macho culture. Again, this reinforces Marshall's findings (Marshall 1984) that women often mute their femaleness in order to gain acceptance and success in the male-dominated world of business. This particular woman felt that she had now found an outlet for this aspect of herself, as both male and female colleagues expected her to show emotion in relation to her son, and perceived this to be acceptable behaviour. Other women spoke of becoming 'more tolerant of people's idiosyncrasies' and of themselves and their inability to fulfil the 'superwoman' role of the perfect wife, mother and professional businesswoman. There were some highly-positive aspects to this new tolerance:

I think it makes you much more sympathetic to everybody around you . . . when you're working with people and they're maybe not behaving as you would like, I think you've got a greater experience bank within yourself to draw on, to try and interpret and be generous, perhaps, to the sort of things that they're doing.

Again, this was a common feeling among the women whom I interviewed. They were trying to treat their children as individuals, with respect, patience and tolerance, and found themselves translating this behaviour into the workplace. On the other hand, this newly acquired patience and tolerance was not extended indefinitely, to the extent where it would become dysfunctional at work:

> As a working woman with a child you do have to do a lot, you have to be very organized, and you have to achieve quite a lot, and you have to be very strong, and when you see people around you being less strong . . . and [despite wives providing back-up support] they *still* can't do the job right . . .

This particular woman left the sentence unfinished, so her specific response to such people and situations was not defined, but her irritation and frustration came across strongly! I did not, therefore, get an impression of women who were now prepared to be infinitely patient and tolerant of others who were ineffective, but of women who were more prepared to allow others to do things in their own way, and who would try to understand their differing motivation and approaches. One woman did, however, express some doubts as to whether her new tolerance was entirely positive, concerned that what she described as her 'intolerant edge' about racism, sexism and organizational politics had been diminished. However, she also spoke of her irritation with some of the pettiness of organizational politics, feeling that she no longer had time to spend on 'time-wasting' tactics. This led me to wonder whether, in fact, her intolerance about certain issues had really been lost.

Only one woman was unsure whether she had learned anything that resulted directly from motherhood, though she then gave me one example of how she felt she had changed. Much of what had been learned, as has been shown, was relevant and beneficial to the work organization and the women were generally quick to make this connection for themselves during our discussions.

## COMBINING WORKING WITH MOTHERHOOD

### The experience of returning to work

All the women I interviewed chose to return to work early and did not take their full period of maternity leave. Several were working part-time or from home two months after their babies were born, and most returned to work full-time within three to five months. In some cases this was because they wanted to get, what they termed, 'time for myself' by re-establishing contact with the outside world of work, but there also seemed to be pressures, exerted by their workplace, influencing them to minimize any possible disturbance that their time away might cause. Again, this supports Marshall's findings (Marshall 1984) that women at senior management levels experience difficulty in leaving and returning to their jobs and that they take the responsibility for managing any problems, either at work or at home, which being a working mother creates.

However, all these women were determined to return to work, despite the fact that they now saw it as having less importance in their lives. One woman's explanation of this was typical: 'Because I couldn't imagine not working . . . because I loved my job, a lot of my self-esteem was bound up in being a working person'. Despite new-found additional sources of identity, work still featured strongly in their self-image, bringing satisfaction and fulfilment of a particular kind.

So, given that these women were keen to return to work and had made considerable efforts to maintain contact with work during their reduced period of maternity leave, what did they experience on their return? Their reports were very mixed, with some, as might be expected, receiving considerably more interest and support than others. Whether or not they received support seemed to be highly dependent on their particular boss and their relationship with him (in every case the boss was male).

In several cases women perceived that their organization did not seem inclined to believe their continued commitment to work. One woman's experience provides an interesting example of this. She was working for a major retailer renowned for its staff welfare policies and practices, yet she found that there was an assumption that she would not return to work. She had to make contact with her employer and drive the process – even then she was given a three-month attachment to another department, indicating that there were still reservations as to whether she would stay. (This was after over fifteen years service with this company!) She commented somewhat drily that this hadn't made her feel valued as an individual. Despite her under utilization, she found that there was no willingness on the company's part to change the situation. Eventually, her determination and perseverance persuaded the company to utilize her skills and she was appointed to a senior management position.

Another woman experienced difficulties in her efforts to be

taken seriously on her return to work. She had negotiated that she would work on a part-time basis, while maintaining her status and responsibility for the management of her function. However, she commented that 'I was having to justify being a relatively senior woman manager and working part-time. It was as if my professionalism was diminished in most people's eyes'. Interestingly enough, it was not just with male colleagues that she encountered difficulty. Some women were disapproving and unsupportive, not appearing to view her situation as setting a potentially useful precedent for themselves and other female colleagues, or as a creative response to her circumstances by the business. She became very aware of the tenuous nature of her position, made additionally difficult by the fact that the two individuals with whom she had negotiated her new contract had now left the organization.

A third woman had also experienced some difficulty on her return:

> There hasn't been any support . . . either an encouragement to come back, or an encouragement to stay back, or to cope on a day to day basis . . . its a question of 'you've got the responsibility, you do it'. Sometimes there's not even the interest.

Again this situation existed despite the fact that she had worked in this company for some years and was a valued senior manager.

The other three women in my research sample had a somewhat different experience of returning to work. One worked as a director in a small company and felt that she was well known and respected by the chairman, who had been interested and supportive while she was away from work. Another woman had approached her previous boss and negotiated a part-time contract with him, working 115 days per year at the same managerial level as before. She was welcomed back, and because of her boss's influence there was general acceptance of her working part-time at this level. However, since then there had been a major reorganization, which meant that she was now working for someone else. She now felt extremely vulnerable and demotivated, and was additionally conscious that this could be misinterpreted as being due to the fact that, as a mother, she was therefore no longer committed to her work. A third woman had had, in some ways, a similar experience to these two, in that her boss had been supportive of her return to work. When she had told him of her pregnancy she had been very nervous, as she had no statutory right to maternity leave, having quite recently joined the company. He had been concerned to see what they could do to work things out and she had a plan, minimizing the time when she would be away and the impact on the company, already prepared to discuss with him. In addition, once he became really convinced that she would return to work, he also upgraded her position. However, she commented that even this boss (who seemed more enlightened than many) was sometimes intolerant of her desire to leave early (by which she meant 5 p.m.) on a Friday, despite the fact that she typically worked long hours and some weekends, and travelled abroad on a regular basis!

From this examination it can be seen that a very mixed picture emerges. Some were not made to feel valued or valuable, despite the fact that they were established and capable managers who had been with their companies for some years. It is interesting to note that, of those women who returned to generally unsupportive environments, two have now taken voluntary redundancy and the third is actively considering leaving her job. I cannot believe this is entirely coincidental. However, by already prejudiced people, those who leave will undoubtedly be seen as bearing out their theories that working mothers lack commitment. Even if such women do not leave, how many may be under utilized and demotivated as a result of such treatment? It is also interesting to see that, where there was support, this was the result of the attitude of the individual woman's boss, his relationship with the woman, and his personal knowledge and appreciation of her ability to perform her role effectively. It seemed to be less a result of company policy and precedent. While such stories offer some encouragement, they also sound a warning, as they suggest that the strongest influence on such situations is that of the individual boss. This leaves companies reliant on the attitudes of individual (often male) managers.

**Pressures and satisfactions**

Although the actual experience of returning to work was very different for each woman, there was a high level of agreement about what constituted both the pressures and the satisfactions of being a working mother.

The main pressure experienced by these women was the lack of time with which to meet all the different demands which were made of them and which, for the most part, they wanted to meet. One woman roundly dismissed the popular notion of quality time, indicating that ultimately, low quantity of time given to personal relationships would adversely affect the quality of those relationships. Conversely, she found that when she took a week off work in order to spend some time with her daughter the whole family became more relaxed. Another woman voiced a similar experience, commenting that home now felt 'like a well-oiled business' rather than a place where she could expect to feel regenerated after a hard day's work. She wondered how long she and her husband could keep going in this situation. Another woman, who regularly travelled abroad on business, found the inevitable travel delays very frustrating, especially when they meant that she was not home in time to see her son before he went to bed. In addition, she spoke of the constant tiredness experienced as a result of these pressures on her time, and her inability, because of this very pressure, to catch up on her sleep. All this would seem to corroborate the fact that the stress of integrating family and work life is most acute for working mothers (Forrest 1989) since typically women still take more responsibility for the home.

In addition, the practicality of arranging and maintaining good childcare was another source of pressure experienced by these women. Several talked about the fact that they were not getting quite what they wanted for their child from their current arrangements, and that this in turn placed additional pressure on them. One woman explained that, if she continued to have doubts about her childcare arrangements, she would have no alternative but to leave her employment. Additional problems were experienced in trying to find childminders or nannies who were prepared to work long hours and to be flexible, particularly when many women's work involved them in spending time away from home overnight. As one woman pointed out, in some ways they were trying to replicate the family support network that no longer exists in a practical sense for those women who have moved away from the parental home town. Where problems of whatever sort existed in relation to childcare arrangements this was seen to exacerbate the 'emotional tug' between work and home that was experienced by women.

Several women had anticipated that not being prepared to work such long hours as previously might produce its own pressure, in that their work performance might suffer. However, due to their enhanced organizational and planning ability, this hadn't in fact happened. This sort of pressure was only felt by one woman, now working part-time, who experienced some frustration that she couldn't progress work as quickly as she had previously done. However, she agreed that maybe her view was coloured by expectations of herself which were no longer appropriate now that she worked part-time.

Although these women undoubtedly felt under pressure from attempting to successfully combine the two demanding roles of mothering and working, amongst others, they nevertheless also experienced strong levels of satisfaction. The 'intellectual stimulation and challenge' which was gained from work and which was different from the satisfaction gained from helping a child to grow and learn was seen as a very positive benefit by all:

> You're part of two units . . . I feel I'm contributing to the business . . . in a service environment . . . When I'm at home I get that sort of satisfaction from feeling that I'm contributing to the environment, to life, in a different way.

It was also seen that each of these roles could enhance the other – some women felt that they enjoyed their children more because they weren't always with them and that being a mother brought, as one put it, 'another dimension to me and my work'. She talked of her attempts to reassure some women from her National Childbirth Trust group about their impending return to work: 'Nothing has been taken away from us, but so much has been added . . . I'm seeing sides of myself that I really didn't think were there . . . I find it very enriching all round'.

So, as a counterbalance to some strong pressures, there was also a powerful sense of satisfaction and achievement gained from being able to operate successfully in two very different worlds.

### Women's perceptions of their future work lives

I was also interested to find out how women perceived their working future. The experience of becoming a mother and being forced to confront the decision about whether and how to continue working seemed to prompt these women to ask themselves the questions about themselves, their purpose, their family and home life, and the pattern of their work and career which Charles Handy

(Handy 1985) suggests we should all be asking if we are to operate effectively in the future world of work. In addition, research shows (Gallos 1989) that women between the ages of 30 and 40 who have achieved professional success typically begin to question what success really means to them, particularly when they may be confronted with the personal and interpersonal cost of that success. Although a couple of the women in my research sample were younger than this, it appeared that the experience of combining work with mothering had prompted them to consider these same issues.

So, what were the results of such self-questioning for these women? Two women, who had returned to what they experienced as generally unsupportive work environments, had volunteered to take redundancy when this option became possible. For one, some time spent at home with her daughter had acted as the final catalyst, giving her a different outlook on work: 'Work had to have something to give me, not just me to give it'. When she made the decision to leave she had not envisaged giving up work, but saw it as an opportunity to look around and consider what it was that she really wanted for herself. She envisaged that a flexible working arrangement, such as working part-time for a polytechnic or business school, and combining this with some consultancy, would provide what she was looking for. The other woman who had also opted for redundancy was in the process of establishing her own consultancy business. She had decided that running her own business would bring her 'freedom, choice and control' and the best way of getting what she wanted – a balanced life.

Two other women were also looking to develop flexible working arrangements, with more control over how and when they worked. One also saw her work future as being a flexible combination of college or university work with some consultancy. The other wanted to establish her own public relations agency. Although she saw this as a longer-term venture, she had already sounded out her boss about the possibility of working part-time in her current position and combining this with freelance work which could be done from home.

Another woman was in the process of deciding whether she would continue to work. She recognized the possible implications of this decision for her career – anticipating that after a break she would probably have to return to a less senior position. However, she hoped that by the time she returned, companies might be prepared to support her re-entry into the work-force.

Even the one woman who envisaged remaining in her current position was very clear about the priorities in her life. She wanted to have another baby at some stage in the future. Despite her commitment to her work, she was clear that her personal relationships were even more important to her. She felt confident that she could make her work, pregnancy and child-rearing fit together again, and that any disruption experienced by her company would be relatively minor when compared to the length of her working life.

These women's perceptions of their working futures seem to indicate that women are beginning to rethink what success means to them and are challenging traditional male-dominated notions of what this is (Gallos 1989; Marshall 1984, 1989). None of these women saw their career as the most important thing in their life, despite all that they gained from working. Neither did they see the major life-style options (for example, work, marriage and other important personal relationships, and motherhood) as mutually incompatible. They were looking to combine these life-style options in different ways, moving away from both the traditional stereotype of the wife and mother, and the more recent image of the professional 'superwoman'. They were making conscious choices about how to integrate these different roles within their lives, taking personal responsibility for their futures in their search for a balanced and fulfilling life. The move out of organizations which some foresaw, to establish what Handy calls a portfolio of activities (Handy 1985) or their own business (a trend noted by Armstrong 1989; Gallos 1989 and Marshall 1984), was one which they envisaged would give them more control over their work and its impact on other areas of their lives.

## IMPACT ON PARTNERS' WORK LIVES

Having explored women's experiences of combining working and mothering I want to refer briefly to their partners' work lives. I looked at this issue primarily from the perspective of the women I interviewed.

Several women found that their partners, while initially very supportive, gradually reverted to more traditional forms of behaviour: 'It was very much a partnership, very sharing . . . that eroded over time . . . I think he basically has an attitude that his job is more important than mine'. One man had taken a promotion which necessitated his working away from home all week, putting his career, albeit temporarily, as the main priority.

On the other hand, a couple of women (including one who worked part-time) reported that their partners were taking an equal share of parental responsibility. One woman commented that her husband's work colleagues were 'incredulous' when he refused to stay late to work on an important presentation, as she was working away from home and he was responsible for picking their son up from the child-minder. She was concerned that such behaviour might influence his career prospects, even though he took care to ensure that the effects on his work were minimal. Another was concerned that, as her husband was about to change his job, his new company might undervalue him if he continued to share these responsibilities since this behaviour would not fit with their norms and expectations. She anticipated that he would come under increased pressure to conform. Sekaran and Hall (1989) have noted that there are more pressures exerted on men to conform to organizational norms than on women. In the face of such pressure it is perhaps not surprising that men's behaviour often belies their attitudes, and that in practice it is generally women who take primary responsibility for childcare and who, where conflict exists, adjust their working lives to accommodate family pressures (Wajcman 1981; Falkenberg and Monachello 1980).

## LEARNING FROM THIS RESEARCH

My research indicates that, contrary to commonly-held belief, women's work performance is not adversely affected by the experience of becoming a mother and combining mothering with working. It shows instead that women can enhance those skills and abilities which have already contributed to their professional success.

Looking back at what has emerged from this research convinces me that we as women have much to learn from each other. In trying to create our own definitions of success we will, by definition, be going our own way. It is therefore particularly important that we are mutually supportive of each other and the different directions which we take, rather than being judgemental of those women who choose alternative paths. While some women in this research study did experience valuable support from other women, others found that their female colleagues were equally, and sometimes more, unsupportive or judgemental of them than their male colleagues.

In trying to live and work according to our own personal views of success, it is also important that we talk with others in similar situations and form mutual support groups so that, if our path is not the majority one, we do not end up feeling unsupported and isolated. The opportunity to discuss an issue of central importance in their lives certainly seemed to be a factor motivating women to take part in this research, and some commented that they were looking forward to reading about other women's views and experiences via this paper.

In my experience of working with women managers on their development, I have found that one of the major issues which many face is a lack of confidence in their own abilities. This research shows the importance of recognizing and valuing all our experiences and the learning which they can give us, and of looking for the linkages between what we learn in our personal lives and the work situation.

This research has also highlighted for me the fact that many of the difficulties encountered by women in trying to combine work with their personal and family lives are also experienced by men, especially by those men who want to take an active role in parenting or family life. I therefore see the issues raised by this research as having pertinence for all those who work in organizations who want the flexibility and freedom to develop other areas of their lives, without this adversely affecting their professional success.

## REFERENCES

Antonis, B. (1981) 'Motherhood and mothering', Cambridge Women's Studies Group, *Women in Society: Interdisciplinary Essays*, London: Virago.

Armstrong, P. (1989) 'Is there still a chairman of the board?', *Developing Women in Management*, special issue of the *Journal of Management Development* 8, (6): 6–16.

Boud, D. and Griffin, V. (1987) 'Introduction', D. Boud and V. Griffin (eds) *Appreciating Adults Learning*, London: Kogan Page.

Falkenberg, L. and Monachello, M. (1989) 'Can organisations respond to the role overload in dual-earner families?', *Developing Women in*

*Management*, special issue of the *Journal of Management Development*, 8 (6): 17–22.

Forrest, A. (1989) 'Women in a man's world', *Developing Women in Management*, special issue of the *Journal of Management Development* 8, (6): 61–8.

Gallos, J. V. (1989) 'Exploring women's development: implications for career theory, practice, and research', M. B. Arthur, D. T. Hall and B. S. Lawrence (eds) *Handbook of Career Theory*, Cambridge: Cambridge University Press.

Griffin, V. (1987) 'Naming the processes', D. Boud and V. Griffin (eds) *Appreciating Adults Learning*, London: Kogan Page.

Handy, C. (1985) *The Future of Work*, Oxford: Basil Blackwell.

Marshall, J. (1984) *Women Managers: Travellers in a Male World*, Chichester: John Wiley.

Marshall, J. (1989) 'Revisioning career concepts: a feminist invitation', M. B. Arthur, D. T. Hall and B. S. Lawrence (eds) *Handbook of Career Theory*, Cambridge: Cambridge University Press.

Massarik, F. (1981) 'The interviewing process re-examined', J. Rowan and P. Reason (eds) *Human Inquiry*, Chichester: John Wiley.

Rowan, J. and Reason, P. (1981) 'On making sense', J. Rowan and P. Reason (eds) *Human Inquiry*, Chichester: John Wiley.

Sekaran, U. and Hall, D. (1989) 'Asynchronism in dual-career and family linkages', M. B. Arthur, D. T. Hall and B. S. Lawrence (eds) *Handbook of Career Theory*, Cambridge: Cambridge University Press.

Wajcman, J. (1981) 'Work and the family: who gets the best of both worlds?', Cambridge Women's Studies Group, *Women in Society: Interdisciplinary Essays*, London: Virago.

## Chapter 9

# Management learning and the white male heritage

*Richard Boot*

This paper describes my attempts to make sense of the field of management learning and my own practice within it. It is a field in which I have been working, one way or another, for about two decades. But only comparatively recently have I tried to make sense of it in terms of my own, and its, white maleness.

The starting point for this particular line of thinking was an insight that came to me as a result of my involvement in a general management development programme for a large local authority. The explicit focus of the programme was on the nature of changes required in management in order that the organization might be able better to respond to the increasingly turbulent context within which it was operating – a familiar story. What was different, however, was that race and gender were explicitly built into the design as general management issues that needed addressing throughout rather than being marginalized into equal opportunities 'slots'. While it is not appropriate for the purpose of this paper to go into all the details of the programme, one aspect of its design is fundamental to the insight to which I have referred.

It was a large programme, the formal part of which consisted of a number of different types of meeting taking place over several months. The participants were divided into four groups, according to race and sex, for the duration of the programme. There was a white women's group working with a white female consultant, a black women's group working with a black female consultant, a black men's group working with a black male consultant and a white men's group working with me as consultant. These groups met sometimes on their own, sometimes all together and sometimes with each of the other groups separately. The rationale was that it would be possible to explore the significance for organizational change of the processes between these groupings, the processes within the groupings and the relationship between the two.

It was the starkness of this separating out into these differences, and in particular the way this seemed to avoid the common blurring of the distinction between the dynamics of gender and the dynamics of race, that stimulated new ways of thinking. And it was the thoughts and feelings provoked by comparing my experience of my group, including myself, with my experience of the black women's group that was the source of my insight. I think this comparison was so central because it felt as though, in some ways, through my whiteness I was part of the same process as the white women and through my maleness I was part of the same process as the black men. This comforting sense of common ground, however illusory, was not available to me in my relationships with the black women. This heightened my sense of difference. The difference was most noticeable in orientation to power. They had an explicit strategy of finding their own internal sources of power and using these as the basis for engaging with the world. This seemed quite evident in the way they related to the rest of us. Their personal power was undoubtedly the dominant source of creative energy in the total group. The white men, on the other hand, had a more external orientation not only to power but also to their own learning. I experienced them as having a deadening effect, not only on me but also on the processes of the total group.

As I reflected upon, fleshed out and tidied up the insight in order to communicate it to others, it became a more elaborate framework couched in more familiar language. It provided me with a new clarity about the nature of management learning and what was required for its development. As I shall explain, however, the clarity did not last for long. For this reason I prefer to start by presenting the insight in its initial raw form which can be represented diagrammatically as in Figure 9.1.

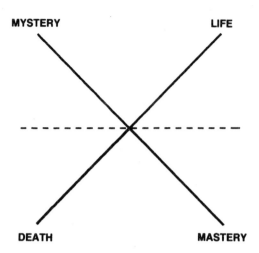

*Figure 9.1*  The initial insight

At its most basic the insight was the meaning I gave to the contrast I experienced between those terms above and those terms below the dotted line. It had both a personal significance in terms of my own 'pathology' and a professional significance in terms of my understanding of the organizational processes I was working with and trying to change. At a personal level, I was aware that a major theme in my own biography has been the continuing attempt to master death. When contrasting this with my experience of the black women, I came to associate this fixation 'below the line' with my white maleness. They seemed, in terms of what I was projecting on to them at least, to be working 'above the line', from a position that was more about being at one with the mysteries of life.

At a professional level it seemed to me that the same could be said of the field of management learning. It too seemed to be characterized by concerns about mastery and death but these concerns manifested themselves in a very different language. This is the language I found myself using as I tried fleshing out the insight into a more communicable (and rational) form.

As I reflected upon the concepts of management and learning together, my thinking allowed the term management to connote the processes of power and the term learning to connote conceptions of knowledge and knowing. So I started thinking 'what does that cross in my diagram mean to me as a white man in terms of knowledge and power?'

Taking knowledge first, it seemed to me that the quest for knowledge could be characterized by an emphasis on objectivity, analysis and quantity, and is typically broken down into separate subjects or academic disciplines. Underpinning this approach to knowledge is the scientific method which, according to one definition, enables 'prediction and control beyond the level of common sense'. The whole point of knowledge, then, is to gain greater control over the world. In essence, it is the desire ultimately for complete mastery of the world.

This seemed, however, in opposition to an approach to knowledge or, perhaps more appropriately, knowing, which is about the quest for harmony or union with the world. Here the emphasis is upon subjectivity, intuition, quality and holism. The essence here is the desire to understand or enter into the mysteries of the world.

These two approaches can be represented by Figure 9.2.

**KNOWLEDGE**

| FOR UNION (MYSTERY) | Holism  Subjectivity | Quantity  Analysis | FOR CONTROL (MASTERY) |
|---|---|---|---|
| | Intuition  Quality | Objectivity  Academic disciplines | |

Figure 9.2  Two approaches to knowledge

My experience is that university business schools and much of training practice are based upon, and structured according to, the right-hand end of the continuum.

Looking at power in a similar way, I found myself considering two faces of power – the power to destroy and the power to create. The former emphasizes division and competition and gets enacted through the processes of hierarchy and control – the structure and process of most of our large organizations. The latter is about the processes of empowerment and emphasizes connection and co-operation. It is typically organized on a smaller scale in terms of networks with an emphasis on informality and, most radically, no boss. Suma Wholefoods might be a good example. In the language of the original insight, I am talking about the distinction between power founded on death (the power to destroy) and power founded on life (the power to create). This can be represented as in Figure 9.3.

| TO DESTROY | Hierarchy | Control | | Connection | Co-operation | TO CREATE |
| DEATH | Division | Competition | | Empowerment | Networks | (LIFE) |

*Figure 9.3* Two approaches to power

When I combined this continuum of power with the continuum of knowledge, I arrived at what I believe is the current picture of management learning (see Figure 9.4).

In this picture of management learning, management is typified by hierarchy, control, division and competition, both internally and externally to organizations. The term 'death' here seems appropriate because organizationally it is about the ability to destroy other organizations in competition and internally it too frequently leads to the destruction of the humanity of the members of the organization – a kind of death. The core process is

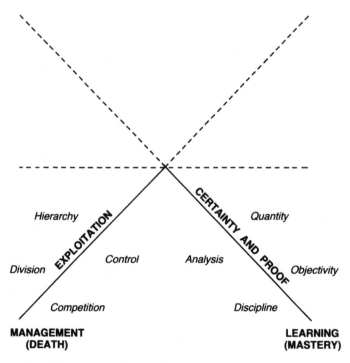

*Figure 9.4* The current picture of management learning

exploitation. Externally it is exploiting the environment, which is often spoken of positively in terms of making maximum use of resources. Internally it is the exploitation of human 'resources' also used as a positive term.

Similarly, in this picture of management learning, learning as institutionalized in business schools is typified by the emphasis on quantification and the division of the world into subjects. So, for example, those undertaking an MBA are likely to find themselves spending much of their time studying the world broken down into accounting, marketing, operations management, organizational behaviour, and so on. And the institution is likely to be organized into faculties and departments. The core process here seems to be the search for certainty and proof.

I choose the term white male 'heritage' because I believe that I, as a white man, have personally inherited these conceptions of knowledge and power. I don't believe, however, they are intrinsic to me but they do influence how I operate and are a part of who I am – my received identity. I also believe that they are what the industrialized world, created predominantly by white men, has inherited. It is full of organizations based upon mastery and death which, in the quest to master the world run the risk of bringing about its death. This is 'global insanity' supported by old criteria for success – growth, bottom line, and so on – and knowledge and power mediated through old organizational structures (see Figure 9.5).

I thought perhaps the hope was in environmentalism and the 'greening' of industry but I became cynical about that because the concept of environment still requires us to regard ourselves as separate from the world. The world is what is around us. We are in our environment. We can either invest in or exploit it but we are not part of it. In this managerialized, or should I say politicized, version of 'green' language, environment and ecology are used as synonyms. I prefer, however, to differentiate the terms. For me ecology refers to a total interrelated system and does not privilege human beings.

The insight, then, gave me a sense of what I needed to be doing personally and professionally. I was to work on moving the world of management learning above the dotted line in Figure 9.5. This meant attempting to establish new criteria for success (personal, professional and, perhaps most significantly, organizational) and new processes of organizing (rather than just playing around with structures). All of this was to be based on the values and ways of

*Figure 9.5* Global sanity and the white male heritage

being that I had come to associate with the black women. Great! I had a clear vision and a new dogma. All I had to do was to stick to them and everything I did in my work would be sound.

After a while, however, the inherent problems with this position began to emerge. I realized it was a false clarity. At a personal level I was happy to put more energy into cherishing the female within me. And at a professional level I was happy to encourage the people I worked with to explore new ways of managing and organizing based upon what some people have referred to as the female principle. But I heard a voice which was asking 'What about me as a man? Will this brave new world require me to deny my masculinity?'

I started considering these questions in two ways. Professionally, given the assumptions about power and knowledge

I saw as currently underpinning management learning, I concluded that I needed to address the concerns of those who currently represent the locus of power – white male managers. I needed to be able to respond satisfactorily to the, sometimes explicit, frequently implicit, line of argument I am confronted with when working with men – 'Why should I change? What's in it for me? Are you saying that I have to give up all the things that I like about being a white man in the modern world? No way! Why should I? I can only see what I am being told I must let go of, not what I can hold on to'.

Also, of more personal significance, I realized that I was perpetuating a simplistic good/bad dichotomy. In this case I was left with woman=> good, man=> bad. But I don't experience myself as bad. I experience all these things as my heritage but I don't experience them as me. Neither, while accepting modern organizations as predominantly male constructions, do I believe they function unequivocally to the advantage of all men. So I now find myself faced with quite a different and, at the moment, less clear task. This is finding an approach to management learning which is based upon 'good man' and 'good woman' in partnership. I acknowledge that this is the language of stereotypes but it is a very stereotypical heritage I am dealing with. I believe it is necessary to find a language which can honour the difference and is not based on big negative concepts like death and destruction, attached to which are all the other ideas like hierarchy and control. It would enable us men working in management learning to see more than the single daunting task of moving not only ourselves but the cohorts of white men with whom we work 'across the dotted line'.

The task becomes that of establishing a positive professional identity which is clearly male and establishing positive organizational processes which are clearly male which can work in equal partnership with those that are clearly female. In trying to represent this diagrammatically I became aware of another troublesome aspect of the task. It may well be that, in order to move towards this positive male image we shall have to let go of the glorified form of the female principle and acknowledge that it too has a degenerate form (see Figure 9.6).

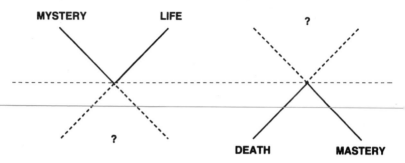

*Figure 9.6*  The task ahead

While I do not have a template to guide me in this task, nor, indeed do I think I aspire to one, there are a number of things about which I'm becoming clearer. The task cannot be accomplished by a glorification of the 'female principle' and a suppression of the masculine within us – the 'new man' approach. Nor can it be achieved by a glorification of masculinity and a suppression of the feminine within us – the 'wild man' approach advocated by the disciples of Robert Bly. Both of these represent a denial of the diversity within us. Unless we can acknowledge and accept that inner diversity, I believe we are ill equipped to establish equal partnerships within the even greater diversity outside of ourselves.

So what does this mean in slightly less abstract terms? For me, a useful starting point would be establishing a greater awareness and understanding of what it means to be a man at work. I'm not thinking here of high order theorizing by enlightened academics, of which there is an increasing amount. I'm thinking of talking and listening to ordinary men, from dustmen to directors, black and white, about their experiences. In some cases the process may well help them articulate experiences which hitherto had been hidden even from themselves. The point would not be to write it all up as 'research findings' for publication in a learned journal but to make it available in as accessible form as possible to any men and women who believe there must be better ways of organizing collective activity than those that predominate at present.

More important, however, than this, I believe, is the need for men and women to talk and listen to each other about what it feels like to be a man or a woman at work. The process will be complicated, not only by the difference in those experiences and the different ways of expressing them, but also by all the pre-existing stereotypes that each group holds of the other. More problematically, the right to define the reality of organizational experience has traditionally been the privilege of men, but more recently it seems as though the right to define the reality of all gender experience has become the privilege of women. In the dialogue which is necessary for the establishment of an equal partnership, I believe neither men's nor women's reality should be privileged.

# Chapter 10

## Female entrepreneurs – success by whose standards?

*Sue Marlow* and *Adam Strange*

### INTRODUCTION

The last fifteen years have seen the emergence of an 'Enterprise Culture' in which entrepreneurial behaviour, particularly the start-up of new small firms, has been afforded a central role. Indeed, the small firm sector is now a major focus for policies of economic regeneration and employment creation throughout the developed world (Storey *et al.* 1987). As Birley (1989) notes of the British case, 'increasingly, all sectors of the population are being urged to consider self-employment' (p. 32), going on to draw attention to the plethora of schemes which encourage and facilitate new business start-up, for example, Enterprise Allowance, TEC (Training and Enterprise Council) programmes, Graduate Enterprise, Firm Start, Ethnic Minority Business Initiative, Women's Enterprise Development Agency. The British experience is paralleled throughout the major economies of the world (Crossick 1986; D'Amato 1986; Goffee and Scase 1987; Thompson and Thompson 1990).

One consequence of the growth of the enterprise culture is the considerable academic resources which have been spent researching entrepreneurship, made manifest as new business start-up. From this base, business growth, operating problems and small firm failure have also been the subject of great investigation (Storey *et al.* 1987). Until recently, however, this research has been largely gender blind. Major studies of the small firm sector carried out in the 1970s and early 1980s (for example the Bolton Report 1971; Storey 1982) did not consider gender as a variable which might influence the process of business formation or the experience of enterprise ownership. As Holmquist and Sundin (1989) state, 'entrepreneurial theories are created by men, for men and are applied to men' (p.1), the implication being either that women do not own small firms, or that those that do act no differently from men. The lack of academic analysis of gender-related issues reflects a male-dominated approach which presumes that women act from similar motivations and look for similar rewards from entrepreneurial activity as their male counterparts.

It is even more difficult to understand the omission of gender discrimination from the research agenda of business ownership, given that studies of segmentation in the labour market had focused clearly on the issue of gender from the 1960s (Doeringer and Piore 1971), whilst feminists have drawn attention to women's subordination in social, economic and political terms for centuries (Wollstonecraft 1792; Hamilton 1909; Rowbotham 1973). Given that business ownership is clearly an occupation which generates an income for the entrepreneur (and is classed as an occupation by the Department of Employment) there has been a lamentable lacuna in the academic research arena regarding the female experience of enterprise ownership. As recent figures indicate that between 1981 and 1989, female self-employment rose by 81 per cent compared to 51 per cent amongst men and, moreover, women now constitute 24 per cent of the self-employed in Britain, there can be little justification for the exclusion of gender-related discrimination from the analyses of issues surrounding small firm ownership (Daly, 1991: 112).

This lack of consideration of female entrepreneurship has ensured that the decision-making processes of funding agencies and policy-makers have been informed almost entirely by analyses of the experiences and actions of male business owners. Consequently, women are judged by parameters which, we would argue, do not take account of extraneous factors which are extremely pertinent to women, for example, gender-based labour market discrimination and domestic responsibilities. Such constituent factors can produce fundamental differences in motivation between men and women who undertake business ownership, which have significant implications for the way in which business success is defined by the entrepreneur herself.

This chapter focuses specifically upon the interaction between gender influences and the attribution of 'success' to small firms. Existing studies commonly define success in accountancy-based terms, such as profitability, turnover and key financial ratios (Chaganti and Chaganti 1983; Hornaday and Wheatley 1986;

Thomas and Evanson 1987). The theme of this chapter, however, is that any assessment of success for small firm ventures should take account of why men and women begin their businesses, what problems business ownership overcomes and generates for the owner and, specifically, what the firm owners actually wish to achieve for themselves.

In this chapter we will be, firstly, considering the motives which predispose men and women to enter self-employment; secondly, arguing that definitions of performance and success traditionally employed in small business research are inappropriate to the study of many ventures, and in particular to the study of the majority of female enterprises; and concluding with the view that not only is gender a crucial variable in the assessment of business performance, but that small firm ownership does not, in fact, offer escape from labour market discrimination for women.

## REASONS FOR CHOOSING BUSINESS PROPRIETORSHIP

It is commonly recognized that individuals' motives for seeking self-employment are numerous and diverse. Research (Goffee and Scase 1985; Cromie 1987) indicates that, superficially, men and women share some common areas of motivation for undertaking business ownership (job dissatisfaction, desire for autonomy, and so on). However, although both men and women were looking for autonomy through proprietorship, Goffee and Scase (1985) found that women wished specifically to escape the male domination of employers and husbands. Similarly, although Cromie (1987) found that men and women were similarly motivated by the desire for autonomy and by dissatisfaction in their previous job, women placed significantly more importance on the needs of childcare and feelings of longer-term career dissatisfaction. Men were found to focus more clearly upon financial gain as a strong motivator towards self-employment. Both studies, however, found that contributing towards women's decision to enter self-employment were experiences of discrimination in the waged labour market specific to their sex.

It is clear that, despite positive legislation and initiatives such as 'Project 2000', women still experience discrimination within the waged labour market because of ascribed social characteristics (Hunt 1988). A useful analytical framework to explore labour discrimination within a market economy is the dual labour market theory where Doeringer and Piore (1971), argue that the labour market consists of two major elements, a primary and secondary sector, where:

> jobs in the primary market possess high wages, good working conditions, employment stability, chances of advancement, equity. . . . whereas secondary market [jobs] tend to have low wages and fringe benefits, poor working conditions, high labour turnover, little chance of advancement and arbitrary supervision.
>
> (Doeringer and Piore 1971: 165)

Research indicates that women and racial minorities are a major constituent of the secondary labour market (Beller 1982; Craig *et al.* 1982; *Feminist Review* 1986). This arises as individuals are ascribed characteristics based upon stereotypical images of the groups to which they are assigned. Thus it is presumed that, as women are largely responsible for domestic labour and childcare, they are less reliable employees with a primary commitment to the home rather than the waged labour. Consequently, women are judged as a group to have a volatile attachment to employment and, as they take time out, or disappear altogether from the labour market due to the demands of 'family formation', to be a poor investment as an employee. Moreover, because of the difficulty some will experience achieving promotion premised upon organizational norms of unbroken service, it is concluded that women are less able than men (West 1982).

Evidence from a survey by the Institute for Employment Research (1985) concludes that the period of 'family formation' leads women to undergo severe downward occupational mobility with an extremely limited opportunity for recovery. The recovery is so limited because the majority of women re-entering the labour market after 'family formation' do so as part-time workers in order to accommodate childcare, domestic labour and waged work. Elias (1988) reflects many other commentators (Doeringer and Piore 1971; West 1982) when he comments that 'part-time jobs are concentrated within a narrow band of occupations, principally in areas of low-skill personal service work . . . [or] at the lowest hierarchical level within the vertical structure of an occupation group with disproportionately fewer fringe benefits' (Elias 1988: 101).

But, disregarding structural social hurdles, there is no evidence to suggest that within the population ability to undertake primary sector occupations is affected by either sex or race.

The dual labour market approach has been subject to extensive critical analysis, focused particularly upon the usefulness of a dichotomous division of the labour market given the complexity of the modern economy (for a more extensive discussion and critical analysis, see Craig *et al.* 1982). It is argued that rather than distinct sectoral division, there is a continuum of conditions from primary to secondary labour markets, with areas of overlap constantly fluctuating according to labour market conditions, such as levels of unemployment, trade union strength, and so on, all of which affect sector parameters. Thus, in tight labour markets women will be drawn into primary sector occupations where provision will be made to accommodate alternative demands upon their time. However, in accordance with the theory of a reserve army of labour (Marx 1956), this sector of the working population will be the most vulnerable during times of recession, whereupon social characteristics, such as the presumed unreliability of female labour because of their primary affiliation to the domestic sphere, will be drawn upon to facilitate and justify labour shedding.

An alternative critique of the dual labour market theory suggests that the division of labour between sectors with differentiated rewards is an efficient use of human capital. Indeed, there is seen to be a reciprocal relationship between the family and the labour market, where part-time work and jobs which do not demand a high level of personal commitment enable women to 'fit' waged work around domestic tasks. The neo-classical economists, Mincer and Polachek (1980), suggest that 'foregoing the market-orientated human capital of mothers is part of the price for acquiring human capital in children, and, more generally a price exacted by family life' (p. 203). This makes a massive presumption that market conditions dictate social organization, that family life with a male partner offering financial support is natural and available to every woman, that domestic labour is primary for women, and that the rearing of the next generation makes women's rights as waged labourers expendable.

The interaction between the economic and social organization of society is highly complex, but we would refute the notion that it is acceptable or necessary for women to forfeit equality in labour to ensure the next generation of labourers, an argument critically examined by Mackintosh (1982). Land (1980) argues convincingly against the notion that most men earn a 'family wage', whilst empirical studies of women in waged work (Pollert 1981; Cavendish 1982; Westwood 1986) support Land in concluding that women's wages are not the euphemistic 'pin money', but are essential to the family to maintain an acceptable standard of living. Moreover, it is not a minority of women in our society who are engaged in waged work. In 1985 the Institute for Employment Research found that only 18 per cent of women fitted the stereotypical 'housewife' models; clearly the presumptions, upon which Mincer and Polachek draw concerning contemporary social conditions promoting efficient use of human resources are based upon false premises (Institute of Employment Research 1985: 24).

There have been attempts to redress the structural inequalities women face within the labour market, mainly through a series of legislative acts attempting to make the labour market more equitable. However, the legislation has largely proved to be ineffective; for example, the Equal Pay Act (1976) applied only to those women who could compare their job to a man's job with the same employer and prove that the only source of differentiation was the gender of the employee. The 1984 amendment to this Act established the principle of equal pay for work of equal value, but it is not clear whether part-time and full-time work can be compared, with the onus being upon the individual to prove her case through complex legal procedures. Research (Lonsdale 1985) establishes that discrimination against women within the labour market cannot be effectively countered by legislation alone. The ghettoization of women into secondary sector employment makes the concept of 'like work' comparisons with primary sector employment irrelevant.

It can be seen that women form a substantial element of the secondary labour market because of the need to accommodate waged work with domestic labour, which restricts choices in employment. For those women without families or domestic responsibilities, for whom this accommodation is not necessary, the expectation is that they will eventually conform to the stereotypical image of women, which prioritizes the domestic sphere.

## WOMEN IN THE SMALL BUSINESS LITERATURE

Self-employment offers one solution to women whose careers have been interrupted or cut short by childcare, and is one form of waged work which allows greater flexibility to accommodate domestic tasks. Thus Vinnicombe (1987) identifies business start-up as an alternative which offers a 'coping strategy' in response to such limitations (together with working part-time or not at all). The attractiveness of proprietorship as an employment strategy for women with children has also been illustrated by Hertz (1985) in the United States. From her research sample she found that only 39 per cent of female executives were mothers, compared with 74 per cent of those who were self-employed (Hertz 1985: 33). Furthermore, from a study of over one thousand female proprietors in Sweden, Holmquist and Sundin (1989) found that the ability to combine domestic and economic roles was the most often cited single motive for women undertaking business ownership.

Stanworth *et al.* (1989), however, challenge this view of female entrepreneurship as a subordination response, or a reaction against dependence upon men, arguing that this could be a 'premature consensus'. It is suggested that the studies upon which these conclusions are based depend upon samples with a bias towards single, divorced and separated women (Watkins and Watkins 1984; Goffee and Scase 1985; Cromie 1987; Carter and Cannon 1988), and thus leads to an inaccurate representation of the 'real' situation.

Birley (1989) lends some support to the critique developed by Stanworth *et al.* (1989), as she finds few differences between the motivations of male and female entrepreneurs:

> Of the four motivations identified by Goffee and Scase (1985), three, avoiding low-paid occupations, escaping supervision, and the constraint of subservient roles (in the incubator organisation) – are directly comparable . . . It would seem that females are motivated by the same need for money, wish to be independent and identification of opportunities similar to their male counterparts.

Such arguments as those outlined by Birley (1989) are useful, as they remind us that women cannot be treated as an homogeneous group. Indeed, as we have noted, the trend in small business research is to treat all women as 'honorary men' and we should not reflect this type of group assessment by presuming that all women share similar motivations for business start-up. Whilst it cannot be denied that previous research may be limited by methodological difficulties, the arguments developed within this chapter are based upon solid evidence from labour market studies (Cockburn 1983; Rubery 1988; *Low Pay Review* 1987) which confirm that women are discriminated against as a group within the employment market. Thus, whether married, single or divorced, business ownership is one clear accommodation tactic, amongst others, to side-step discrimination in employment.

It is not disputed that, at least on the surface, motivations for business start-up may in some respects appear similar for both men and women, but critically, the experiences underlying these motives are very different. If the existing evidence from the female entrepreneurship studies is informed by the extensive analysis offered by the labour market theorists (above), it is a coherent conclusion that the position and role of women within society currently and historically predisposes them to a set of reasons for pursuing self-employment which is unique to their sex.

If, as it is argued, social and economic pressures prompt women to undertake business ownership, it is likely that women will have differing expectations of the experiences of entrepreneurship than men. If such expectations are met, for example, combining waged labour with remaining at home, and at least sufficient profits made to keep the business viable, we would describe the business as successful. Yet so often, business success is equated with business performance. In fact many firms which are fulfilling the ambitions of their owners are neither growing, in accounting terms, nor acting as significant employers. This, we suggest is often the case with small firms owned by women, and we now turn to review the manner in which business success is measured in existing literature, and whether such measures are always appropriate for women-owned businesses.

## BUSINESS SUCCESS

Kelmar (1990) reports the results of a literature search to determine how small business success and failure have been measured in previous studies. The search resulted in the detailed examination of forty chapters addressing the question of success, and sixteen on failure. From this Kelmar finds that the indicators of 'growth' (business, organizational, employment, productivity) and increased sales are the most-frequently-used measures of business success. In studies of failure, financial indicators such as bankruptcy and the calculation of key financial ratios were predominant. As Thorpe (1989: 1–11) notes:

> The normative models so often used in disciplines such as marketing, accounts and general management almost always view success from the point of view of an external agency. Success, depending upon whether you are a venture capitalist, a bank manager or a local authority is viewed in terms of jobs created, or wealth created.

Even these objective measures are not directly comparable, and are certainly not interchangeable as alternative indicators of performance. In practice, however, success or failure is a much more individual experience than can be reflected by across-the-board application of such measurement criteria. As Thorpe goes on to argue, '. . . the owner manager and his business are one and the same' (p. 4), with the fortunes of the two being inextricably linked. It follows, therefore, that the success or failure of a venture should be assessed, at least initially, in terms of the founder's own motives for setting it up. The aims and expectations of all proprietors cannot be assumed to be similar. Indeed, one person's failure may be another's success (Kelmar 1990). This is not a situation which can be adequately reflected by uniformly applied accountancy-based measures.

It is especially important that this question of definitions of success should be resolved in future studies of female proprietors. As has already been suggested, self-employment performs an important role for many women, which cannot be measured in these traditional terms. All businesses must be financially viable on some level in order to continue to exist. Beyond this, however, an enterprise which functions effectively as a 'coping strategy' for one or more women must also be seen as being 'successful' in terms of the reasons for which it was set up. As Carter and Cannon (1988) found, 'Women generally regarded success in terms of how well the business met individual needs rather than in conventional terms of profitability and income gained' (p. 50).

## SELF-EMPLOYMENT AS A LIBERATING EXPERIENCE FOR WOMEN

As a final point, it is important to note, however, that it is unlikely that business ownership will prove to be successful as a liberating experience for many women, given that those who choose this option in order to accommodate the demands of domestic labour are, by definition, still undertaking a dual role. Being self-employed is by no means an undemanding way of life, and female entrepreneurs can usually expect little assistance from other family members with their domestic tasks, with the result that they find themselves pulled in two directions, between the competing demands of home and work. Meanwhile, discrimination remains a problem for women in self-employment just as in employment, with the area of finance provision being particularly notable in this respect (Carter and Cannon 1988). Bank managers are still reluctant to fund female ventures, particularly those which stray beyond traditional feminized occupations.

In addition, if we review the sectors in which women-owned businesses predominate, they are found in the areas we have described as secondary sector in the employment market. Hakim (1987) finds that 29 per cent of female-owned firms are in consumer services (for example, hairdressing), and whilst 39 per cent are in manufacturing, 60 per cent of these businesses make clothing (Hakim 1987: 4). Holmquist and Sundin (1989), with a large sample of over 1000 women-owned firms, found the majority to be concentrated in personal services, catering and small retail, Thus, the low-paid, low status, tenuous nature of employment is reflected in low profit, highly-competitive areas of business owner-ship for women. The enterprise culture is not heralding new choices or new forms of freedom for the majority of female small firm owners.

## CONCLUSIONS

Women are constrained in their choices in the employment market by their responsibility for domestic labour. Due to the nature of the waged labour market, women find themselves marginalized in the competition for primary sector employment, and disadvantaged in achieving career progression.

Thus, self-employment is an attractive proposition in as much as it allows women the opportunity to accommodate the conflicting demands of domestic and waged labour. Although it has been argued that men and women share some common motives for business start-up, women's experience of subordination colours and influences their motives. For men, self-employment is an individual response to an individual situation. For women, it is an individual response to the effects of group stereotyping, based upon presumptions arising from gender discrimination.

If, as is suggested, the reconciliation of the competing demands of waged and domestic labour is a major factor in women's decisions to undertake business ownership, achievement of such an accommodation must be seen as an important indicator of a successful business. Current policies aimed at small firm owners presume constraints and goals for business ownership which, at present, are inappropriate for female entrepreneurs. Women may have strong ambitions to be successful small firm owners in terms of profit, growth and employment. However, the barriers of social and economic discrimination experienced by women as a group over many years, mean that these are difficult to achieve. Policy-makers and advisers in the area of small businesses must take account of such factors, if they realistically wish to assist women. For example, time management for those involved in accommodating domestic and waged labour should be a policy issue. Likewise, 'networking' is a 1990s catchword, but business 'networking' for women will include support groups for women business owners who share similar problems related to accommodating conflicting domestic and business demands.

As a group, women have a legacy of negative discrimination, which dictates that certain fundamental motives for business ownership are specific to their sex. As such, the issue of gender must be afforded serious attention in any assessment of business success. This is not to deny that businesses, regardless of the gender of the owner, have to make sufficient profit to remain viable but rather to suggest that current definitions of business success are too narrowly focused to the exclusion of other important extraneous variables such as gender.

## REFERENCES

Beller, A. (1982) 'Occupational segregation by sex: determinants and changes', *Journal of Human Resources* 17 (3) 26–37.
Birley, S. (1989) 'Female entrepreneurs: are they really any different?', *Journal of Small Business Management* 2 (2): 32–46.

Bolton, J. (Chairman) (1971) *Report of the Committee of Inquiry on Small Firms*, Cmnd 4811, London: HMSO.

Carter, S. and Cannon, T. (1988) *Female Entrepreneurs: A Study of Female Business Owners, Their Motivations, Experiences and Strategies for Success*, Department of Employment Research, chapter no. 65, London: HMSO.

Cavendish, R. (1982) *On The Line*, London: Routledge & Kegan Paul.

Chaganti, R. and Chaganti, R. (1983) 'A profile of profitable and not-so-profitable small businesses', *Journal of Small Business Management* 21 (3).

Cockburn, C. (1983) *Brothers: Male Domination and Technological Change*, London: Pluto Press.

Craig, C., Rubery, J., Tarling, R. and Wilkinson, F. (1982) *Labour Market Structure, Industrial Organisation and Low Pay*, Cambridge: Cambridge University Press.

Cromie, S. (1987) 'Similarities and differences between women and men who choose business proprietorship', *International Small Business Journal* 5 (3): 43–60.

Crossick, S. A. (1986) 'E.C. plans policies on small business', *Europe* 256: 417–22.

Daly, M. (1991) 'A decade of growth in enterprise', *Employment Gazette* (March) London: HMSO.

D'Amato, A. (1986) 'International trade in focus: the White House Conference on Small Business', *Review of Business* 8 (2): 316–31.

Doeringer, P. and Piore, M. (1971) *Internal Labor Markets and Manpower Analysis*, New York: Health Lexington Books.

Elias, P. (1988), 'Family formation, occupational mobility and part-time work' in A. Hunt (ed.) *Women and Paid Work*, London: Macmillan.

*Feminist Review* (1986) (ed.) *Waged Work: A Reader*, London: Virago.

Goffee, R. and Scase, R. (1985) *Women in Charge: The Experiences of Female Entrepreneurs*, London: Allen & Unwin.

Goffee, R. and Scase, R. (1987) (eds) *Entrepreneurship in Europe*, London: Croom Helm.

Hakim, C. (1987) Research Design, Strategies and Choices in the Design of Social Research, London: Allen & Unwin.

Hamilton, C. (1909) *Marriage as a Trade*, London: The Woman's Press.

Hertz, L. (1985) *The Business Amazons*, London: Andre Deutsch.

Holmquist, C. and Sundin, E. (1989) 'The growth of women's entre-preneurship – push or pull factors?', EIASM Conference on Small Business, University of Durham Business School.

Hornaday, R. W. and Wheatley, W. J. (1986) 'Managerial characteristics and the financial performance of small firms', *Journal of Small Business Management* 24 (2) 53–67.

Hunt, A. (1988) (ed.) *Women and Paid Work*, London: Macmillan.

Institute for Employment Research (1985) 'Review of the economy and employment 1', University of Warwick, Coventry.

Kelmar, J. H. (1990) 'Measurement of success and failure in small business – a dichotomous anachronism', chapter presented at the 13th Small Firms Policy and Research Conference, Harrogate, 14–16 November, 1990.

Land, H. (1980) 'The family wage', *Feminist Review* 6: 55–77.

Lonsdale, S. (1985) *Work and Inequality*, London: Longman.

*Low Pay Review* (1987) 'Low pay in Britain'.

Mackintosh, M. (1982) 'Gender and economics: the sexual division of labour and the subordination of women', in K. Young, C. Wolwowitz and R. McCullagh (eds) *Of Marriage and the Market: Women's Subordination in International Perspective*, London: CSE Books.

Marx, K. (1956) *Capital 1*, London: Lawrence & Wishart.

Mincer, J. and Polachek, S. (1980) 'Family investments in human capital: earnings of women', in A. H. Amsden (ed.) *The Economics of Women and Work*, Harmondsworth: Penguin.

Piore, M. (1986) 'On the job training in a dual labor market', in A. Weber *et al.* (eds) *Public-Private Manpower Policies*, Coventry, Industrial Relations Research Unit, University of Warwick.

Pollert, A. (1981) *Girls, Wives, Factory Lives*, London: Macmillan.

Rowbotham, S. (1973) *Hidden From History*, London: Pluto Press.

Rubery, J. (1988) 'Structured labour markets, worker organisation and low pay', *Cambridge Journal of Economics* 2: 17–36.

Stanworth, J., Stanworth, C., Granger, B. and Blyth, S. (1989) 'Who becomes an entrepreneur?', *International Small Business Journal* 8 (1): 11–12.

Storey, D. J. (1982) *Entrepreneurship and the New Firm*, London: Croom Helm.

Storey, D. J., Keasey, K., Watson, R. and Wynarczyk, P. (1987) *Small Firms in Britain*, London: Croom Helm.

Thomas, J. (III) and Evanson, R. V. (1987) 'An empirical investigation of association between financial ratio use and small business success', *Journal of Business Finance and Accounting* 14 (4).

Thompson, S. C. and Thompson, M. C. (1990) 'Policy: how it benefits small business', *Practising Manager* (Australia) 11 (1): 29–42.

Thorpe, R. (1989) 'The performance of small firms: predicting success and failure', chapter presented at the 10th UK Small Firms Policy and Research Conference, Durham University, 1987.

Vinnicombe, S. (1987) 'Drawing out the differences between male and female working styles', *Women in Management Review* Spring 7 (2) 5–16.

Watkins, J. and Watkins, D. (1984) 'The female entrepreneur: background and determinants of business choice – some British data', *International Small Business Journal* 2 (4): 21–31.

West, J. (1982) (ed.) *Work, Women and the Labour Market*, London: Routledge & Kegan Paul.

Westwood, S. (1986) *All Day, Every Day*, London: Pluto Press.

Wollstonecraft, M. (1792) *A Vindication of the Rights of Woman*, Harmondsworth: Penguin, 1978.

Chapter 11

# Why women leave senior management jobs
## My research approach and some initial findings

*Judi Marshall*

This chapter provides an interim report from an interview study of women who have chosen to leave senior management jobs with no immediate career plans. It is an account of the research approach and methods used, with an outline of initial findings. Some implications for training and development will be explored.

## INITIATING THE PROJECT

I had been thinking about doing this research for several years. The idea came from a test question I was often asked when giving public talks on women in management. A senior manager, usually male, would cite a case of a woman who had risen to senior ranks in their organization, but then left. People often had only a confused idea of why she had done so, I was told. I was asked to explain, and to comment on women's apparent ambivalence about the senior positions to which they had ostensibly been aspiring.

I would hear similar stories from women directly or through networks, but with a rather different gloss. Typically, after prolonged periods of struggling to achieve an identity she valued and of feeling under pressure, the woman would decide to take control of her life and leave. It was usually a celebration of personal power, a positive step, rather than confusion or being unable to cope. I had also wanted to leave employment at some times, so this theme related to my own personal process, as much research does (Marshall 1992).

A few years ago I had some time off work for family reasons, and as I returned I became excited about pursuing the topic of women leaving as a research study. I wanted to tell the stories of the women concerned from their perspectives, as these did not seem to be understood. The interpretation that these women had somehow been inadequate for organizational life seemed to dominate.

As I prepared to return to work I found myself devoting more and more time to the research proposal, giving it priority over other, supposedly more urgent, tasks. This seemed like research I had to do. As I began to talk to other people its wider interest was confirmed, and I was encouraged to take the topic on.

I realized from the outset that not all women managers leave organizations; that most stay, and some, although perhaps as yet not many, thrive. So I am dealing with a small subgroup. None the less they are interesting. I see them as representing a test case, not only for what happens to some women who are organizationally successful, but also for how to make sense of women's experiences if their voices are still relatively marginal in employment.

I encouraged myself to start the project at a busy time in my life by applying for a small research prize from Routledge Press. I was lucky enough to be awarded this. From the outset it was important to me to do the study in a way which does not erode my life too much – an intention with plenty of obvious relevance to the research theme. I have therefore tried to let the research take its time, not forcing myself to do things when I am too busy with other activities. The project has therefore happened in phases, and it is as if people have come to me to make it happen rather than that I have had to push. This is particularly evident in how contacts have emerged to be interviewed at times when I had time to meet with them. This sense of fit between my energy cycles and those of others involved has contributed to a feeling of rightness and timeliness about the research. At peak times I was making new contacts daily, with a sense of excitement and movement forward. And then there would be lulls, times of gestation.

## RESEARCH APPROACH

My style of research can be broadly labelled 'post-positivist'. I do not believe that there is objective knowledge that we discover, or that the researcher should maintain their distance from the issues they study and the people they engage with. Rather I believe that research is done from a perspective – defined by Schwartz and

Ogilvy (1979) as 'a personal view from a distance'. A major aspect of rigorous research practice is trying to be critically aware of my own perspective and how that affects my strategies and sense-making. I also believe in doing *research with people* rather than on people. I therefore invite others involved in the study to join me in making sense of their experience.

I wanted this to be a qualitative study, telling the stories of about a dozen women in some depth. In due course I shall write a book from the data, to be published by Routledge. I started out by drafting an invitation, explaining that I was interested in women who reach middle to senior level organizational positions, and so have shown considerable commitment to career development, and then decide to leave for reasons other than to pursue their careers. I noted that this categorization was somewhat ill defined, but that I wanted to let what did happen to women emerge through the research process rather than set out with narrow preconceptions.

I mailed out copies of the invitation to a wide range of people who might know suitable candidates. I also talked about my research in passing to friends and contacts. The research topic seemed to strike a chord with many people and I soon had many relevant conversations. Suitable people to talk to were also recommended to me. Then came the process of tracking them down. As they had left organizations some were not easy to trace; a few we never did find. Most people on my contact mailing list were chosen specifically because they had access to particular wider networks. In two instances I sent out information about the study to contacts asking them to circulate it to networks to which they belonged. Both initially misinterpreted my letter because they had recently left organizations in circumstances which made them suitable participants. They wondered how my letter had been so appropriately timed!

My research field-work is to be in phases. Initially I am interviewing people individually. I shall then prepare a draft of their story and offer it to them for comment and amendment. We shall work together to achieve a telling which seems appropriate to us both. As a further stage I shall invite all the people I have interviewed to meet for a day to address issues which have emerged from the first phase of research. In this way I hope also to benefit from the sense they make in interaction with each other. At the time of writing I have interviewed eight people and have made initial contact with several others.

## MAKING CONTACTS AND DEVELOPING IDEAS

I am using a process of emergent sampling. I started from the core idea of talking to women who leave senior jobs for reasons other than career progression, for whom leaving is the primary motivation. I vaguely assumed that most would then spend time 'at home', as this had happened to several of the people I had previously heard about. I soon realized that this assumption could be a thinly-disguised version of 'woman's place is in the home'. Having myself spent time at home and then returned to my previous job may also have shaped my thinking. I soon decided to relax any ideas of what women do 'after leaving', only holding to the interest in people who felt that they *had* to leave. In this way I let the sampling process inform me of what people did, and help me map the territory. It seems people leave for a variety of reasons, and in a variety of ways. After leaving, their lives are very open to change; new opportunities might soon reshape their initial intentions.

I have let the research process inform me about the topic I am studying, which is rather different from many forms of traditional social science research in which the topic area has to be defined in advance. Had I controlled the sampling more in advance, however, I would have learnt much less.

The eight interviews I have conducted so far have been guided by four broad topic headings:

- a brief review of career and life history;
- the job and organizational situation;
- the decision to leave and process of leaving; and
- general views on being a woman in employment and managing identity as a woman manager.

Within each topic area I have identified possible specific questions. The interviewee and I have typically shared the resulting checklist, using it as a prompt if necessary. All interviews have been tape recorded and fully transcribed.

I have found the interviews interesting, stimulating and often moving. People have generally been keen to reflect about, and make sense of, their experience, and so in most cases it has felt like a shared journey of exploration. Telling their story fully has been an emotionally-powerful event for some people. The interview has helped them explore their current feelings. One ex-manager was surprised and delighted to note the positive tone in which she told her story and to realize that she had now left much of the pain of the events behind. Another realized how upset she still was, but found the interview helped her address these feelings. Several have said explicitly that they are handing their story over to my care because they cannot tell it publicly themselves but think it should be heard as it is significant for women generally.

## REVIEWING RELEVANT LITERATURE

As a parallel strand of the research I am collecting potentially-relevant literature. Some is clearly focused on women leaving organizations, far more covers associated themes such as management styles, power, organizational culture, career patterns, and critical commentaries on contemporary gender relations. At the moment the research feels relatively unbounded conceptually. Analysing and recounting the managers' stories will determine the intellectual approaches I later take to sense-making.

There is some recent literature, from the United States and Canada particularly, which talks about women 'bailing out' of employment, women 'quitting' and 'corporate attrition', and therefore is closely related to my study. It is interesting that corporate life is so clearly the reference point and norm against which women's behaviour is judged, as these labels for the phenomenon show.

MBA graduates are providing interesting samples, because they offer populations of women and men with equal qualifications, who are expected to be both able and career-committed. Given this base, it is interesting to find that women show a higher drop-out rate than men from employment, although just how big the difference is is open to debate. Certainly such findings raise concern and comment. Those taking an effectiveness perspective, who do not question the desirability of current organizational life, ask whether women are therefore making best use of an MBA education and the 'equality' it offers them. Alternatively, some people suggest that organizational cultures have done little to change deep-seated male-dominated values as more women enter and that MBA and other women live with the unresolved tensions (Gordon 1991). Choices of interpretation are obviously important here.

Taylor (1986) reported on a *Fortune* follow-up study of men and women who had received MBAs in 1976 from '17 of the most selective business schools' (p. 17) in the USA. The study found that 30 per cent of the women MBAs described themselves as self-employed or unemployed ten years later, compared to 21 per cent of the men. Additional telephone interviews with people in these categories suggested that the initial figures over-estimated women's employment and under-estimated that of men.

There is also journalistic material suggesting that both women and men are leaving. There may therefore be some life-stage issues which are leading this generation to question employment, or the type of high-commitment career they have initially followed, as they reach mid-life. Also, some studies are finding that men are as likely to quote work–family conflict and wanting more time with their children as potential reasons for leaving jobs as are women (Korabik and Rosin 1991).

When the literature tries to explain why some women leave, it often talks about them putting family before career. Schwartz's (1989) suggestion that there should be 'mommy tracks' for women who have children, and are therefore assumed to have moderated their career aspirations, has generated much discussion and heat. But the picture does not seem as simple as this. Certainly some women leave for family reasons, especially to cope with having pre-school children. But most see this situation as temporary, as Rosin and Korabik (1990) found in a survey of 391 Canadian women with MBA degrees. (The sample's work experience ranged from one to twenty years, with a median of seven; two-thirds had reached middle or senior management jobs.) But there seems to be at least another distinct, and significantly-sized, group who leave because of dissatisfaction with the organization environment, office politics, and limited career opportunities (Korabik and Rosin 1991). It is interesting to note that in the latter study nearly a quarter of the female sample were seriously considering leaving their jobs, suggesting that the potential for turnover was high.

From my brief engagement with this literature so far it seems that there is no one reason why women leave, that men are concerned about work–family conflict, that some men also wish to leave employment or change its nature, and that many of the women who do leave will do so only temporarily. I also note how surprising it is to some commentators to find that women are not leaving to be mothers, and that they have dissatisfactions with the organizational world.

## LIMITS TO INVITING CRITICAL FEEDBACK

Researching gender and management means entering a minefield of interpretation. In many ways this project is about interpretation, about affirming that of the women concerned, and answering back to dominant voices who doubt their commitment to employment, suitability and so on. Early in the research I was feeling very bold about engaging with other interpretations of the data I would present. There seemed a danger of not taking these sufficiently into account. I therefore devised a research plan which involved showing my first draft of the book to a panel of carefully-chosen 'critical readers', people who would represent particular viewpoints and might have alternative, challenging, interpretations of my material. Stereotypes which immediately came to mind were very traditional male personnel managers, post-modernist theorists, women who claim that women are never at a disadvantage in employment and simply need to learn to play the game, sympathetic feminists working on management theory, and highly radical feminists. The book would then incorporate dialogue with these readers' comments.

Exciting as this idea seemed at the time, and I still think it of value for a different piece of work, I realized that I was opening my boundaries too much, potentially making me and the women managers too vulnerable to public reactions. Instead I have now reaffirmed the purpose of the book as being to find an internally authentic voice for the women's experiences. I need to offer appropriate protection for this to develop, rather than expose the stories prematurely to alternative sense-making. Within that boundary I can carry a watching consciousness of other perspectives into the study. As women's voices are still often silenced or misinterpreted, any writing about women needs, I believe, both to be able to stand its ground *and* to use dialogue in productive ways, so as not to become ideologically rigid.

## RESEARCH IS ALSO A PERSONAL PROCESS

As I hinted earlier, the topic area has some personal relevance to me. This I would expect as I believe that much research is founded in personal process (Marshall 1992). As part of the study I shall seek to maintain my awareness of how my resonances with the emerging issues affect my sense-making. I am, for example, keeping research notes, and discussing my work with various individuals and groups, especially the research group at Bath whom I can trust to challenge me rigorously as well as be supportive. Personal process aspects of the research will be a further strand in the final writing. For some early reflections see Marshall (1992).

## THE PARTICIPANTS: ELABORATING THE MEANINGS OF 'LEAVING'

In my initial invitation I described several groups of people I wanted to contact. My core group were 'people who have left or are leaving senior organization positions without other immediate career plans'. I also wanted to include 'others who have left for a mix of motives, have been forced to leave, or want to leave but have not yet decided to'.

As well as carrying out the eight interviews previously referred to I have also had initial contacts with several others. The transcripts of our meetings are each about thirty pages of single-spaced typing in length. I have not yet analysed the material in any depth. What I shall offer here is therefore some brief information about the people I have met, to show the range of circumstances involved; and initial impressions of the data which are emerging.

The people I have spoken to so far come from nursing, personnel, local government, public relations, service industries and banking. They range in age from mid-thirties to mid-fifties. Four are married, two live with partners, one is divorced and one is single. One is a lesbian. One has grown-up children. None so far has young children, so this group's decisions to leave have not been motivated by this kind of family-work conflict. Dissatisfaction with the cultures of the organizations they worked in and with their immediate job situations and disillusion with the appeal of being organizationally senior were the reasons most gave for leaving. For some there was also the feeling that they wanted to rest, to live without the continual time demands of employment.

Two women were asked by others to leave (but they also shared the general dissatisfactions above). One explains her dismissal as the result of an organizational backlash. She was the major change agent for organizational development work envisioned by the chief executive and herself. The intention was to move to more collaborative, open, ways of working, particularly empowering an occupational group which had previously been relatively undervalued. The change processes had been under way for about eighteen months and were bearing fruit. At that point established power-holders in the organization started moving against her politically, isolating her and using personal attacks to undermine her credibility. The chief executive gave her his full support privately, but would never stand up for the changes or her in public. Eventually, the day after he had again pledged his full support in private, she was dismissed. Another manager had been ill for some time previously, but had then recovered. Organizational and industry changes were making her working environment less congenial. The company was looking for staff cutbacks. She, the only woman at her level, was the only manager to be offered early retirement. Many male colleagues also wanted to leave, but were not offered help to do so. Some have since left of their own accord, taking significant financial penalties in doing so. In this case, special treatment was favourable in many ways. Two other women were taking advantage of their companies' current redundancy schemes to realize plans they already had to leave.

Some interviewees have been in the process of leaving as I met them, others did so a year or more before. I have therefore benefited from freshness in some accounts and retrospection in others. The next destinations for the managers vary widely. Two are next taking time at home. One is travelling for six months and plans to set up a business on her return. Another took time out and developed her own consultancy, only to be head-hunted into a chief executive position within a year. Two are involved in academic study, seeing this as an opportunity for reflection and reorientation. Two found other jobs to go to, one making a career change in the process, before acting on their decision to leave.

I do not believe that these situations are unique to women. Men too leave organizations, and for a mix of reasons. But I do think it worth examining women's experiences in depth, especially as so few of them have so far reached senior positions, and what women, in all their diversity, want from employment and organizational life appears to be in the process of development and change.

## RECURRING THEMES: SOME INITIAL IMPRESSIONS

Standing back from the interviews I have done, my feeling was of great variety in the women's stories. Reviewing each briefly, however, I was surprised to find that there are some recurring themes in the material, ones shared by three, four or more people. There are also many differences. In this section I shall therefore describe some of the apparently common threads; they are as yet highly tentative, but none the less interesting. They reflect issues some successful women managers encounter, and we can consider whether current training and organizational development activities do actually address them.

The recurring themes, in no particular order of significance, are shown in Table 11.1. Several of the sample had experienced *illness* in the year or so before leaving. Most of these had had weeks or months off work; some described their physical and emotional defence systems as significantly eroded. Most had recovered before finally deciding to leave. The illness had, however, typically heightened their awareness of the pressures and dissatisfactions in their job and work environment. They had realized that what they were doing was not wholly healthy for them.

*Table 11.1* Recurring themes in women managers' stories: initial impressions

| |
|---|
| **illness** |
| **tiredness** |
| **control** |
| **being undermined** |
| **being organizationally successful for age** |
| **re-evaluating own worth and values** |
| **working on childhood themes** |
| **feeling good about decisions** |
| **weight gain and loss** |
| **anticipating leaving** |
| **securing valuable financial deals** |
| **returning to employment** |

A linked theme was *tiredness* and wanting a rest. Several people said that they just wanted to stop, to take stock, and that they

would then see what to do next. I was reminded of the phrase
'very often being very tired' (p. 182), which had emerged in my
interviews with women managers in a previous study (Marshall
1984) as a common description of their lives.

*Control* was also often discussed. Some people wanted more
control over their lives, to be in charge rather than living to the
dictates of other people and organizations. Others wanted to give
up control, to give up telling themselves what to do every day.
The latter saw life after leaving as an adventure of doing things
they previously had too little time for, such as gardening, and
trying new things simply for the experience.

In their descriptions of the job contexts they left, several of the
managers talked about *being undermined*, and being continually
challenged by others in ways which had contributed significantly
to their tiredness. They felt tested out, some very overtly, others
more covertly, and made to prove themselves acceptable and
credible in male-dominated cultures. Some talked of the strains of
having to create an identity and establish their status anew in each
interaction, pressures they thought were seldom placed on men.
These processes had meant that they had not felt affirmed in their
chosen identity, and had had to struggle to maintain a sense of self
they valued. Even those who saw themselves as organizationally
marginal, and did not expect to be accepted, found that the
resulting lack of any affirmation as people had affected them.
Facing such situations had contributed significantly to the managers'
weariness, and had eroded their energy for their jobs.

Quite a few participants were *organizationally successful for
their age*. This had several repercussions. First, the opportunities
ahead, particularly for women, were decreasing, and they could
see their careers slowing down. Second, their peers were often
older, white, males with little experience or apparent acceptance
of women as equals. With increasing status had come more
conflict, pressure and isolation. Third, despite their success, some
managers were not particularly self-confident. This story is familiar
from other research studies. They did not have a strong self-image
from which to fight back against combatitive colleagues.

Reflecting on these struggles had not motivated the people I
talked to to become tougher, but to doubt the value of the system
in which they had become involved. They began *re-evaluating their
own worth and values*. This was another recurrent theme. Several
interviewees were reviewing their lives and coming to radically

different formulations of what they wanted from life and career. For some this was associated with a blossoming of experimentation, changing their style of dress, trying new daring activities, travelling. I wonder if those who moved quickly back into committed employment can maintain this self-exploratory energy, or will have to set their personal questioning aside again for now.

A few appeared to be *working on childhood themes* in this process of reflection. For some people it seemed that messages they had grown up with – to be perfect, achieve and so on – had been satisfied by mid-life. Now they were wondering what to do next; they were preparing to reformulate their dreams based more on their own motivations. Several talked about issues from their childhood and early family life that they now wanted to explore. Two were undertaking major journeys to reconnect with family members. I had not asked for this sort of material, but was struck by its power, particularly for three of the people I met.

Most of the participants *felt good about their decisions* to leave and good about themselves in the process. To do something so 'unusual' they had had to be thorough in their self-analysis, and willing to stand by their decision-making in the face of general views on the importance of employment and seniority. The clarity of expression most brought to the interview was further testimony to the depth of their self-reflections. A few mentioned *weight gain and loss* as a factor linked to their comfort with their decision-making. In employment they had tended to put on weight. Having decided to leave, these people started losing weight, spontaneously, feeling healthier and more positive in their self-image as a result. One woman wondered if putting on weight had somehow given her more feeling of 'presence' in a difficult organizational situation, a possibility supported in theoretical literature (Orbach 1978).

Most interviewees had not made their decision to leave instantaneously. Several had *anticipated leaving*, and their promise to themselves that they would eventually do so had made staying under pressure tolerable. One manager had imagined that she would work for about twenty years and was now reaching the end of that vision of herself. Others had experienced stressful times and promised themselves that they would sort things out, re-prove their ability and competence, and *then* leave. Another sign that leaving was not typically a sudden exit or retreat were the *valuable financial deals* some managers had struck with their organizations.

Even though they were yielding, deciding to withdraw, they had handled the negotiation powerfully, maintaining their sense of self-worth, unwilling to let the organization ignore their financial rights.

All but one of the eight 'leavers' have *now returned to employment or intend to do so*. This finding supports those who suggest that many women now see paid work as a significant and relatively continuous part of their lives. Employment offers a forum for growth and development. Being employed is also now a financial necessity for many women. This was revealed as I looked for the sample for this study. One contact who initially thought she knew several appropriate candidates later reported back that they were all staying in employment because they needed their pensions. It may be the end of a dream – or yet another myth about women and paid work – if most women now see themselves as no longer able to choose to stay outside the system or leave if dissatisfied. Perhaps more women will then be reluctant to adapt to organizational life-styles they dislike and be stronger voices for reform.

## SOME DIFFERENCES

The stories of the women I have interviewed are akin to densely woven parts of a loosely connected tapestry. Common threads weave in and out, but there is much that is singular and distinctive about each story. At this stage I shall only comment on three apparent differences which are particularly relevant to the core issues of the study. These are: how cautious or risk-taking they were in their decision-making; how open they were with others about their reasons for leaving; and their views on being women in employment.

### Risk-taking and caution

A few managers left with little attention to what would happen next, acting on their need 'just to go'. More had planned their leaving, particularly securing their financial position. For one this was a deliberate counter to the behaviour of a friend. The latter had acted on impulse, pleased only to leave, and had soon met severe financial difficulties but been unable to return to employment.

## Openness about decision-making

Some people had left a sense of mystery behind them. They had given few or only superficial reasons for going, and people (according to my initial informants) had consequently felt unclear, speculating. These managers said they did not want to expose their decision-making, did not expect to be understood, and wanted to take the route of least visibility or upset. Others had been open with some groups of staff, those with whom they felt some affinity. Within specific arenas they had been more in control of telling their truth. One manager had, for example, made her leaving a celebration, reaching out to people who had supported her in the organization, paying attention to the leaving process in ways which made her feel honest and connected, whilst also clearly severing a connection she found unhealthful.

## Views on women in employment

Most of the people I interviewed would not define themselves overtly as feminist. They were wary of this label, feeling that it is a dismissive category when applied by others, and that feminists have done much to harden or polarize issues of gender. They did not see 'feminist' as a viable identity for a senior woman manager. A few did identify with feminist issues, and had used theoretical ideas about gender and power in organizations to inform their ways of understanding and acting. Most commented on the negative stereotypes of feminism in employment and the pressure on women not to identify with its issues.

## NEXT STEPS

My next tasks are to complete the further interviews and find appropriate forms to write the stories which are the core of the study. I am exploring writing possibilities, wanting to avoid portraits which stereotype or simplify. Two aspects of current importance in my deliberations are language and vulnerability.

As I have already said, interpretation and honouring voices are issues at the heart of this study. How I express the stories and our analyses of them, especially what language I use, is particularly critical. For example, so much of the language in this area affirms employment as a major life activity, and moving upwards as a standard of progress. Even by talking about women managers as 'leaving', I create employment as the reference point. I shall need new and re-visioned words and phrases to describe what is happening. I shall also need to guard against taking for granted current 'common sense' about organizations, employment and the relative value placed on different forms of life pattern. Inviting critical comment on my draft writing will help me stay alert to such issues.

Participants' confidentiality is difficult to ensure in a study such as this, which aims to tell in depth the stories of a small group, each with a distinctive account to give. Several interviewees have said that they cannot tell their stories publicly, but would like them to become known as they seem important for women at the moment. They want them to be told powerfully rather than hidden. Toning down the stories to achieve anonymity would greatly reduce their impact and potential value. I am therefore considering 'fictionalizing' the accounts in some way, to disguise personal details but free me to tell the more fundamental meanings that I and the interviewee consider important, to tell 'the truth' as we see it. Doing so will raise interesting methodological issues, but is compatible with recent trends to appreciate the constructed nature of all knowledge.

## IMPLICATIONS FOR TRAINING AND DEVELOPMENT

It is premature to look for more than tentative indications of implications at this early stage of the research. The picture portrayed so far is of managers who are outwardly successful, but whose identity and legitimacy are frequently challenged in everyday interaction, making them feel undermined. The demands of resisting such challenges may well contribute to their feelings of stress and tiredness, and to experiences of illness. Much established training and development work with women managers is related to these power and identity issues and to stress management. The question of whether popular initiatives such as assertiveness training 'merely' help women adapt to male-dominated cultures and so legitimate the latters' aggressive, competitive, independence-oriented ethos is increasingly being asked. Alternatives, based more on introducing and legitimating co-operative strategies, are unlikely to be viable unless the specific organizational culture is open to such changes, as some now are.

There are obvious implications from this material for organizations to address how their patterns of culture put women at a disadvantage and under pressure. But these exhortations have already been made frequently, with limited effect. Responsibility for achieving change tends more often to be attributed to women. Whilst I feel that cultural change is clearly needed I shall not, therefore, rehearse these arguments here.

Another strand in the data is the depth of personal reflection in which the managers have engaged, and their re-evaluations of meanings of employment and success. Their self-perceptions and career expectations are certainly more open and flexible than most normative, linear approaches to career planning. Employees with such values find their organizational commitment is doubted, although they may well stay longer in posts than others who are more traditionally ambitious and move for career advancement. The language of negotiation between individual and organization, and the range of opportunities on offer, would have to be expanded to accommodate the potential depth of these discussions.

It is possible that some of the managers would have been able to pursue more of their personal reflection within their organizations, given appropriate development opportunities and a suitably open culture. Mid-life brings significant re-evaluations for many men and women, and can change attitudes to work and career. Organizations may be unable to benefit from the potential generativity of this time if people are expected outwardly to 'maintain appearances'. Women who reach senior positions relatively young may feel particularly isolated and reluctant to express their concerns, doubting whether male colleagues or seniors will understand or sympathize, and knowing few women in similar situations.

## CLOSING REFLECTIONS

One of the fascinating features of this study has been the interest shown by a wide range of people with whom I have casually discussed it. I feel confirmed in my view that these managers and their stories are 'test cases' in a variety of ways, worthy of further attention.

# REFERENCES

Gordon, S. (1991) *Prisoners of Men's Dreams: Striking out for a New Feminine Future*, Boston: Little, Brown and Company.

Korabik, K. and Rosin, H. M. (1991) 'Corporate flight of women managers: moving from fiction to fact', paper presented at the Western Academy of Management, Santa Barbara CA, March.

Marshall, J. (1984) *Women Managers: Travellers in a Male World*, Chichester: Wiley.

Marshall, J. (1992) 'Researching women in management as a way of life', *Journal of Management Education and Development* 23 (3): 281–9.

Orbach, S. (1978) *Fat is a Feminist Issue*, London: Paddington Press.

Rosin, H. M. and Korabik, K. (1990) 'Marital and family correlates of women managers' attrition from organizations', *Journal of Vocational Behaviour* 17: 104–20.

Schwartz, F. N. (1989) 'Management women and the new facts of life', *Harvard Business Review* 89 (1): 65–76.

Schwartz, P. and Ogilvy, J. (1979) *The Emergent Paradigm: Changing Patterns of Thought and Belief*, Analytical Report 7, Values and Life Styles Program, Menlo Park, CA, SRI International.

Taylor, A. (1986) 'Why women are bailing out', *Fortune*, 18 August, 16–23.

# Chapter 12

# Women-only management training – a past and present

*Breda Gray*

The participation of women and men on an equal basis at decision-making level continues to be seen as a desirable goal in the 1990s (Chinery-Hesse 1993). However, at the current pace of women's movement into decision-making positions, it will take another 475 years before women and men are represented in equal numbers at the higher levels of political and economic power (Ducci 1993). Women-only management training (WOMT) forms part of a 'positive action drive' to help increase the numbers of women in management (Pepptalk 1993). Yet, the development of single-sex management training for women raises many questions about how women's advancement is defined and about the complex relationship between training and women's career development (Goodale 1993).

In this chapter I focus on WOMT in Britain and the USA. Although WOMT is many-faceted and takes a variety of forms, my purpose in this chapter is best achieved by looking at WOMT in general. (For an overview of the variety of management development and training directed at women managers, see Marshall 1991.) I suggest that WOMT has been influenced more by a combination of demographic changes and the requirements of business than by feminist politics and theories. While WOMT may have been influenced by feminist views about equality and women's independence in the 1960s and 1970s, complex developments in theories and practices within feminism in the 1980s and 1990s have contributed little to the design and content of WOMT programmes in these two decades.

## WHERE TO BEGIN?

The 'life history' of WOMT has not been recorded. We know little about the circumstances that gave it birth, the main influences on its growth and development, its struggles and its successes. My exploration of the literature on WOMT finds much activity but little reflection on these activities. There is no evidence of a teenage identity crisis about its purpose or where it 'fits in' in the world. To understand WOMT in the 1990s I need to know about its past, for 'in returning to the past I am talking about the present' (Hearn 1992: 9). WOMT in the 1990s is like a lost child, argued over by its supporters and its opponents, unsure of its identity, with little sense of its past and few plans for the future.

It may be that WOMT is a post-modern phenomenon. It appears to have no definitive identity but includes many identities depending upon circumstances and requirements; has no theoretical allegiance but draws upon many disciplines and sources; engages in many and changing relationships with political, economic and social movements; has a fragmented 'history', and fluid meanings.

While this may well be the case, in this chapter I force the development of WOMT into a narrative form, partly for convenience of presentation but mostly because I want to understand the phenomenon of WOMT in some context. I want to give it an identity that can then be contested. My search for a more integrated picture might be seen as reducing the complex and changing nature of WOMT to a simplified whole. However, I am uncomfortable with the decontextualized, unreflective and pragmatic representation of WOMT in most of the literature and reflected in my experience of participating in women-only management training programmes. This lack of context seems to allow WOMT to sit on the fence and to avoid engaging with wider personal, social and political issues affecting women and men.

In my exploration of the context in which WOMT has developed, I focus mainly upon western feminist thought and equal opportunity initiatives because I see potential interrelationships between these developments and the growth of WOMT. This chapter represents *my* perception of how WOMT has developed, based on my experiences, reading and selection of significant influences. I start by exploring the assumptions that underpin some women-only management training programmes based on my experience of participating in these programmes. I do this to personalize my discussion and to make my ambivalent attitude towards WOMT explicit from the beginning. I go on to discuss some of the contextual factors that may have influenced the development of WOMT since 1960.

The chapter is structured by a chronological/narrative framework which relies on the identification of themes relating to women in work and in management in each of the past four decades. The themes spill over from one decade to another; as Gibson Burrell and Jeff Hearn emphasize in their discussion on sexuality of organization, rather than an unfolding narrative there are 'reversals, circularities, incomplete beginnings and unfinished ends' (Burrell and Hearn 1989: 15). By using a chronological framework I do not want to suggest that WOMT has evolved smoothly; instead I hope that my use of a structured framework highlights some of the circularities and discontinuities in its development.

## WOMEN-ONLY MANAGEMENT TRAINING PROGRAMMES – SOME ASSUMPTIONS

The decision to attend my first women-only management training programme was influenced by feelings of isolation in my job, dissatisfaction with the amount of my time absorbed by work, contradictions and conflicts between what I saw as managerial responsibilities and personal values. I was at a crossroads; I wanted the training programme to help me to become clearer about what appeared to be a choice between a career and having a life! My experience of participating in women-only management training programmes has been mixed. I learned some management skills, made friends, reflected endlessly on the problems for women in work organizations and drew up action plans for when I got back to work. However, there was little time for questioning contradictory and conflicting thoughts and emotions. For example, enthusiasm for women's success at work drowned out discussion about the costs to women themselves.

In my view, the presence of women in management brings an opportunity for change in work patterns and within work organizations. I see WOMT as having the potential to facilitate and support these changes. Yet my experience of participating in women-only management training programmes was that these programmes often reinforce the status quo. This experience appears to be linked to the seemingly-unquestioned assumptions upon which these programmes were based. I list six of these assumptions here as they account for some of my ambivalent feelings about WOMT.

### 'Success is measured by reaching senior levels of management in organizations'

I was reminded on WOMT programmes that 'women can reach the top' and that the 'mastery' of skills such as assertiveness, negotiation and financial planning would equip me to overcome the barriers along the way. Because these programmes are about women achieving in management, the underlying assumption is that real success and achievement relate to position in the organizational hierarchy and the associated financial and status rewards. While broader definitions of success are explored, it is difficult to question the implicit assumptions on which WOMT programmes are based. For example, on one programme a participant's suggestion that reducing working hours to spend more time with important people in her life could be defined as success was greeted with momentary consideration – 'if only' – before the tyranny of the hierarchical ladder took over again.

### 'If the barriers to women's advancement are identified then appropriate strategies can be developed to overcome these barriers'

Because many WOMT programmes are implicitly based on this assumption, much time is spent on how organizations, men, systems, structures, domestic responsibilities, and so on block women's way to the top. The view seems to be that if the barriers are identified then they can be overcome. The resounding list of 'barriers' recounted on women-only management training programmes leave me with overwhelming feelings of inertia and hopelessness. I want to ask other questions, to examine the politics of women in management in relation to men, life in general, non-managerial women, family responsibilities, economics and the power dynamics in these areas.

### 'Women need separate space to share their experiences so that they can develop confidence to tackle discrimination at work'

Women-only training programmes are portrayed as 'progressive' because they are seen as providing for the particular training and support needs of women. While the growth of WOMT programmes in recent years reflects the demand from women managers for development and training, it may also indicate that sponsoring organizations see WOMT programmes as unthreatening. They are sometimes seen as meeting women's particular training needs in such a way that dominant cultures in work organizations are not challenged. This portrayal of WOMT programmes suggests that they meet some of the training and support needs of women managers while also meeting organizational needs to 'contain' issues relating to gender and sexuality.

### 'Women are responsible for changing gender relations and sexual dynamics at work'

As work organizations have been developed largely without women's participation at managerial levels, it is not surprising that many women's experiences and priorities are omitted from traditional ways of organizing and managing: 'Commonsense notions, such as jobs and positions, which constitute the units managers use in making theory, are posited on the prior exclusion of women' (Acker 1991: 175).

As more women move into work organizations and management positions they often find themselves acting as innovators or change agents. Many women, therefore, have two jobs at work, the actual job for which they are employed and the job of trying to change the organization so that their priorities are incorporated or at least recognized. Rita Mae Kelly (1991) suggests that women tend to see power as a means of promoting change. Power and change are fundamental to WOMT but are rarely addressed in depth due to the demands of more skill-oriented goals.

### 'Women can have it all'

Popular culture in the early 1990s promotes the idea that women can have it all – a high-powered job, happy personal relationships, time for recreation, keeping fit, eating healthily and so on; yet the reality for most of us is different. 'Having it all' is portrayed differently for men in that there is less emphasis on being the perfect parent and expectations in the domestic sphere are lower than they are for women. In my experience the assumption that 'women can have it all' frequently goes unchallenged on WOMT programmes.

**'There is a unity of interests amongst women managers so there can be solidarity and support between women on WOMT programmes'**

Comfortable gender stereotypes about women and men give women-only training groups a sense of female solidarity even when individual members break these stereotypes by their behaviour on training programmes. The emphasis on solidarity and providing a supportive environment frequently means that differences often go unacknowledged and competition between women is played down. It is hard to see how a 'supportive' environment based on an uncontested consensus can be truely supportive and nurturing. Instead, it may serve to gloss over differences, power differentials, women's own assimilated sexist attitudes and prejudices, ambition, competitiveness, hierarchical thinking. This assumption is supported by the further assumption that women managers are heterosexual, white, and middle class. Ethnicity, race, colour, and class rarely enter the analysis of women's experiences of organizations, management and learning.

While the assumptions discussed above are challenged by feminist writers (Phillips 1987; Barrett 1992; Walby 1992; Tasker 1991; McNeil 1991, Newman 1991) and those concerned with sexuality and organization (Hearn and Parkin 1987; Hearn *et al.* 1989), most writers and trainers interested in WOMT do not appear to be engaged in these debates. Richard Boot and Michael Reynolds (1984) see management trainers as influencing the training and development process in such a way that 'the natural order is maintained'. These processes, they argue, are not due to conspiracy or malevolence, but to the operation of dominant ideologies in everyday life. Training is also restricted by market forces which affect the viability of training programmes.

For WOMT to engage actively in feminist discourse about capitalism, heterosexism, racism and patriarchy in the workplace, dominant ideas about men, women and management would have to be challenged. This could be threatening to organizations as they are currently constituted. The piecemeal incorporation of some feminist theories into WOMT can give the appearance of a more radical approach but avoid facing up to the existence of possibly irreconcilable differences and contradictions. Because very little has been written about the factors influencing the development of WOMT it is difficult to understand the dominance of certain assumptions in practice and in the literature. I try to remedy this by looking at some of the contextual features affecting the development of WOMT.

## WOMT – A BIOGRAPHICAL OVERVIEW

Calas and Smircich (1990) point out that the production of literature on women in management (WIM) coincided with what has become known as the 'second wave' of the women's liberation movement associated with the 1960s and 1970s. I have therefore chosen to construct a biographical account of WOMT from the 1960s to the 1990s by examining some of the insights of feminist thinking and their relationship to the development of WOMT. Although 'feminism' is a contested term (Porter 1992), I see feminism as being concerned (albeit in different ways) with the eradication of sexism and sexist oppression, and therefore central to an analysis of the context in which WOMT has developed.

My purpose in writing this chapter is to provide more of a biographical overview than a detailed history. Although I have taken the so-called 'second-wave' feminist movement as my starting point, my interpretation of the terms 'first wave' and 'second wave' is that they are 'convenient terms for identifying certain recent clusters in women's activities' (Kaplan 1992: 7) rather than representing the view that womens' activities have taken place only recently and in a chronological pattern. Women have probably always been involved in activities which could be seen as feminist, however, as feminist historians point out, women's activities are rarely recorded (Kaplan 1992). This is particularly true for black women and is perpetuated by the absence of a detailed analysis of race and gender within the professions (Sokoloff 1992).

## THE 1960s – COMING TO TERMS WITH WOMEN IN MANAGEMENT

### Background

Between 1949 and 1963 there was low unemployment in most European countries. This was a period of 'entrepreneurial euphoria . . . uninterrupted by crises' (Postan 1967: 62,89, in Kaplan 1992: 12). In the USA, women's labour force participation grew from 17 to 30 per cent between 1950 and 1960 (Evans 1989). Gisela Kaplan suggests that the broadening of women's career and educational choices in the 1950s and 1960s (despite much discrimination), and the activities of the civil rights movements in Europe and the USA led to an increased awareness amongst women of injustice and sexism.

The 'second wave' of the women's movement is said to have emerged in the late 1960s (Chafetz 1990). It was led by middle-class women whose thinking about paid work was influenced by Betty Friedan's book, *The Feminist Mystique*. Betty Friedan (1963) presents work outside the home as central to women's liberation because she perceived paid work as offering independence from men. However, for many women who were already in the paid work-force (mainly working-class women of whom a high proportion were black), work was far from liberating. bell hooks points out that 'Even though the notion of work as liberation had little significance for exploited, underpaid working women, it provided ideological motivation for college-educated, white women to enter, or re-enter, the work force' (hooks 1984: 96).

For bell hooks (1984) the focus of feminism in the 1960s was on 'careerism' and the pursuit of high-paying positions. Many feminists in the 1960s believed that those who worked were 'already liberated' (hooks 1984).

## Women in management

A few women progressed up the managerial hierarchy and literature on women in management became available (see Appendix). This literature did not analyse the condition of all women in paid work nor did these writers seek a collective approach to the improvement of conditions for all women workers. Janet Saltzman Chafetz (1990) suggests that women who assumed non-traditional roles changed their comparative reference group from women to men. Women managers, while discriminated against on the basis of their sex, also saw the opportunity for personal economic gain within the capitalist system. They may have perceived themselves as 'liberated' due to their status in the paid work-force. If WOMT in the 1960s reflected this view it would have been concerned with helping women in management to maintain or improve their position in relation to men.

A *Harvard Business Review* article in 1965 entitled 'Are women executives people?' explores perceptions of the role of women in the higher echelons of business management in the 1960s and describes it as 'an emotionally charged topic' (Bowman *et al.* 1965: 16). In their survey of 2,000 male and female executives, Bowman *et al.* (1965) found agreement amongst respondents that only 'exceptional women' could hope to succeed and that the 'home-job syndrome' was a major block to women's success. The majority felt that equal opportunities legislation was not necessary. There was some disagreement between the male and female executives about whether women should be feminine or act like men; men had a slight preference for the view that a woman executive should act like 'a lady'. One male executive advised: 'Look like a woman, work like a dog and think like a man' (Bowman *et al.* 1965: 170).

The debate about women's presence in management positions in the USA focused initially on whether women wishing to succeed in management should be treated as 'people', an ungendered term for being treated as men. Gender differences, sexuality, and power dynamics were being challenged by women taking on managerial positions. However, as long as a woman continued to 'look like a woman', then, at least on a sexual level, existing patriarchal power dynamics could be maintained in the workplace. These remain familiar themes in the 1990s.

Meanwhile in Britain during the 1960s women were also beginning to take on senior positions at work. As in the USA women began to consciously see networking as useful in career terms (Segerman-Peck 1991). Although the United Kingdom Federation of Business and Professional Women had been in existence since 1938, by the 1960s women managers in the UK felt a need for a network specifically for women managers. In 1969 a professional management association for women was established called 'Women In Management'. The main goal of this association, which still exists today, is to provide relevant training and support to members in their professional roles.

## Training for women managers

Training, development and support was a central concern for women managers in the USA and in Britain. The Bowman *et al.* (1965) study in the USA suggested that there was resistance to training and developing women managers because of their high rates of turnover. Felice Schwartz (1989), in an article on the cost of employing women, refers to a recent study by one multinational company which showed that the turnover rate in management positions is '2½ times higher among top-performing women than it is among men', indicating that turnover amongst women managers continues to be high in the 1980s and 1990s. Women's satisfaction with success in the workplace does not appear to be improving despite the increase in women-only management training programmes since the 1960s.

Women's concern with training and advancement at work in the 1960s fitted in with feminist views of the day. The impetus for women in management to set up networks and demand the right to training was probably influenced by the active and visible role of the women's movement. Janet Giele characterizes this aspect of women's activities in the 1960s as follows: 'Informal support groups established communication and trust among women from diverse backgrounds. Formal groups investigated women's educational job opportunities' (Giele 1992: 9).

Feminist theories being developed in the late 1960s tended to emphasize women's common experience of oppression and male domination in the form of patriarchy as affecting every aspect of women's lives (Franklin *et al.* 1991). This perception of women's experiences still dominates much WOMT.

## 1970s – SOLIDARITY FOR EQUALITY

### Equality in theory and practice

Although women have expressed concern about sexual discrimination for centuries, the concept of 'equality' did not gain political and occupational significance until the twentieth century (Kelly 1991). Equality legislation covering discrimination based on gender was greatly influenced by the race equality legislation (see Appendix). The discourse on equality that took place in the 1960s expanded to include gender and gained more institutional acceptance in the 1970s with the passing of equal opportunities legislation in Europe and the USA and the setting up of the Equal Opportunities Commission in Britain. (The Equal Employment Opportunity Commission (EEOC) was established in the USA in 1964 (see Appendix)). The UN Decade for Women (1976–85) also made equality one of its three main aims.

Equality legislation is based on the notion of the fundamental equality of all human beings, and therefore, the right of each individual to equal treatment (O'Donovan and Szyszczak 1988). However, equal opportunities legislation, policy and practice has been constructed within the framework of work patterns and organizations developed by men for men. Within the legislation men remain the standard. The position and behaviour of men is largly unchanged, while the aim of the legislation is to bring women 'up to' the standard of men. It is assumed that workplaces, managerial jobs and work organizations are 'gender neutral' (Alvesson and Billing 1992).

As 'equality' is an abstract concept it is frequently discussed outside a particular context. There is an assumption that it is value free and that a certain standard and certain processes for achieving that standard are acceptable to all. For example, a female applicant for a job may bring a different perspective to how the job might be defined or carried out arising from her gendered experience of the world. However, her only chance of getting the job is to accept the position as it is defined and demonstrate her ability to achieve the predefined tasks competently. Her particular contribution, 'history', context, perception and knowledge are irrelevant. Indirect discrimination as highlighted in this example was brought to public attention in the 1970s:

> As a stream of young graduates entered business and pro-
> fessions after the mid 1970s, they met more subtle forms
> of discrimination than their predecessors had experienced.
> They found themselves in a world that proclaimed equality of
> opportunity but defined career paths in the rhythms of a male
> life cycle.
>
> (Evans 1989: 308)

Despite the existence of equal pay legislation in Europe since the 1970s (see Appendix) women currently earn up to 30 per cent less than men in all EEC countries (*Crew Reports* 1992). The limited effectiveness of equal opportunities initiatives in Britain is evident from recent British reports on earnings and the composition of the labour force. These reports suggest that the biggest cause of the disparity in earnings between women and men is occupational segregation (New Earnings Survey 1992), while the key influence on women's participation in the labour market is childcare responsibilities (Labour Force Survey 1991). Because

Equal Opportunity legislation, as it stands, does little to address the relative value attributed to different jobs, or the interrelationship between home and work responsibilities, it can have little impact on women's position in the labour force. The pursuit of equality involves conflicts of interests and difficult negotiation because it ultimately involves a redistribution of power.

Women are defined as equal to men in the public sphere but continue to be seen as different from men in the private domain. Rational procedures are introduced to deal with 'private' issues such as childcare, in order that 'public' work life can remain untainted by the emotional, unpredictable and messy nature of many 'private' concerns. In the mid- and late 1970s flexible working hours and part-time employment were introduced by the US Federal Civil Service and these became popular 'work – family' policy issues in the USA (Pleck 1992). However, these kinds of initiatives are aimed mainly at women and do little to challenge gendered division of labour between home and the workplace.

As a way of overcoming some of the difficulties with the idea of equality O'Donovan and Szyszczak (1988) suggest that we move away from the notion of equal treatment to giving and receiving equal concern so that each person is taken account of in her or his own environment. Cynthia Cockburn recommends incorporating differences instead of aiming for equality by aiming for 'parity between the two sexes, separately specified, comprising human kind' (Cockburn 1991: 28).

Merle Thornton (1986) provides a potential focus for WOMT when she suggests that we start to address the achievement of equality by seeing women as knowers. She emphasizes women's difference from men and suggests that sex equality 'does nothing in itself to explore new societal forms which build on the distinctive gender characteristics of women' (Thornton 1986: 97). This approach might make it possible to move beyond the 'reactive position' in which women are placed by the notion of equality. She sees this being achieved by celebrating women's knowing, creating alternative theories and identifying the gaps and spaces in what is known.

## Affirmative action

While equality of opportunity legislation in Britain and Europe focuses on procedures, pay and equal treatment in general,

Affirmative Action (AA) programmes in the USA recognize women's unequal starting point and establish measurable integration goals, timetables and quotas for the advancement of women and minorities (Carr-Ruffino *et al.* 1992). Affirmative Action (AA) programmes have been in existence in the USA since 1941, when they were first introduced to prohibit race discrimination; AA was extended to include sex discrimination in 1964 (Carr-Ruffino *et al.* 1992). Some studies suggest that many women's careers and economic statuses improved in the 1970s due to AA initiatives. This is particularly true for already more advantaged women (Sokoloff 1992). The enforcement of AA was relaxed in the 1980s when a number of Supreme Court decisions undermined the implementation of AA (Carr-Ruffino *et al.* 1992). Affirmative Action programmes were introduced in Australia in the 1980s (see Appendix).

Christine Wieneke sees AA programmes as having the potential to restructure work relations and remove hierarchical levels, but warns that this is difficult to achieve because AA 'in this form attacks too obviously the interests of the power brokers' (Wieneke 1992: 138). She also emphasizes that for women to gain any equal treatment in the workplace there must be changes outside paid work. I discuss the progress of AA in the 1990s later in this chapter.

## Androgeny

The concept of androgeny was adopted in the 1970s as a model to help facilitate women's access to senior positions. The ideal of androgeny which regards gender difference as a social construct and seeks to annihilate sex roles (Rothfield 1990), was also seen as having the potential to reorder unequal sexual and social relations (Ferguson 1991). It provided an alternative vision of equality in which the 'ideal professional' would be a combination of the instrumental masculine self and the more expressive female self (Kelly 1991). Despite this seemingly equal combination of feminine and masculine, Ann Ferguson (1991) sees androgeny as privileging masculinity and adding femininity as a complement. The concept of androgeny is further weakened by its reliance on traditional stereotypical notions of feminine and masculine characteristics. Although androgeny might have provided a framework for WOMT, its degendering effects, and its implicit valuing of characteristics traditionally associated with masculinity, meant that it did not gain widespread support.

## Sexual harassment

In the 1970s some women in the USA began to draw attention to sexual harassment at work (Cockburn 1991). Initially the US courts saw sexual harassment as a private matter and refused to provide protection under the Civil Rights Act, however, guidelines were eventually issued by the Equal Employment Opportunity Commission holding employers responsible for sexual harassment (Gutek 1989). Sexual harassment did not become a matter of concern in Britain until 1981 when a trade union, the National Association of Local Government Officers (NALGO), recognized sexual harassment as a legitimate topic for union action (Wise and Stanley 1987). Debates about sexual harassment at work drew attention to the gendered and sexualized nature of organizations as well as heterosexism in workplace culture (Cockburn 1991). Equality cannot be seen simply as a matter of equal pay or opportunities as long as heterosexual dynamics remain unequal and sexual harassment continues.

## Equality and women-only management training

Despite the opening up of discourse about the public/private split and sexual dynamics at work, WOMT continued to focus mainly on achieving equality with men and success in the workplace. The dualistic definitions of masculine and feminine identities in the 1970s emphasized sameness amongst women and amongst men. WOMT was seen as providing space and mutual support for women managers whose experiences and concerns would be similar. The debate about equality tends to reinforce this dualism thereby reducing the possibilities of change for men, women and organizations. Mats Alvesson and Yvonne Due Billing suggest that

> more women adapting to male norms and becoming managers is hardly in itself contribution to equality between the genders, unless it is complemented by more men obtaining positons requiring 'female' socialization. Equality is hardly achieved by a one-sided adaptation of the one sex to the standards of the other.
>
> (Alvesson and Billing 1992: 80)

Yet, the assumption that the achievement of managerial positions is in the best interests of women seems to be related to the hope placed in the equality initiatives of the 1970s and the view that

> To the extent that women are absent from high-level management positions, women are not characterised in terms of power, status, and leadership ability.
>
> (O'Leary and Ickovics 1992: 9).

Rosabeth Moss Kanter's (1977) influential study on men and women in US corporations found that the smaller the minority of women in management positions, the greater their chances of being isolated and stereotyped. She calls these few women (less than 15 per cent) 'tokens' because they come to represent all women. These findings added weight to the argument for more women in management in the 1970s. WOMT supported this aim. However, Kanter's emphasis on increasing the numbers of women in management as a strategy for change has since been challenged. Janice Yoder (1991) suggests that an increase in 'lower status members' threatens 'dominants' and a backlash takes place in which discrimination is increased and opportunities for advancement are reduced. Yoder asks if the 'glass ceiling' could be a symptom of this backlash.

## 1980s – DIFFERENCE AND INDIFFERENCE – THE DEMOGRAPHIC TIME BOMB AND MANAGING DIVERSITY

### Difference

Equality and the view that women need to prove themselves in the workplace continue to influence discourse on gender, work and management in the 1980s and the 1990s. However, the emphasis in feminist literature on women's common experiences was challenged in the 1980s by single women, black women, lesbians and others. For these women different kinds of oppression are interdependent and interact. The focus of attention shifted from commonality to 'difference', both between the sexes and within the categories of men and women. In the late 1970s and early 1980s difference between men and women was discussed by women writers in the field of psychology. By the mid-1980s some feminists and post-modern thinkers (Weedon 1987; Fuss 1989) were beginning to define 'difference' in broader terms, seeing it as central to our understanding of western society in the late twentieth century.

There was a move away from equal treatment to special treatment of women when psychoanalytic theorists emphasized differences between women and men. Jean Baker Miller (1986) rejected androgeny by developing a theory of women's psychology. She suggested that the particular qualities that women possess such as tenderness, co-operativeness, and ability to nurture are consistently devalued by both women and men. Carol Gilligan (1982) and Mary Belenky *et al.* (1986) celebrated women's particular morality and ways of knowing. These and other writers at the time (Dinnerstein 1978; Chodorow 1978; Daly 1978) moved the focus away from political concerns with sex roles and equality to an exploration of more psychologically-based gender differences. Vicky Hutchings highlights one of the dilemmas raised by the debate about equality and difference when she asks 'Are we fighting to be the same or to have our distinct female qualities as valued as male ones?' (Hutchings 1992: 16).

Meanwhile, other writers questioned the binary oppositions between women and men (Weedon 1987; Fuss 1989) and highlighted the need to take the context and specificities of peoples' lives and culture into account (Giroux 1992). The view that gender and sexual identities are socially constructed gained popularity. For example, Catherine MacKinnon points out that 'sex in nature is not a bipolarity, it is a continuum; society makes it into a bipolarity' (Mackinnan 1989: 233). While 'difference' in this broader sense was beginning to be discussed in the 1980s, the view of difference as being different to white male predominated in practice.

### The demographic time bomb and managing diversity in the USA

In the 1980s, ideas about 'difference' as a way of understanding changes in the demographic make-up of the workplace gained popularity in the USA. The 1980 US Census revealed a shift in employment demography. Women and minority group men composed 51 per cent of the job market with women accounting for 44 per cent (Seymour and Voss 1988). In 1992, 47 per cent of the work-force in the USA were native white males, while over the following 12 years 85 per cent of new entrants to the work-force will be women, minorities and new immigrants (Betters-Reed and Moore 1992). Women are seen as representing the largest growth sector in the US labour force (ibid.).

These demographic facts led to a discussion of 'difference' which focused on women and minorities and 'difference' in the workplace was defined as 'different from white male'. This definition guided the development of 'managing diversity' strategies in the USA. Roosevelt-Thomas (Executive Director of the American Institute of Managing Diversity Inc.) put forward his view that there is a need to move beyond equal opportunities and affirmative action programmes because these initiatives cannot ensure the 'upward mobility of *all* kinds of people, including white males' (Roosevelt-Thomas 1990: 108). He goes on to define managing diversity as getting 'from a heterogeneous workforce the same productivity, commitment, quality and profit that we got from the old homogeneous workforce' (Roosevelt-Thomas 1990: 109).

The assumption seems to be that the 'we' are the white men who will manage and set the agenda for the diverse work-force of the future. He goes on to say that managers must ask themselves 'does it work as smoothly, is morale as high, as if every person in the company was the same sex, and race and nationality' (Roosevelt-Thomas 1990: 109).

These questions assume that homogeneity is best and that the task for managers of the future is to ensure that a diverse workforce comes up to this standard. These assumptions reflect early approaches to incorporating immigrants in the USA and Britain, for example, assimilation and integration. 'Diversity' is seen as a problem that needs to be resolved. Roosevelt-Thomas and others in the USA (Hanamura 1989; Greenslade 1991) promote a strong managerial approach which involves defining, planning, organizing and controlling 'difference'. In my view, this approach represents a move by the current stakeholders of power in organizations, to prevent any fundamental change resulting from the increased numbers of 'different' people in the workplace. Issues of power, privilege, dominant norms and oppression are glossed over. The possibility of shared experiences is played down by the emphasis on 'difference'. This may be because the potential power of group identities in organizations may be seen as threatening to existing hierarchies.

By developing management systems specifically for managing

diversity, including employee surveys and awareness training, Roosevelt-Thomas suggests that people will be enabled to reach their full potential. He does not tell us what happens when, in order to reach their potential, unanticipated or 'unacceptable' change is required. Women in management and others defined as different do not appear to have a voice in the development of this new approach to dealing with difference. In contrast, Christine Williams (1992) found that in the case of men entering predominantly female professions, gender is constructed as a 'positive' difference. She describes their experience as being like stepping on a 'glass escalator' as compared to women manager's experience of the 'glass ceiling'. Bonita Betters-Reed and Lynda Moore (1992) suggest that the women in management literature fail to address diversity and power shifts between women in the workplace: 'Essentially, the current women in management research and writing strongly suggest that the term "Women in Management" means *white* women in management' (Betters-Reed and Moore 1992: 34).

Valuing differences involves the transformation of organizations rather than adapting them or people (Betters-Reed and Moore 1992). Catherine MacKinnon (1989) suggests that the issue is not that difference is not valued but that difference is defined by power; 'inequality comes first; difference comes after' (MacKinnon 1989: 219). Despite much public discussion about diversity in the workplace in the USA, the status of African American workers deteriorated in the decade between 1980 and 1990 (Malveaux 1992). Questions arise about how WOMT can analyse and engage with power relations in the workplace.

### The demographic time bomb and the 'business case' for women in management

As in the USA, the projected demographic changes in the labour force are also a central concern in Britain. By the year 2025 the projected rate of growth of the elderly population in Britain is such that 'every ten economically active citizens will support four pensioners and three children' (Hamnett *et al.* 1989). It is estimated that by 1995 there will be a 1.2 million reduction in school-leavers in Britain (Davidson 1991) and women are projected to take the largest proportion of new jobs.

These demographic facts have led to women in Britain and the USA being seen as 'a wasted resource'; a resource that should be maximized over the coming decades. This perspective plays down women's economic contribution through unpaid work in the home (Truman 1992). While 'making better use' of women in the paid work-force is emphasized, little attention is given to how children and elderly people's care needs are to be provided for. Despite these unanswered problems, demographic factors were invoked in the 1980s to make a 'business case' for women in management.

**Women's contribution to management**

At the same time, another case was being made in the 1980s for more women in management based on the particular characteristics that they bring to the job (Rosener 1990). For example, Valerie Hammond (1992) refers to Stuart Crystal in the UK who specifically recruited women managers for production because of the interpersonal skills associated with women. This kind of case is made on the basis that these characteristics are exactly what are needed in management in the environment of the 1980s and 1990s: 'As the work force increasingly demands participation and the economic environment increasingly requires rapid change, interactive leadership may emerge as the management style of choice for many organizations' (Rosner 1990: 125).

There are a number of difficulties with the case for women in management being based on the 'different' contribution of women in the workplace. First, the characteristics of management as divided into two neat categories, one of which is allocated to men and the other to women, is problematic. This bipolarity between the sexes means that both women and men in management are confined to predetermined behaviours. Second, by suggesting that women have a particular style the many differences amongst women and amongst men are overlooked, thereby reducing opportunities for learning and change. Third, there is the danger that women will lose out when trends in management styles change. This bipolar view of women and men's contribution to management leaves little room for exploring MacKinnon's view of sex as a continuum and how gender is socially constructed.

## A public profile for women-only management training

The first European Conference on women in management took place in 1983 and the European Women's Management Development Network was established in 1984. In Canada, a Women in Management Programme was established at the National Centre for Management Research and Development, University of Western Ontario in 1987. In 1989, the Department of Labour in the USA established the 'Glass Ceiling Initiative' to investigate the phenomenon of 'the glass ceiling' in corporate America (see Appendix). These initiatives emphasized development and training for women managers and gave WOMT a more public profile in the 1980s. However, it is not clear how WOMT contributed (if at all) to debates about equality and difference in this decade. It is worth noting that the boom in MBA programmes in the USA and Britain in the 1980s took place without any attention being paid to the particular needs of women managers. These programmes took place independently of, and uninfluenced by, WOMT programmes. Equally, the mostly male management gurus (with the exception of Kanter) of the 1980s ignored gender and sexuality in organizations and management.

The emphasis on equality which I have associated with the 1970s involves a language of universality and homogeneity characteristic of modernism. The concept of 'difference' which became prominent in the 1980s focuses on heterogeneity and specificity reflecting post-modern views of the world. The shift of emphasis from equality and solidarity towards difference and particularity may be linked with the growth of possessive individualism in western countries during the 1980s. In his discussion of post-modernism and feminism, Henry Giroux (1992) warns that the emphasis on difference can lead to individualism. He asks whether it is possible to develop an understanding of difference that changes rather than reproduces prevailing power relations. Despite my characterization of WOMT as a 'post-modern' phenomenon at the beginning of this chapter, I now think that it incorporates elements of both modernist and post-modernist thinking. For example, there is an emphasis on commonality of experience while the specific career interests of the individual are also emphasized. If like feminism, WOMT is concerned with change, then the development of a theory of difference that also allows for a politics of solidarity will be important (Giroux 1992).

## Antifeminism/postfeminism

In any discussion of the 1980s it is important to note the rise of antifeminism. In 1981, Betty Friedan, the mother of 'second wave' feminism, criticized feminism for its 'direct and confrontational' politics in her book *The Second Stage*. Other criticisms were made by Germaine Greer (1984) and Camille Paglia (1990). Antifeminism or 'the backlash', as it is also known, is analysed by Susan Faludi (1991) and Tania Modleski (1991). Antifeminist discourses led to the use of the term 'post-feminist' to characterize some of the thinking about feminism in the 1980s. Deborah Rosenfelt and Judith Stacey suggest that 'postfeminism demarcates, revises and depoliticizes many of the fundamental issues advanced by Second Wave feminism' (Rosenfelt and Stacey 1987: 77).

They identify a shift in the personal needs and priorities of those women who supported second wave feminism. Some of these changes are reflected in post-feminist rhetoric which expresses

> an uneasiness with the quality of contemporary life for working women . . . the loneliness of women without families, the frustration and exhaustion of mothers who also must or wish to work, and the anxiety of single mothers trying to reconcile heterosexual adult relationships with maternal responsibilities.
> (Rosenfelt and Stacey 1987: 79)

Feminists criticize post-feminism for reflecting pro-family ideology and its lack of concern with class, race or sexuality. Post-feminist rhetoric probably reflects the experiences of particular groups of women but fails to consider others. I think that post-feminist discourses echo many of the concerns raised by participants on women-only management training programmes. Although their opportunities might have improved as a result of the activism of second wave feminism, they now have other concerns such as reaching top levels of management and juggling family and work responsibilities. They question the relevance of feminism in their lives.

## 1990s – POST-FEMINISM/POST-MODERNISM/POST-WOMT TRAINING?

Ideologies of individualism and enterprise culture run alongside pro-family and heterosexist themes within post-feminism. The contradictions within post-feminism probably reflect the struggles of many women managers and other women in the 1990s. Feminism is often seen as hindering women's path to success. Instead of taking a feminist stance, women are encouraged by post-feminist rhetoric to choose the brand of femininity that will most aid their progress in work organizations. Themes of 'mobility, opportunity and self-help' focus on individual women's careers and ignore structural inequalities affecting women (Newman 1991). These themes reflect dominant ideologies in business and the ethos of many WOMT programmes (see assumptions earlier in this chapter). If this is the case, WOMT is influenced more by dominant business ideologies than by feminism.

Post-feminist discourses focus on 'gender relations' rather than 'women' as the key area of concern. These discourses often promote the notion of 'dialogue' between women and men. The view that dialogue is possible is based on the assumption that there is equality between the sexes and elides 'the question of power asymmetry' (Modleski 1991: 6). Yet, if there is no space in which women and men can express their different experiences and jointly address the 'muddle in the middle', how can the burden of bringing about change be taken off women's shoulders? When women and men get close to talking to each other conflict often arises and communication gets stuck. If communication between women and men were to be successful then both women and men would have to change. I think change is a frightening prospect for women as well as men. The development of training programmes for both women and men managers which focus on gender relations and equality is a recent phenomenon. These programmes are a source of data about women and men learning together and are worthy of close monitoring and evaluation.

## Organization of the work-force

Post-feminist ideology has arisen at a time of change in the capitalist system and in the organization of work. Scott Lash and John Urry (1987) point to changes in the organization of the work-force as reflecting the 'disorganized capitalism' of the late 1980s. This is characterized as bringing about the 'increased importance of service industry for structuring social relations (smaller plants, a more flexible labour process, increased feminization, a higher mental component etc.)' (Lash and Urry 1987: 6).

These changes involve the development of flexible core and periphery workers (Allen and Truman 1992), encompassing arrangements such as subcontracting, temporary contracts and part-time work (Walby 1990). This flexibility will lead to an increased casualization of women's work in Europe (Truman 1992). Part-time employment and self-employment form part of this picture of work-force flexibility and we know, for example, that already in Britain 90 per cent of part-time employees are women. Yet, it is questionable whether this so called 'flexibility' represents any change in the working conditions of women whose work has always been casual, insecure and part-time.

Huw Beynon (1992) characterizes the 1980s as a period in which the pace of work increased and greater commitment was demanded by employers. There is no sign that this has changed in the 1990s, and women are expected to rise to the challenge. Hisrich (1990) suggests that one way for women to reach the top is to gain experience by setting up their own businesses and then bypassing the corporate ladder by 'parachuting' in from above (in O'Leary and Ickovics 1992: 26). Self-employment amongst women in the USA grew by 28 per cent between 1980 and 1983 (Kelly 1991). Female self-employment in the UK increased by 70 per cent in the ten-year period between 1982 and 1992 with women now making up around 25 per cent of the self-employed in the UK (Campbell and Daly 1992). Labour Force Surveys (1981–91) in the UK show that self-employment is higher among those of Asian origin compared to the white population and that the self-employed from ethnic minorities create more employment for others than do their white counterparts. Many of the issues relating to women in self-employment are addressed by a number of writers in this volume (see chapters by Judi Marshall, Sue Marlow and Adam Strange, Jo Knight and Sue Pritchard).

### Which women succeed?

Recent evidence suggests that successful women are from middle-class backgrounds, have a grammar school education, an early sense of independence, self-sufficiency and the motivation to excel (White *et al.* 1992). The same study found that 'high flyers' are still expected to conform to a male model of a successful career. They also experience work overload and a deficit in energy. These women have to manage the tension between work and the family which is only partially resolved by the market:

> a market in which middle-class women buy the labour of working-class women; in which white women buy the labour of black women; and in which enterprise for women means the creation of businesses which essentially service other women in a way which offers no challenge to the sexual division of labour. . . . the family and domesticity are added to list of things we have to manage to be a successful *woman* manager.
>
> (Newman 1991: 252)

These labour market arrangments feed into a growing income gap between women. Yet this growing disparity in incomes and working conditions amongst women is not on feminist or WOMT agendas in the 1990s. Instead, the feminist debate in all industrial countries is about 'whether to choose family, career or a combination of work and family roles' (Giele 1992: 10).

## Work and family friendly?

The dominant trend since 1970, according to Janet Giele 'has been toward a pattern of multiple simultaneous roles' (Giele 1992: 10). She sees the juxtaposition of family and work life as bringing about two kinds of changes: first, a change in family forms due to attempts to role share in the home between women and men, and second, a demand for 'quality of life as well as economic advancement and access to power' (Giele 1992: 22). The latter change is epitomized by Suzanne Gordon's (1991) proposal for a 'national care agenda' in the USA. This policy would give higher priority to leisure and family life (Giele 1992). Arlie Hochschild (1989), in her study of working parents and the double burden of domestic and paid labour for women, identifies the chief problem as being the home and not work. Her findings call for flexibility and changes at home.

Patricia Hewitt (1993) asks if 'full-time, life-time employment – 40 hours for 50 weeks for 40 years' is really what we want. If women and men want more control over their life-styles in the 1990s, then flexible employment arrangements including career breaks, jobshares and flexitime would appear to offer more security than part-time work for which pay, promotion prospects and training are poor. To ensure that flexibility works fairly,

Patricia Hewitt calls for a 'new legal framework of "fair flexibility",
based on the principle of equal treatment for all employees,
whatever their hours' (Hewitt 1993: 23). Yet, these proposals are
based on an assumption that 'flexibility' will be available to all.
The question remains 'flexibility' for whom?

### Affirmative Action programmes for women managers in the 1990s

Women are being encouraged to commit themselves to work
organizations via 'family friendly' (Hochschild 1989) work arrangements and by promises of professional advancement. In the 1990s
Affirmative Action initiatives specifically aimed at women in
management are being implemented in the USA and in the
UK. The 1991 American Civil Rights Act (see Appendix) established a 'Glass Ceiling Commission' to make recommendations
on the barriers to women's advancement. It is also charged with
increasing the opportunities for development and advancement of
minorities and women into management and decision-making
positions in business.

In 1991 'Business in the Community' (a voluntary organization)
launched 'Opportunity 2000' in the UK. This initiative involves
the setting of voluntary targets for improving women's progress in
member organizations. By 1992 around 25 per cent of the working
population (141 organizations) were covered by this campaign.
This initiative represents a weak form of affirmative action as there
is no requirement to join the campaign nor is there any requirement to achieve specific targets. It is seen as a long-term campaign
in which 'the wasted talent of women' can be utilized in the
workplace and employers are encouraged 'to treat women and
equal opportunities as a mainstream business issue' (Lady Howe
1992). The first year review of Opportunity 2000 found that almost
all of the member organizations provided some training designed
to increase women's opportunities at work. However, the need to
improve access to such training was noted. It is difficult to predict
the effects of these initiatives on women's positions in organizations. They could be seen as missing the point when there is
much evidence to show that many senior women managers are
leaving work organizations (Marshall, in this volume; Hardesty
and Jacobs 1986; Taylor 1986; Maynard 1988). Time will test the
commitment to change in favour of women's advancement behind
the Opportunity 2000 initiative.

## Women-only management training in the 1990s

Tolerance for women-only activities may be limited if the notion of 'gender relations' rather than 'women' continues to take priority. I see some merit in focusing on 'gender' and developing training programmes for women and men managers because I think that communication between women and men is central to the advancement of women manager's welfare at home and at work. I expect that mixed gender management training programmes dealing with gender, equal opportunities, sexuality and management practices will expand in the future. Equally, the growth of men's groups and literature on masculinity in the 1980s and 1990s (Morgan 1992; Hearn 1992; Rutherford 1992) suggests that the time is also ripe for men-only management training (MOMT), focusing on gender and sexuality issues as they affect men manager's management experiences and practice.

While the progress of WOMT might appear to be sluggish when we look back over the decades, this is, in itself, important evidence in coming to understand the nature of WOMT. The processes by which WOMT has developed and grown throws considerable light on the processes involved in facilitating women's development and visibility. Perhaps the 1990s is a time for WOMT to take stock, to record the largely oral data that exists on women's experiences as managers and to identify directions for the twenty-first century.

## CONCLUSION

In this chapter I challenge the seemingly dehistoricized and depoliticized nature of WOMT. I tried to construct a kind of 'historical' account of the context in which WOMT has developed, at a time when post-modern thinkers hail the end of 'history' and the end of the gender class of 'women'. I hoped that an exploration of WOMT in the context of other movements and initiatives aimed at women's advancement would explain the predominance of certain assumptions in many WOMT programmes. However, I found that I could not easily make connections or identify patterns or processes. It is as if WOMT developed parallel to and influenced by feminism and equal opportunities initiatives rather than in engagement with them.

The relationship between business and feminist interests is not an easy one, yet these interests come together within WOMT which tries to contain the tension between the centre and the margins. By aiming to reach senior positions in their work organizations, women managers belong in the centre. WOMT is mainly aimed at facilitating women's progress in mainstream work organizations. Yet, once management and women are explicitly coupled as they are in WOMT there is a shift to the margins and the activities of WOMT are devalued. The gains of WOMT have taken place in the context of marginalization and WOMT appears to collude with this process of marginalization. MBA programmes have chosen to avoid addressing both business/management interests and the interests of women managers together, thereby avoiding the tensions which exist within WOMT.

I started my journey by outlining the assumptions that seem to dog many WOMT programmes. These assumptions include WOMT's narrow definition of success, including the notion that women can 'have it all'; the belief that if the barriers to success could be identified strategies could be developed to overcome them; the idea that all women managers' work experiences are similar and that women have to take responsibility for changing work organizations. It is as if these became the 'acceptable' assumptions which enabled WOMT to continue to be tolerated and funded within patriarchal and heterosexist work organizations. This may also explain why, although influenced by the women's movement in the late 1960s, WOMT largely avoided taking an overtly political stance in relation to the development of women managers.

By focusing on obstacles to women's development, WOMT concentrates its energies on opposition forces, those things that resist women's efforts and define women as victims (Newson 1991). It seems important to shift the focus to forward motion, whatever direction that takes, so that women managers become agents in their own learning and in their choices at work. Women in management are highly visible in the 'public' domain. Much has been written about men's influences on 'public' space and how the public in turn constructs masculinities (Hearn 1992). WOMT could be instrumental in exploring how the activities of women managers redefine public spaces and how women, in turn, are being constructed differently in the public domain.

My experience of trying to contextualize WOMT raises questions (similar to those raised within feminism) about the respective roles of theory, politics, pragmatism and the personal in educating and training women managers. WOMT includes all of these but appears to be driven mainly by the pragmatic aim of facilitating individual women's achievement in work organizations. Women participants on WOMT programmes have much to contribute and to gain from engaging and struggling with the personal, political and the theoretical. My experience of trying to contextualize WOMT within feminist and other discourses suggests that theories of management, feminism, equality and others are unable to incorporate the contradictions and broad territory on which the experiences of women in management take place. Many of the experiences of women in management fall between theories and cannot be easily contained in one explanatory system. Perhaps our efforts to fit experiences into existing theories, or even the theorizing of experience itself, mean that important aspects of women managers' experiences are ignored.

As in feminism, there will always be contradictory projects within WOMT, but these projects and the relationships between them provide a rich source of learning. At present WOMT tries to live within the depoliticizing and limiting spaces of work organizations. One of its goals might be to expand the spaces in which we try to understand women in management. I think that WOMT has colluded with those who have sought consciously or otherwise to contain its influence and effectiveness. If WOMT is to come alive then those involved will have to make difficult and risky decisions about how to confront this collusion.

## APPENDIX

Some dates, events, activities, reports, publications/books and legislation (case law is not included) relevant to women in management since the 1960s. The large number of books/reports relating to women in management published in the 1980s and 1990s makes it impossible to include these here. Instead, references in these decades are limited to some books on development and training for women managers.

### The 1960s

1960:  International Convention against Discrimination in Education (UNESCO) adopted – to be implemented in 1962.

1961:  President's Commission on the Status of Women – reported in 1963 (USA).

1963: TUC Charter for Women at Work (UK).

Equal Pay Act (did not mandate equal access to jobs) (USA).

Betty Friedan, *The Feminine Mystique*, New York: W. W. Norton Company.

Edgar S. Ellman, *Managing Women in Business*, Waterford: Prentice Hall.

1964: Civil Rights Act broadened to include 'sex' as well as race. The Equal Employment Opportunity Commission (EEOC) was established to define and enforce acceptable employment policies and practices in relation to minorities and women (USA).

1965: Race Relations Act (UK); this Act was introduced to balance tough immigration controls; the act outlawed racial discrimination in public places and established the Race Relations Board.

G. W. Bowman *et al.*, 'Are women executives people?' in *Harvard Business Review*, Vol. 43, NO. 4. July/August.

1966: National Organisation of Women (NOW) established to campaign for legal and educational reform (USA).

1967: Abortion Reform Act. (UK).

Affirmative Action extended to women – Executive Order 11375 – companies receiving federal contracts required to take positive steps to recruit and train women and minority men (USA).

1968: Ford strike by sewing machinists for equal pay for women (UK).

Race Relations Act (UK) also enacted to balance further immigration controls; this act made it unlawful to discriminate on grounds of race, colour, ethnic or national origin in relation to housing, jobs and the provision of commercial and other services (UK).

1969: 'Women in Management' – a professional management association set up for women in the UK. Goals: to provide relevant training and development to members and to support members in their professional roles (UK).

**The 1970s**

1970: Equal Pay Act (UK) – passed but not to take effect until December 1975.

First Women's Liberation Conference at Ruskin College, Oxford (UK).

President's Task Force on women's rights and responsibilities (USA).

Cynthia Epstein Fuchs, *Women's Place: Options and Limits in Professional Careers*, Berkeley: University of California Press.

1971: Conference on Women's Challenge to Management sponsored by Columbia University Graduate of Business (USA).

Michael Fogerty, *Women in Top Jobs: Four Studies in Achievement*, London: Allen & Unwin.

1972: Equal Employment Opportunities Act (USA).

Douglas C. Basil, *Women in Management*, Cambridge Mass: University of Cambridge Press.

Michael Fogerty, Rhona Rapaport and Robert Rapaport, *Women and Top Jobs: The Next Move*. London: Allen & Unwin.

1973: Eli Ginzberg and Alice M. Yohalem (eds), *Corporate Lib. Women's Challenge to Management*, Baltimore: Johns Hopkins University Press.

1974: 'Ligue Française pour le droit des femmes', founded by Simone de Beauvoir (France).

Industrial Society established the 'Pepperell' development course for women managers and professionals (UK).

First British National Lesbian Conference.

TUC's Women's Rights Conference and adoption of Working Women's Charter (UK).

1975: Sex Discrimination Act (UK) – established the Equal Opportunities Commission to assist enforcement of the legislation.

Wages for Housework Demonstration, London (UK).

Virago Publishing Company launched (UK).

Equal Credit Opportunity Act (USA) – allowed women equal ability to obtain credit.

International Year for Women (UN).

1975–1985: UN Decade for Women.

Equal Pay directive (75/117/EEC) covered all aspects and conditions of remuneration (EEC).

1976: Equal Treatment Directive (76/207/EEC) – based on the principle of equal treatment for men and women in every respect, for example in access to employment, training, etc. (EEC).

Race Relations Act (UK) – extends the definition of discrimination by differentiating between direct and indirect discrimination; abolished the Race Relations Board and established the Council for Race Relations (CRE).

1977: Rosabeteth Moss Kanter, *Men and Women of the Corporation*, New York: Basic Books (USA).

International Colloquium on Women in Management. INSEAD Fontainbleau – Aim: To help companies meet the challenge to traditional personnel practices raised by the need to give equal opportunities to women employees.

1978: Pregnancy Discrimination Act (USA) – prohibits employers from discriminating on the basis of pregnancy.

City Women's Network established in the City of London. (UK).

Margaret Hennig and Anne Jardim, *The Managerial Woman*. London: Marion Boyars Publishers Ltd.

Women's Press established (UK).

Organisation of Women of African and Asian Descent established (OWAAD) (UK).

TUC Charter on Facilities for Under Fives (UK).

1979: Convention on the elimination of all kinds of discrimination against women adopted by the UN (to come into force in 1981).

Equal Treatment Social Security Directive (79/7/EEC).

S. V. Langrish and J. M. Smith, *Women in Management: Their Views and Training Needs*, Training Services Division of Manpower Services Commission, Sheffield (UK).

Child benefit payable to the person with day to day responsibilities for children (UK).

## The 1980s

1980: Commission of European Communities, 'European Women in Paid Employment' produced a report entitled 'Practical Approaches to Women's Management Development' edited by Valerie Hammond.

Ashridge Management College, *Employee Potential: Issues in the Development of Women*, London, Institute of Personnel Management (UK).

Amendment to New South Wales Anti Discrimination Act (1977) requiring Affirmative Action for specific groups including women (Australia).

1981: Convention concerning Equal Opportunities and Equal Treatment for Men and Women workers (UN).

Civil Rights Commission issued a formal statement 'Affirmative Action in the 1980s; Dismantling the Process of Discrimination' (USA).

Greenham Common Women's Peace Camp established (UK).

1982: European Commission Action Programme for Equal Opportunities, 1982–5 – focus on women playing a more active role in economics, politics and social life.

1983: Equal Pay Act (UK) extended to cover work of equal value. (Resulted from action of European Commission against the UK.)

First European Conference on women's management development. This conference initiated the establishment of a European Women's Management Development Network.

1984: European Women's Management Development Network established.

Equal Pay (Amendment) Regulations – same pay and conditions for women and men doing totally different work, as long as jobs have equal value in terms such as decision making, physical and mental effort (UK).

Second equal pay strike at Fords (UK).

Pepperell Unit established within the Industrial Society to provide a range of training and development courses for women (UK).

Workplace Nurseries Campaign set up (UK).

1986: Ministerial Group on Women's Issues established in UK.

Sex Discrimination Act (UK).

Women in Management Review & Abstracts launched. (Published in association with the Equal Opportunities Commission.)

Federal Affirmative Action (Equal Employment Opportunity for Women) Act, Australia (application of this Act evaluated in 1991/2 and revealed that quality of AA programmes would have to improve for women to achieve equality with men at work).

The European Commission's Second Action Programme for Equal Opportunities (1986–90) stressed more equitable sharing of family, occupational and social responsibilities between women and men.

1987: Department of Labour (USA) published report – *Workforce 2000* – focused on demographic changes in the work-force and increased importance of minorities and women to the American economy.

Women in Management Programme established at the National Centre for Management Research and Development, University of Western Ontario, London (Canada).

1989: Glass Ceiling Initiative – Department of Labour investigation of glass ceiling in corporate America.

Stonewall group set up to campaign for 'legal equality and social justice for lesbians and gay men' (UK).

National Alliance of Women's Organisations (NAWO) set up (UK).

Employment Act repeals a range of protective legislation treating women and men differently (UK).

Northern Ireland Fair Employment Act established a framework for achieving equality.

## The 1990s

1990: EEC Council of Ministers resolution on protection of the dignity of women and men at work – covers sexual harassment (EEC).

European Women's Lobby set up to promote equal rights and opportunities at a European level (EEC).

TUC and Carer's National Association launch Charter for Carers (UK).

TUC Charter for women at work *Equality for Women within Trade Unions* (UK).

Act for Better Child Care (ABC) enacted in USA.

1991: Opportunity 2000 launched 'to increase the quality and quantity of women's participation in the workforce' (UK).

First *full* degree in Women's Studies validated in UK.

NHS Management Executive set up a Women's Unit (NHS is the largest employer of women in Europe) (UK).

'Women in Management' (UK) set up a European group.

The European Commission's Third Equality Action Programme (1991–5); encourages collaboration between the Commission, member states and social partners; covers childcare and sexual harassment; for discussion of the programme see *Social Europe: Equal Opportunities for Women and Men* available from EC Office for Official Publications, L-2985, Luxembourg.

Department of Labour (USA) produced their *Report on the Glass Ceiling Initiative*.

Civil Rights Act (USA) reversed the effect of some of the US Supreme Court decisions which narrowed protection against discrimination in employment. The Act established a 'Glass Ceiling Commission' (to make recommendations concerning elimination of barriers to advancement of women and minorities and increasing opportunities and developmental experiences for women and minorities) and a National Award for Diversity and Excellence in American Executive Management.

1992: Department of Labour (USA) produced report entitled *Pipelines of Progress – A Status Report on the Glass Ceiling*.

Liz Willis and Jenny Daisley, *Developing Women Through Training, A Practical Handbook*. London: McGraw Hill International Ltd.

The Institute of Management and British Home Stores research report published *The Key to the Men's Club – Opening the Doors to Women in Management* (1,500 women members and 800 male members of the Institute of Management were surveyed) (UK).

Transfer of responsibility for all women's issues from Home Office to Department of Employment. Appointment of working group to advise the Employment Secretary on issues relating to women (UK).

Cabinet subcommittee on women's issues established in UK (The Ministerial group set up in 1986 did not have Cabinet status) (UK).

New Earnings survey (UK) revealed that women earn 21 per cent less than men. Found that this disparity is mainly due to occupational segregation (gap between earnings amongst the widest in Europe) (UK).

Tenth individual Directive within the meaning of Article 16(1) of Directive 89/391/EEC – introduced measures to encourage improvements in the safety and health at work of pregnant workers and workers who have recently given birth or are breast feeding. Includes provision for minimum of 14 continuous weeks of paid maternity leave and protection from dismissal during pregnancy (EEC).

Geraldine Brown and Catherine Brady, Women in management workbook series – three titles – *Are You Ready to Manage?*; *The Sucessful Manager*; *Getting to the Top*, London: Kogan Page.

# REFERENCES

Acker, J. (1991) 'Hierarchies, jobs, bodies: a theory of gendered organisations', Lorber, J. and Farrell, S. A. (eds) *The Social Construction of Gender*, London: Sage Publications.

Allen, S. and Truman, C. (1992). 'Women, business and self-employment: A conceptual minefield', Arber, S. and Gilbert N. (eds) *Women and Working Lives Divisions and Change*, London: Macmillan Academic and Professional Ltd.

Alvesson, M. and Billing, Y. D. (1992) 'Gender and organization: towards a differentiated understanding', *Organization Studies*, 13(12): 73–102.

Ashridge Management College (1980) *Employee Potential: Issues in the Development of Women*, London; Institute of Personnel Management, UK.

Baker Miller, J. (1986) *Toward a New Psychology of Women*, 2nd edn, Boston, Mass.: Beacon Press.

Barrett, M. (1992) 'Words and things: materialism and method in contemporary feminist analysis', M. Barrett and A. Phillips (eds) *Destabilizing Theory: Contemporary Feminist Debates*, Cambridge: Polity Press.

Basil, D. C., (1972) *Women in Management*, Cambridge Mass.: University of Cambridge Press.

Belenky, M. F., Clinchy, B. McV., Goldberger, N. R., Tarule, J. M. (1986) *Women's Ways of Knowing. The Development of Self, Voice, and Mind*, New York: Basic Books.

Betters-Reed, B. L. and Moore, L. L. (1992) 'Managing diversity: focusing on women and the whitewash dilemma', U. Sekaran and F. T. L. Leong (eds) *Womanpower Managing in Times of Demographic Turbulence*, London: Sage Publications.

Beynon, H. (1992) 'The end of the industrial worker', N. Abercrombie and A. Warde (eds) *Social Change in Contemporary Britain*, Cambridge: Polity Press.

Boot, R. and Reynolds, M. (1984) 'Ideology in Development', *Management Education and Development* 15, (2): 183–7.

Bowman, G. W., Worthy, N. B. and Greyser, S. A. (1965) 'Are women executives people?', *Harvard Business Review* 43(4) July/August: 14–178.

Brown, G. and Brady, C. (1992a) *Are You Ready to Manage?*, London: Kogan Page.

Brown, G. and Brady, C. (1992b), *The Successful Manager*, London: Kogan Page.

Brown, G. and Brady, C. (1992c), *Getting to the Top*, London: Kogan Page.

Burrell, G. and Hearn, J. (1989) 'The sexuality of organisation', J. Hearn *et al.* (eds) *The Sexuality of Organisation*, London: Sage Publications.

Calas, M. B. and Smirich, L. (1990) 'Rewriting gender into organisational theorizing: directions from feminist perspectives', M. I. Reed and M. D. Hughes (eds) *Rethinking Organisation: New Directions in Organisational Research and Analysis*, London: Sage Publications.

Campbell, M. and Daly, M. (1992) 'Self-employment: into the 1990s', *Employment Gazette*, June: 269–92.

Carr-Ruffino, N., Baach, J. C., Flipper, C., Hunter Sloan, K. and Olivolo, C. (1992) 'Legal aspects of women's advancement: affirmative action, family leave and dependent care law', U. Sekaran and F. T. L. Leong (eds) *Womanpower Managing in Times of Demographic Turbulence*, London: Sage Publications.

Chafetz, J. S. (1990) *Gender Equity An Integrated Theory of Stability and Change*, London: Sage Publications.

Chinery-Hesse, M. (1993) 'Paths to Equality', *World of Work* (the magazine of the International Labour Office) 2: 8–9.

Chodorow, N. (1978) *The Reproduction of Mothering: Psychoanalysis and the Sociology of Gender*, Berkeley: University of California Press.

Cockburn, C. (1991) *In the Way of Women*, London: Macmillan.

*Crew Reports* (1992) 12(4): 12–17.

Daly, M. (1978) *Gyn/Ecology: The Metaethics of Radical Feminism*, Boston: Beacon.

Davidson, M. J. (1991) 'Women managers in Britain – issues for the 1990s', *Women in Management Review and Abstracts* 6(1): 5–10.

Dinnerstein, D. (1978) *The Rocking of the Cradle and the Ruling of the World*, London: The Women's Press.

Ducci, M. A. (1993) 'Women in authority: the ideal and the reality', *World of Work* (the magazine of the International Labour Office) 2: 4–5.

Ellman, E. S. (1963) *Managing Women in Business*, Waterford: Prentice Hall.

Evans, S. M. (1989) *Born for Liberty: A History of Women in America*, New York: The Free Press.

Faludi, S. (1991) *Backlash: the Undeclared War Against Women*, London: Chatto & Windus.

Ferguson, A. (1991) *Sexual Democracy: Women, Oppression and Revolution*, Boulder, Col.: Westview Press.

Fogerty, M. (1971) *Women in Top Jobs: Four Studies in Achievement*, London: Allen & Unwin.

Fogerty, M., Rapaport, R. and Rapaport, R. (1972) *Women and Top Jobs: the Next Move*, London: Allen & Unwin.

Franklin, S., Lury, C. and Stacey, J. (1991) 'Feminism and cultural studies: pasts, presents, futures', S. Franklin, C. Lury and J. Stacey (eds) *Off-Centre Feminism and Cultural Studies*, London: Harper Collins Academic.

Friedan, B. (1963) *The Feminine Mystique*, New York: W. W. Norton Company.

Friedan, B. (1981) *The Second Stage*, New York: Summit Books.

Fuchs, C. E. (1970) *Women's Place: Options and Limits in Professional Careers*, Berkeley: University of California Press.

Fuss, D. (1989) *Essentially Speaking Feminism, Nature and Difference*, New York: Routledge.

Giele, J. (1992) 'Promise and disappointment of the modern era: equality for women', H. Kahne and J. Giele (eds) *Women's Work and Women's Lives: the Continuing Struggle*, Boulder, Col.: Westview Press.

Gilligan, C. (1982) *In a Different Voice: Psychological Theory and Women's Development*, Cambridge, Mass.: Harvard University Press.

Ginzberg, E. and Yohalem, A. M. (eds) *Corporate Lib.: Women's Challenge to Management*, Baltimore: Johns Hopkins University Press.

Giroux, H. (1992) *Border Crossings Cultural Workers and the Politics of Education*, New York: Routledge.

Goodale, G. (1993) 'What training for career advancement?', *World of Work* (the magazine of the International Labour Office) 2: 8.

Gordon, S. (1992) 'A national care agenda', *Atlantic Monthly* 267(5) (January): 64–68.

Greenslade, M. (1991) 'Managing diversity: lessons from the United States', *Personnel Management*, December: 28–32.

Greer, G. (1984) *Sex and Destiny: The Politics of Human Fertility*, London: Secker & Warburg.

Gutek, B. A. (1989) 'Sexuality in the Workplace: Key Issues in Social Research and Organisational Practice', Hearn *et al.* (eds) *The Sexuality of Organisation*, London: Sage Publications.

Hammond, V. (1992) 'Gender: what does the research tell us?', *Management Development Review*, 5(1): 6–7.

Hamnett, C., McDowell, L. and Sarre, P. (eds) (1989) *Restructuring Britain – the Changing Social Structure*, London: Sage Publications.

Hanamura, S. (1989) 'Working with People who are Different', *Training and Development Journal*, June: 110–14.

Hardesty, S. and Jacobs, N. (1986) *Success and Betrayal: The Crisis of Woman in Corporate America*, Toronto: Simon & Schuster.

Hearn, J. and Parkin, W. (1987) *Sex at Work: the Power and Paradox of Organisation Sexuality*, Brighton: Wheatsheaf Books.

Hearn, J., Sheppard, D. L., Tancrad-Sheriff, P., and Burrell, B. (eds) (1989) *The Sexuality of Organisation*, London: Sage Publications.

Hearn, J. (1992) *Men in the Public Eye*, London: Routledge.

Hennig, M. and Jardim, A. (1978) *The Managerial Woman*, London: Marion Boyars.

Hewitt, P. (1993) 'Time's up for 9 to 5', *New Statesman and Society*, 15 January, 23.

Hisrich, R. D. (1990) 'Entrepreneurship/intrepreneurship', *American Psychologist*, 45, (2): 209–22.

Hochschild, A. (1989) *The Second Shift: Working Parents and the Revolution at Home*, New York: Viking.

hooks, b. (1984) *Feminist Theory from margin to center*, Boston: South End Press.

Howe, E. Lady, (1992) 'Opportunity 2000', *Equal Opportunities Review*, 41 (Jan/Feb): 20–7.

Hutchings, V. (1992) 'The Woman Question', *New Statesman and Society*, 11 December: 16–17.

Kanter, R. M. (1977) *Men and Women of the Corporation*, New York: Basic Books.

Kaplan, G. (1992) *Contemporary Western European Feminism*, London: Allen & Unwin.

Kelly, R. M. (1991) *The Gendered Economy: Work, Careers, and Success*, London: Sage Publications.

Labour Force Surveys 1981–91, 'Women and the labour market: results from the 1991 Labour Force Survey' in *Employment Gazette*, September 1992: 433–459.

Langrish, S. V. and Smith, J. M. (1979) *Women in Management: Their Views and Training Needs*, Training Services Division of Manpower Services Commission: Sheffield (UK).

Lash, S. and Urry, J. (1987) *The End of Organized Capitalism*, Cambridge: Polity Press.

MacKinnon, C. (1989) *Towards a Feminist Theory of the State*, Cambridge, Mass: Harvard University Press.

Malveaux, J. (1992) 'Foreword', N. J. Sokoloff, *Black Women and White Women in the Professions*, New York: Routledge.

Marshall, J. (1991) 'Women Managers', A. Mumford (ed.) *Gower Handbook of Management Development*, 3rd edn, Aldershot, Hants.: Gower.

Maynard, R. (1988) 'Thanks but No Thanks', *Report on Business Magazine*, February: 26–34.

Modleski, T. (1991) *Feminism without Women Culture and Criticism in a 'Postfeminist' Age*, New York: Routledge.

Morgan, D. (1992) *Discovering Men*, London: Routledge.

McNeil, M. (1991) 'Making and not making the difference; the gender politics of Thatcherism', S. Franklin *et al.* (eds) *Off-Centre Feminism and Cultural Studies*, London: Harper Collins Academic.

New Earnings Survey (1992) Part A, London: HMSO.

Newman, J. (1991) 'Enterprising women: images of success', S. Franklin *et al.* (eds) *Off-Centre Feminism and Cultural Studies*, London: Harper Collins Academic.

Newson, J. (1991), '"Backlash" against feminism: a disempowering metaphor', *Resources for Feminist Research*, 20 (3 & 4): 90–7.

O'Donovan, K. and Szyszczak, E. (1988) *Equality and Sex Discrimination Law*, Oxford: Basil Blackwell.

O'Leary, V. and Ickovics, J. R. (1992) 'Cracking the glass ceiling: overcoming isolation and alienation', U. Sekaran and F. T. L. Leong (eds) *Womanpower Managing in Times of Demographic Turbulence*, London: Sage Publications.

Paglia, C. (1990) *Sexual Personae: Art and Decadence from Nefertiti to Emily Dickinson*, New Haven: Yale University Press.

Pepptalk, (1993) *The Pepperell Network Newsletter*, April/May: 3.

Phillips, A. (ed.) (1987) *Feminism and Equality*, Oxford: Basil Blackwell.

Pleck, J. H. (1992) 'Work–Family policies in the United States', H. Kahne and J. Z. Giele (eds) *Women's Work and Women's Lives: the Continuing Struggle*, Boulder, Col.: Westview Press.

Porter, D. (1992) 'Introduction' in D. Porter (ed.) *Between Men and Feminism*, London: Routledge.

Postan, M. M. (1967) *An Economic History of Western Europe 1945–1964*, London: Methuen & Co.

Roosevelt-Thomas, R. (1990) 'From affirmative action to affirming diversity', *Harvard Business Review* 68 (2): 107–17.

Rosener, J. B. (1990) 'Ways Women Lead', Harvard Business Review 68, (6): 119–25.

Rosenfelt, D. and Stacey, J. (1987) 'Second thoughts on the second wave', *Feminist Review*, 27: 77–95.

Rothfield, P. (1990) 'Feminism, Subjectivity, and Sexual Experience', S. Gunew (ed.) *Feminist Knowledge Critique and Construct*. London: Routledge.

Rutherford, J. (1992) *Men's Silences: Predicaments in Masculinity*, London: Routledge.

Schwartz, F. N. (1989) 'Management, women and the new facts of life', *Harvard Business Review* January/February: 65–76.

Segerman-Peck, L. (1991) *Networking and Mentoring: A Woman's Guide*, London: Judy Piatkus (Publishers).

Seymour, D. T. and Voss, G. C. (1988) 'Equality for women?', Business Horizons 31 (6): 10–13.

Sokoloff, N. J. (1992) *Black Women and White Women in the Professions*, New York: Routledge.

Tasker, Y. (1991) 'Having it all: feminism and the pleasures of the popular', S. Franklin *et al.* (eds) *Off-Centre Feminism and Cultural Studies*, London: Harper Collins Academic.

Taylor, A. (1986) 'Why women managers are backing out', *Fortune* August: 16–23.

Thornton, M. (1986) 'Sex equality is not enough for feminism', C. Pateman and E. Gross (eds) *Feminist Challenges: Social and Political Theory*, Sydney: Allen & Unwin.

Truman, C. (1992) 'Demographic change and "new opportunities" for women: the case of employers' career break schemes', S. Arber and N. Gilbert (eds) *Women and Working Lives Divisions and Change*, London: Macmillan Academic and Professional.

Walby, S. (1990) *Theorizing Patriarchy*, London: Basil Blackwell.

Walby, S. (1992) 'Post-post-modernism? Theorizing social complexity', M. Barrett & A. Phillips (eds) *Destabilizing Theory: Contemporary Feminist Debates*, Cambridge: Polity Press.

Weedon, C. (1987) *Feminist Practice and Poststructuralist Theory*, Oxford: Basil Blackwell.

White, B., Cox, C. and Cooper, C. (1992) *Women's Career Development: A Study of High Flyers*, Oxford: Basil Blackwell.

Wieneke, C. (1992) 'Does equal opportunity legislation and practice serve the women's movement? A case study from Australian higher education', H. Hinds *et al.* (eds) *Working Out New Directions for Women's Studies*, London: Falmer Press.

Williams, C. L. (1992) 'The glass escalator: hidden advantages for men in "female" professions', *Social Problems* 39 (3): 253–68.

Willis, L. and Daisley, J. (1992) *Developing Women Through Training: A Practical Handbook*, London: McGraw Hill International.

Wise, S. and Stanley, L. (1987) *Georgie Porgie: Sexual Harassment in Everyday Life*, London: Pandora Press.

Yoder, J. D. (1991) 'Rethinking Tokenism: Looking Beyond Numbers', *Gender and Society* 5 (2): 178–92.

# Name index

# Subject index